Being
Married
♥ Happily
Forever

Being Married *Happily* Forever

Love
Tova

TOVA

G. P. PUTNAM'S SONS

New York

Being Married ♡ Happily Forever

22 Secrets, 12 Strategies, and 8 Compromises

Tova Borgnine

G. P. Putnam's Sons
Publishers Since 1838
a member of
Penguin Putnam Inc.
200 Madison Avenue
New York, NY 10016

Library of Congress Cataloging-in-Publication Data

Borgnine, Tova.
Being married happily forever : 22 secrets, 12 strategies,
and 8 compromises / Tova Borgnine.
p.   cm.
ISBN 0-399-14321-1
1. Marriage. 2. Husbands—Psychology. 3. Wives—
Conduct of life. 4. Borgnine, Tova—Marriage.
5. Borgnine, Ernest, date—Marriage. I. Title.
HQ734.B74115   1997   97-26359 CIP
306.81—dc21

Printed in the United States of America

1   3   5   7   9   10   8   6   4   2

This book is printed on acid-free paper. ∞

BOOK DESIGN BY AMANDA DEWEY

To Ernie,
my beloved husband,
whose constant love, caring,
and support helped me
find my voice.

$\mathcal{A}$cknowledgments

❖

There have been so many people who have nurtured both my life and my career. This book would not have been possible without their love, help, and support.

To Mama, for your unconditional love, faith, and support . . . Your words and example have guided me through all the steps I have made and will make in my life. I love you.

To David, my son . . . That I can call you my son is truly a miracle. For us to have a loving and growing relationship, after thirty years apart, is my life's most precious gift. You are my most deeply felt accomplishment. I love you and am truly proud of you.

To Ernie, my husband, for always being there. With you next to me, I know there is nothing I cannot achieve. Thank you for your support, pride, encouragement, and love. Most of all, thank you for filling my life with so much joy.

To Sharon, Nancee, and Cristofer . . . Your laughter and love brighten all of my days. Thanks for bringing us Shelby, Shaelyn, Jeffrey, and Hunter—and, I hope, even more delicious babies in the years ahead.

To all my staff at the Tova Corporation . . . Although I know I don't say it enough, you are doing a great job! You make it all possible. Thank you. Special thanks to my assistants, Peggy Barron and Kathryn Tierney, for their dedication and unfailing loyalty.

To Karen Moline . . . This book would never have become a reality without her vision, support, and Herculean efforts. She gave me the courage to disentangle the memories of my life.

To Peggy and Doug Briggs, Anne and Kirk Douglas, Lydia and Charlton Heston, Barbara and Frank Sinatra, and Cathy and Ed Kangas, for their contributions to this book, as well as to my life, my heartfelt thanks. To all the wise, funny, and gracious women who took the time to fill out the questionnaires I gave them, as well as to all my friends and many acquaintances who patiently divulged details about their lives and husbands. Thank you for your energy and your savvy, which inform so much of these chapters.

To my devoted friends, Brugh Joy and Signe Quinn Taff, whose advice, understanding, and friendship have guided me through good times and bad. To my very good friends, Gail Gross and Pat Mitchell, whose close and lasting friendship I will treasure always.

To three therapists of rare wisdom: Joan Child, LCSW, and Ashley Davis Prend, ACSW, and most particularly Janis Altman, MSW, whose endlessly perceptive insights into human behavior gave me much food for thought and shaped much of this book.

To Phyllis Grann, thank you for your faith and support. Special thanks to Susan Petersen, whose personal guidance, words, and efforts helped immensely to guide me through this book. Also, thanks to Liza Dawson, who provided assistance and encouragement when I needed it. My thanks as well to my literary agent, Madeleine Morel, who has nurtured this project, along with her partner, Barbara Lowenstein of Lowenstein–Morel Associates.

To David Frank Ray, my creative director, whose creative magic and loving spirit have always made me glow. Thank you.

I have been blessed to be a part of the QVC family for over seven years now. I wish to thank the hundreds of friends who make all things possible before, during, and after our *Beauty by Tova* shows, especially Melissa Smith and Ann Marie McCabe. Please know that I love and appreciate you all. Doug Briggs, Darlene Daggett, and the entire executive team have always listened and given me incredible support. You helped make my dreams a reality.

The hosts and producers of QVC are the magic that transfers the energy: Kathy Levine, Judith Crowell, Jane Rudolph-Treacy, Pat De-Mentri, Lisa Robertson, Mary Beth Roe, Dan Hughes, and David Venable are just a few of this incredible team. The tireless staff responsible for broadcasting, sales, and marketing have always given that extra effort which makes QVC number one, from Len Czabator, Tom Armstrong, Roger Elvin, and Tom Okuniewski to Robb Cadigan, P. J. McGrath, Paul Greenholt and Rich Moraski, and Richard Mauer, and the hundreds of hardworking, creative people. And to Dennise Epps Manning, our spokewoman and lovely model who gave life and beauty to my TOVA products. This list could go on but I would be remiss if I did not mention Fred Siegel, who is the dynamic head of marketing, and Ellen Rubin, the passionate leader of public relations and the staff that holds it together. Much love and my sincere thanks for all of your support.

No list of acknowledgments would be complete without my warm appreciation to the gifted staff of my Body, Mind, and Spirit Salon . . . I love you all!

$\mathcal{C}$ontents

◆

Part One:
DATING FOR LIFE

Part Two:

COMMUNICATING WITH
THE MAN YOU LOVE

Introduction

◆

Just last week, I sat with Ernie and watched the sunset for the first time from our brand-new deck. As I thought of how its construction had dragged on for nearly three years, I realized that building a marriage is not unlike what we'd just gone through. You start out with an idea of what you want it to be, but until it's finished, you don't really know what it's going to look like, how hard it might be to get what you want, or how you'll ultimately feel about it.

When Ernie and I got married nearly twenty-five years ago, we didn't know what was going to happen to us. At the time, I thought I could predict our lives together—but I had no idea what was to come! Now, I can happily say, we feel that we've been together forever, that we belong to each other. But it hasn't always been easy, or all fun and games, or the happily-ever-after of fairy tales. It's taken discipline, perseverance, and devotion. From both of us. And especially from me.

You see, Ernie and I made a commitment to each other when we said our marriage vows, but I made another promise to myself: I was going to make our marriage work. I didn't know then what it would take to keep that promise, and I've been figuring out how to do it ever since. This book is the story of what I've learned, why it works for us, and how you can transform your marriage by doing what I did.

I wrote this book because I believe that all women want the same thing: a happy, secure marriage. They want to love and trust their husbands; they want to feel cared for and cherished. Most of all, they want to share their lives fully with someone who appreciates them for all the things they are.

But a wise woman soon learns that with these gifts of love comes responsibility. I believe it's our job as women and wives to teach our men how to be emotionally open, how to be physically close, and how to connect on a soul-deep level with the women they married. This may sound old-fashioned, or out of step with the times, but none of that matters if it's true.

Does this mean letting go of your ego or giving up the fantasy that your husband will always know just what you need? Yes, but it's more than that. Making your marriage work means dealing with what *is,* not with what you wish would be. You can choose to be angry or disappointed or feel like a victim when you don't get what you want from your husband and your marriage. Or you can do what I do: change what *you* can, and learn to nurture this precious relationship with the man you've chosen to love.

It won't happen overnight, but it will happen.

Now, I've told you what I believe women want. What do men want? you may wonder.

Tova's *Secret* 1:

Men want the same things that women want—but they don't know how to get them. So, my dears, it really is up to us to show our beloved men just what to do to get what they want—*and* how to give us what we need.

That's a big promise, I know. But I can say this with conviction because I've lived it. I understood even before we got married that in order to become the best wife I could be, I'd have to work on myself. I never saw this task as a sacrifice or a burden, because I loved Ernie with all my heart.

What I discovered is that every single day of this marriage, I've learned more about *me* than about Ernie. Until I took responsibility for my own needs and for making changes, until I stopped expecting my husband to live up to my fantasies, I often felt powerless and frustrated. Sometimes I felt as if Ernie and I were standing at opposite ends of a room, shouting to each other, "This is *my* half, and you can come into *my* half only when *I* say so!"

Is that how you want to live with your husband? Of course not.

Can you have a happy marriage forever? Yes. It *can* be done.

That simple phrase "It can be done" has always kept me going. I've heard those four words a million times from my mother, but it wasn't until I applied them to my marriage that my life changed completely. What she was trying to tell me was simple: that when you put your heart and mind to anything, you can accomplish so much more than you ever thought possible—even when it seems that the odds are stacked against you.

When Ernie and I were first married, those words were almost like my daily prayer, bolstering my courage to handle everything he threw at me to see how I'd react. There I was, newly wed to someone highly recognizable in Hollywood—Wife Number Five, no less!—and desperate to make my marriage a success. Not only were both of us scarred by our previous relationships (which had left us gun-shy and scared to learn about each other), but I felt as if everyone were looking at me and betting on how long I'd last. I certainly wasn't going to admit I didn't know what I was doing! Instead, I kept telling myself I'd find a way to grow into my new role as Ernie's wife, that I could do it by being true to myself.

Being myself has been the key to my success—in my marriage and in my business. I've been selling my cosmetics and perfumes live on QVC, the number-one television shopping network, for nearly eight years now. Live television is a great teacher, and early on I learned if I tried to be something or someone that I wasn't, everyone would notice it immediately. I had to be myself and hope for the best.

Being myself has brought me in contact with thousands of women who consider me a friend and ally. We share a common bond, these women and I—a deep love for our families and friends. And because I talk so much about my marriage to Ernie, many of these women have called me at QVC or written to me for advice. (One woman really touched my heart by telling me she'd named her darling newborn daughter after me!)

These women have told me again and again they long for simple, easy-to-understand help in making their relationships better. Although I'm not a therapist, I *am* a self-taught expert at listening to people and giving them what they want and need. For years my friends and I have shared our thoughts and concerns about what we wanted from our lives and marriages, and what we've found works best with our husbands.

It's given me such pleasure to distill all the lessons I've learned from my friends, colleagues, and clients into this book. (You'll see that in addition to drawing on my own experiences, I've included stories throughout supplied by many of the women who confided in me.) I hope you'll agree that it delivers clear, helpful, and encouraging advice that will make a real difference in your life.

Let me tell you a story. A few months after Ernie and I began seeing each other, we went to Hawaii on a vacation. While we were there, we did a radio show together, and the guest appearing before us was a professional psychic. She took one look at us lovebirds and said, "By the way, you two have been married seven times before in your previous lives." I took it as a good omen—why not?—but I knew in my heart that what she told us wasn't important. I wanted to be happily married in *this* life to Ernest Borgnine. It was our *future* together that mattered, not the past.

I hope that this book will help you create the marriage you've always dreamed of, a romantic and fulfilling partnership that satisfies you heart and soul. I hope when you finish reading it, you'll say to yourself with a great big smile: It *can* be done.

I know you can do it—because I did!

Tova: Secrets from a Survivor's Scrapbook

◆

Some of you reading this book may be newlyweds, blissfully happy and hoping that your marriage will be a honeymoon that lasts forever. Others may have been married for a few years but have begun to worry that their marriage is at an impasse. And still others may be reading this late at night, glancing sideways from time to time to stare at the snoring lump lying next to them in bed and wondering, *Who is this man I married?*

Perhaps you're also wondering if it's normal to feel that your marriage is like a roller-coaster ride filled with stomach-lurching ups and downs, sometimes nearly careening off the tracks.

Fear not, the answer is "yes," most of us have felt all those sensations. Throughout my nearly twenty-five years of marriage to Ernie, I've experienced them all. And it's taken me all of these twenty-five years to figure out a few strategies, discover some secrets, and come to understand the joy of compromise. My journey has been a personal one, but I hope you'll find your own truths in some of mine.

I'd like to start by sharing a list that summarizes the essence of what I believe in. These nine simple words focus my energies and remind me of what's important in my life. As I explored how I felt about each of them, I began to understand more about the man I married—how to satisfy his needs as well as my own, how to deepen our commitment to each other, and how to manage my expectations and let go of my fantasies.

This list goes with me everywhere. It works magic for me, because these words are like challenges. They represent everything I want to feel and think—about my marriage, my career, and my self. I call them my Borg-Nine Principles.

THE BORG-NINE PRINCIPLES

1. Inspiration
2. Passion
3. Hope to Accomplish Something Worthwhile
4. Risk-Taking
5. Persistence
6. Perseverance
7. Patience
8. Being a Mentor
9. Giving Back

You'll find that I draw on these principles throughout this book, that they influence all that I am and all that I do. Why these particular promises to myself? Each word reminds me of the heart-deep values that make my life worthwhile and wholly satisfying.

INSPIRATION

Inspiration gives you the creative energy for whatever you do with and whatever you feel about your husband. Every morning, you must draw on what inspires you, in order to accomplish something new and wonderful in your life and in your marriage.

PASSION

You must be passionate about whatever it is that inspires you. That means always remembering the passion you first felt for your husband and letting it spark your enduring love—even when he's driving you crazy with his unwillingness to look at a map when he gets lost.

HOPE TO ACCOMPLISH SOMETHING WORTHWHILE

If you don't hope to accomplish something good and true, all of the above doesn't matter. Whether it's in your marriage or in your chosen career, lighting a candle of hope that symbolizes all you dream of doing is vital to making it happen. Start by "hoping" that your love for each other will be strong and steady.

RISK-TAKING

Being passionately in love with your husband and getting married are the riskiest—and most rewarding—tasks you will ever accomplish in your life. But understand this: taking risks is an essential part of moving forward, as a wife, partner, and businesswoman.

PERSISTENCE

In order to consistently evolve, you must be persistent. Persist in the work you have to do to keep your marriage thriving. Persist in your campaign to become the woman you want to be. Never give up on yourself or on the man you love.

PERSEVERANCE

It's not enough to persist in your efforts, you must also persevere. You must be prepared for difficult times but still willing to trust in your dream of happiness, in the man you married, in your own ability to cope.

PATIENCE

Next, you must be patient. Even when you're certain you could do something better or faster, even when your husband insists he knows what he's doing. Especially when your husband really doesn't know— and tries your patience to an extreme. (Patience is not a virtue for nothing!)

BEING A MENTOR AND GIVING BACK

Once you've accomplished whatever you've set out to do, that's when your true work really begins. Because then you must go to numbers eight and nine: become a mentor and give back. Why? Because generous, open women know that if they've been graced with so much, they must, *must* share their wisdom with others. Especially wisdom about relationships. Which, as you may have just guessed, is one of the reasons I'm so happy to be writing this book.

If I could add a tenth word to this list, it would be *now.* Whatever you do, it has to be done *now* or shared *now* or played *now* or worked at *now.* Now is the time to get going and make your marriage work. Your life together can be everything you hoped it would be when you first fell in love, everything you dreamed of when you both said your vows and acknowledged that love.

How I wish I'd had a list like this when I was growing up, nine strong words of wisdom to show me my path. I didn't, though. You might think that because I'm married to a Hollywood star that my life has always been glamorous and fun . . . but it hasn't. I'd like to tell you a few things about a lonely little immigrant girl named Tova . . . and then I hope you'll understand why my Borg-Nine Principles are so important to me.

An American Dream

In 1949, my mother came to America on a freighter, crossing a seemingly endless Atlantic Ocean from Norway. She had seventy dollars in her pocket, a dream of a better life, and me. *It can be done,* she would tell me. I didn't understand what she meant at the time; I was just seven and a half and knew only four words in English: *yes, no,* and *thank you.*

Mine was a difficult childhood. For one thing, I could barely communicate with anyone I met—and I was acutely aware of being an outsider. I'll never forget how, after my very first day of school in Brooklyn, my teacher sent me home with a note telling my mother not to send me back the next day. Instead, she highly recommended I go to a special school. Because I hadn't responded to any of her questions, she thought I was mentally retarded. It never dawned on the woman that I didn't speak her language. (My mother, fortunately, spoke English fluently because she had worked for the American embassy in Oslo for years.)

Because she could find work only as a housekeeper, we lived in the shadows of the families who employed my mother. She understood her position, but I didn't. All I knew was that I had lost my bond with Norway, my language, and my father. It made it hard to trust anyone, or even play with other children.

When I was fifteen, my mother remarried, to a man I called my "wicked stepfather." He was a widower who worked in the lumber business. He was a very, very heavy man, a diabetic who drank a lot. I think my mother married him out of a kind of desperation. We moved to Clifton, New Jersey, where I remember that my bedroom was about as big as a couch. I became very introverted, reading and going to the movies a lot, losing myself in a fantasy world. I dreamed of finding a man who would love me, but I had no real-life role model to show me how to recognize such a man.

In 1959, the summer I was seventeen, I met my first grown-up boyfriend at the Jersey Shore—and he seemed like my dream come true. I was staying with friends and looking for a job. I could barely type, but the son of the owner hired me anyway. Lou worked for the company; he was extremely good-looking, with tons of gorgeous hair, a great build, an engaging manner, and a real twinkle in his eye. (He was also twenty years older, getting divorced, and had four children; let's just say that I was extremely naive.) I developed a massive crush on him, so when he asked me out to lunch, I agreed, then panicked. Would I say the right thing? Would he ask about my awful typing skills? It didn't matter—I must have seemed like a breath of fresh air to him. After several lunch dates, he asked if I would like to go for a ride in his dashing, sleek, and polished speedboat, and I quickly decided he was the one for me.

Once that summer ended, we secretly kept seeing each other. I was eighteen, a senior in high school, and madly in love. We made love for the first time after we had been going out for almost a year. It was his birthday; I was eighteen, and we were hidden away from the world on his boat. I was terrified yet exhilarated, wondering what I was doing. . . . Would he respect me in the morning? Would I respect myself? But there was also a strange kind of pride afterward, that I was a woman at last, that I couldn't go back again. I had given myself to someone I really loved and everything was wonderful.

Until I realized I was pregnant. Nice girls didn't discuss birth control in those days. Nice girls certainly didn't think about condoms. Nice girls didn't do any of this, unless they were married.

Near hysteria, I called Lou. It was Thursday, and he said he'd come for me that Saturday so we could talk. An abortion was completely out of the question. He told me he'd take care of everything, that everything would be fine. That as soon as his divorce was final he would marry me and we would work things out.

He never showed up.

What happened? That night Lou stopped his car in the middle of the parkway and got out. He wasn't so much walking as staring; he'd totally flipped. The police moved his car off to the side of the highway, found Lou's identification, then contacted his father. His parents picked him up, took him to a doctor Friday morning, and by that afternoon he was admitted to a sanitarium, where he spent the next six months.

But I didn't know any of this. All I knew was that Saturday had come and gone and my beloved boyfriend had vanished from the face of the earth. I didn't dare tell anyone about my predicament. I was absolutely devastated. I felt totally alone and abandoned.

I finished my senior year in high school, never admitting to anyone that I was pregnant. I worked that summer as a dental assistant, standing all day on my swollen feet, and hoping somehow it was all a mistake. I was too scared even to go to a doctor. But by September it was obvious, and I had to tell my parents. It was the only time I ever saw my mother cry. What made me feel even worse was her reaction. "How could you? How could you do this to me, how?" she wailed. "Are you trying to kill me?" I had no answer.

It was the only time I saw my mother stand up to my stepfather. When she told him the bad news, all hell broke loose. He wanted to send me off to a home for unwed mothers; when my mother said no, he decided I should be shipped off to Norway, where I could be a burden to my real father. So we called my father, but he replied, by telegram, that I was not welcome in his house.

I had been knocked down twice now: my parents were really unhappy with me, and then my father turned me away. I will admit I thought of suicide. There was nothing to look forward to, and nowhere to run back to. There were so few alternatives for a terrified teenager in 1960. Society is far more forgiving now, and teens in my situation have options I didn't have.

I wanted the baby, but I had no idea how in the world I was going to be able to take care of it. I wanted to protect my child from the loneliness and desperation I was feeling. When I look back, what I remember most is how absolutely petrified I was, how riddled with panic, disillusionment, and humiliation I felt. I was very timid, and I barely spoke. My only real alternative was to give up my baby for adoption.

In the last two months of my pregnancy I blossomed out like a football. I'd go for walks only late at night, when the neighbors wouldn't see me. They all thought I was living somewhere else instead of hidden at home in my tiny room with my huge shame.

My labor took nineteen excruciating hours, and then my baby was born, a beautiful boy. I wanted to call him Bjorn, a Norwegian name that means "fair," although he was ultimately named David. I wasn't supposed to see my baby, but the nurses forgot the protocol for birth mothers and presented me with my newborn. I had to stay in the hospital for three days, and when it was time to leave, for some unknown, devastatingly thoughtless and cruel reason, I was told that I had to dress my baby before giving him to his adoptive parents. That haunted me more than anything. I was shaking as I dressed this adorable little creature who had been conceived with love. He looked up at me with such trust; I almost died at the sight of those enchanting eyes.

I was required to hand him over to his adoptive parents myself. (What a truly sadistic regulation that was!) I had to dress my baby and carry him in my lap as they wheeled me to the door of the hospital, and then see him safely deposited on his new mother's lap.

At that final blow, I shattered into a million pieces, spiraling into such profound emotional shock, such deep heartbreak, it stayed with me for thirty years.

Starting My Life Over

The sharp pain of giving up my baby slowly lessened, and I started to wonder what I could do with the rest of my life. I wanted more education, but I was still so terribly isolated. Some friends had suggested I try to get work as a model. I wasn't sure how to do that, but at least I had a destination: New York. I had photographs taken and by some miracle I got a job as a model in a showroom. It was fun and not too stressful, but it didn't pay enough to live on. So I became the hat-check girl at the Left Bank, a tiny but very successful supper club that was a hangout for jazz musicians, comedians, and the theater crowd. (I'll never forget the night Elizabeth Taylor came in, dragging a full-length sable along with husband Mike Todd. She was drop-dead gorgeous.)

Soon I had saved enough to rent my first apartment, a minuscule studio close to the Left Bank. It had more roaches than you can imagine, but it was mine. I was filled with pride in my newfound independence, and I decided to go to drama school. I was determined to be an actress—me, the great communicator! But it was through drama school that I discovered my true calling. My acting teacher recommended that we learn how to apply stage makeup, so I walked over to a brightly lit shop called the Makeup Center, a well-known haven for Broadway stars, dancers, and models.

As soon as I walked in, I knew this was the place for me. I was like a kid in a candy shop, and couldn't get enough. I started hanging out there all the time (I think I was a bit of a pest!). I would sit for hours watching as the pros went through their paces and were in turn taught by visiting makeup artists. Eventually I summoned up enough courage to ask if I could try it, and I happily jumped in.

There were still times when I could barely pay the rent, days when I wondered if I could afford to eat. My friends and I would go to the Automat, where we made our own tomato soup from ketchup and hot water, laced liberally with the free saltines they always had on the tables.

But I didn't mind. I was living in the most exciting city I knew, and my life had wonderful moments of glamour and excitement. I'll never forget the day I was working on a film called *Love with a Perfect Stranger,* which starred Steve McQueen. I may have been only an extra, but it was still show biz. Too bad they didn't pay me my small fee in cash, because I didn't have a dime on me. I hadn't eaten all day and I was famished. I knew I'd be going to my mother's that night if only to get a proper meal.

But I had no way to reach her when work was over. I didn't even have a dime for a phone call. I decided to go to the Hampshire House hotel, where I knew the doorman. (When I'd saved up some of my Left

Bank tips I would treat myself to the hairdresser there.) It was about a two-mile walk, which really isn't that bad. Unless you're starving.

My pal Chris was on duty, and he greeted me with a smile. "It's so good to see you," he said. "What can I do for you?"

"Well, all I have is a hundred—and I don't want to change it. . . . Do you think you can lend me a dime? I just want to make a quick phone call," I said.

"Of course. Do you want more?"

I assured him a dime was fine, called my mother collect from the hotel, and asked her to please come get me. Then I went back out, gave Chris back his dime, and thanked him.

For pride, I'd do anything.

Another New Beginning

About that time, nearly a year and a half after our baby had been born, I unexpectedly ran into Lou. At first I wanted nothing to do with him because I was still so hurt. But eventually we made our peace with each other. His mysterious disappearance and breakdown had been due in part to a brain injury, a skull fracture he'd sustained in World War II. In times of great mental stress he would suffer what we would now call post-traumatic stress disorder. I was justifiably still quite upset and angry . . . but I had to temper it knowing that he had a genuine reason for abandoning me.

Lou was persistent, and he began to court me again. I'd had a few casual boyfriends, but no one I was serious about. I realized I still loved Lou—my first real love. He was charming, and so outgoing and attractive. When we became engaged, my mother was thrilled.

I think that somehow I needed to be married to justify myself and my life to that point. Now I can see that our marriage was doomed from the start because I wasn't being true to myself and my real needs. But I pushed those thoughts aside, and Lou and I were married in May of 1966. We lived in Point Pleasant, New Jersey, and that August I opened Tova's Touch, my very own tiny makeup boutique in nearby Sea Girt.

(Acting was definitely out of the question—his family flat-out insisted that no actress was going to tarnish the reputation of *this* family. Looking back, it's hard to picture myself as the kind of shy, voiceless woman who would go along with such a demand. It had nothing to do with my wants or my needs, but only their feeling that I would somehow shame them.)

My boutique was a real novelty, decades ahead of its time. I had one chair and one counter, and all the brushes and colors and products from my beloved Makeup Center. (In fact, I was one of the first people to take on a little line called Neutrogena, at that time a small company from California.) I hardly made any money but was close to breaking even. Overhead was low, as I was the only employee. Best of all, Tova's Touch was my unique creation. It wasn't acting, my first career choice, but as a second choice it was pretty fabulous. And the more I worked in my tiny boutique, the more I realized that I had found something that I could do well. It gave me focus and a real boost of self-respect.

At first Lou got a kick out of what I was doing, and was proud to say, "Yes, my wife dabbles in something, but it's nothing serious." Remember, at the time, few men were willing to admit any more than that. A wife could *dabble*—as long as dinner was on the table when he got home.

That attitude wasn't what ended our marriage, though. It wasn't one big thing, something specific or tangible I could pinpoint. I knew only that it wasn't working. Of course, I can see the reason more clearly now.

Tova's *Secret* 2:

If you're not paying attention to your relationships, they can run right away from you.

As our marriage eroded, it wasn't as if either of us were ready to say, "Let's forget it and call this marriage off." There was a lot of low-level friction. I honestly believe that if I'd truly wanted to nurture that relationship, it would have endured. Or it might have. I don't know that for certain, and I never will.

But in 1969, when we had been married three years, I went out west to visit my mother; my wicked stepfather had died, and she had remarried a lovely man. I stayed away a little longer than I'd intended, and Lou was very upset. Because it was not a great time for us—one of the reasons I was in no hurry to go back—I felt as if I needed breathing space. Eventually, though, I went home. Lou picked me up at the airport, and as we were driving home, he started to tell me how he'd had a very nice time while I was away—with a woman in town. Not only that, but he confessed that he'd spent quite a few nights sleeping with her . . . and two of those times were in our bed. It was bad enough that he'd been unfaithful with her, but I couldn't believe he'd punished me by doing it in the sanctity of our bedroom.

It was unforgivable.

I never went home again. When we got near our street, I jumped out of the car and went to stay at a girlfriend's. She went to the house to pick up some of my clothes and things; I vowed not to set foot in it again. Lou tried everything to get me back, he really did. I was still working at Tova's Touch, and I would meet him for lunch sometimes. He was terribly distraught. One heartbreaking time, one of his young sons came with him to lunch, begging me to reconsider and come back, but I was too deeply, profoundly hurt to respond. Lou's adultery in our own bed destroyed something so necessary to my well-being, I just couldn't face dealing with him.

Not long after that, I flew to Montgomery, Alabama, to get a divorce. (It took only three days there.) I went down by myself, a wounded, desperately unhappy woman. From there I was going to go to Las Vegas to stay with my mother and new stepfather. But when I arrived in Montgomery, I called Lou from the hotel. I had gotten cold feet and was all alone and afraid. I talked to him, but he was very cool to me; obviously *she* was sitting right there.

If there had been the smallest opening, if there had been one tiny signal from Lou, I am convinced that I would have said, "Can I just come home and we'll forget about everything that happened?" But he didn't give me that opening. Did he truly want out, or was his pride getting in the way (as mine had), as well as his shame? I'll never know.

My Life Goes On

But I couldn't dwell on the pain. I discovered once more that what's so great and so hard about life is that it forces you to move forward. I couldn't look back. I had to move on. I literally had no choice.

What could I do now? I no longer had a home; I was lonely, deathly afraid, and felt like an absolute failure. When I got up the following morning, after crying so much my eyes were nearly swollen shut (which, by the way, was very cathartic, to let all that emotion out), I decided to start the second half of my life in a completely new arena. I flew to Las Vegas.

I didn't know if I was going to stay for a weekend or a decade. I went to one of the shows at the Tropicana and asked to go backstage. I started talking to the showgirls, who told me that when they needed makeup they had to call New York or California because they had no local supplier. The possibilities were clear, and I started setting things in motion. I still owned Tova's Touch, so I sold everything I had left and closed the shop. I knew I wasn't going back there. I just wanted out, to be done with it.

With my nest egg, I launched two makeup concessions in the beauty salons at Caesar's Palace and the International (now the Las Vegas Hilton). The showgirls and dancers would call me and order what they needed, and I would arrange to deliver it to them. I missed having my own shop, but I was doing well in a business I knew and loved. Not only that, focusing on something new and challenging helped me through the first stages of my divorce.

At first I didn't date at all. I felt too fragile, too vulnerable to let anyone get close to me again. But I often went to see the shows. I was fascinated by the whole scene, the spectacle that is Vegas. That's how I met comedian Marty Allen and his lovely wife, Frenchie. She was an amazing lady, and she and Marty took one look at me and said, "What's a nice girl like you doing in this dust bowl? We must get you out of here." They took me under their wing and invited me to dinner whenever Marty was playing in Vegas. Through them I met some fascinating people, many of whom became my clients, including actress Merle Oberon, whose beautiful, radiant skin (and unique beauty secret) would be responsible for my launching my own skin-care line (more about that later!).

Marty and Frenchie helped build my confidence in a way I'll always treasure. I was still shy, and still grieving for my marriage. But for the first time in a long while, I felt the stirrings of new hope.

When, early in 1972, I told Marty and Frenchie I was coming to Los Angeles on business, they told me they had a date for me. I wasn't really interested, but I didn't want to let them down after all their kindness to me, so I said okay. Marty asked, "Well, don't you want to know who it is?"

He told me my "fix-up" was an actor named Ernest Borgnine.

Unfinished Business—and a Long-Lost Love

Once our relationship began to get serious, I told Ernie about the son I'd given up for adoption, but we never talked about David. Or rather, I was unable to talk about him. For twenty-nine years I locked away the pain and shame I still felt about letting him go. It wasn't until I started seeing a wonderful Reichian therapist and working with incredible teachers that I was even able to relate this story. With their help I finally understood that I could begin to heal only when I began to let go. (Letting go of that sorrow also helped me find my voice.)

That's when I started searching for my son. I had to at least set the wheels in motion. I didn't expect him to want to see me, but I needed to make sure he was okay. As part of the process of healing, I went on what I called a personal pilgrimage to Prescott, Arizona, a truly spiritual place of great natural beauty. As I walked along a trail to a lookout point, I saw a dead bird on the grass. I picked it up with a spoon and did a burial ritual, placing stones over its little grave. As I continued on, I saw the tiniest little butterfly alight on a rose I was holding. (Yes, I firmly believe in symbols!) Later that day, I wrote eighteen pages detailing everything that had happened, and then I burned it all. I burned away all the guilt, burned away all those years of living with unworthiness. It was now time to go forward. How else did I sense I was on the right path? I went to a beauty salon, and when they brought me a cup of coffee, I saw the mug was labeled *To a Great New Mom.*

Not long after that, in March of 1991, I was reunited with my wonderful son, David. Just about thirty years had passed since his birth. No matter how much anger, resentment, and guilt had shadowed both our lives (David knew he'd been adopted, but always felt something was missing), the minute I let go of those emotions, it was almost as if I became a different person, a different spirit. In a way, I walked through a door—and changed irrevocably for the better.

This is why I talk so much about learning to let go. The emotional catharsis of my reunion with my son, after such a long time, helped me come to grips at long last and let me move on. (One of my greatest sorrows is that Lou, who died in 1986, never got to see David, who looks so much like him.)

The Strength of a Survivor

It's amazing what our minds and bodies can do when survival is at stake. In fact, my earliest memory is being scared awake in my crib in Oslo. My father ran into my room and grabbed me out of my bed just before the bombs hit. (I can still see this clearly, as if I were watching a movie in slow motion.) The Germans were blowing up the ammunition dumps in Oslo, and in the process blew up half the city as well. Our entire apartment collapsed, but my father had snatched me away from death in the nick of time.

Sometimes I look back at the first part of my life and shake my head at the struggles I went through and the difficulties I faced. Even though

I lived through them, they almost seem like the ingredients of a novel. But they were real, and the pain I experienced still hurts when I recall those tough times.

Yet I know that if I hadn't endured these traumas, I wouldn't be the person I am. If I hadn't started childhood as the housekeeper's shy daughter, friendless and unable to communicate, if I hadn't felt abandoned by my own father and my first husband, I wouldn't have learned the lessons that have made me so strong.

My struggles have kept me focused and taught me how to live. I believe that my instinct for survival brought me to Ernie and his unquestioning love, and gave me the courage to create my own company. I have a wonderful life now, and I know I can conquer my fears.

Which brings me to another lesson I want to share with you.

Tova's Secret 3:

As you look at the man you married, who sometimes makes you so angry and frustrated that you wonder *why* you married him, remember: **Happiness is all the more sweet because it so often comes after heartbreak.** It's out of pain that we grow and learn.

Let's grow and learn together about loving our men—and loving ourselves.

Part
One

Dating for Life

"After World War II, we were living in a tiny cold-water flat in New York's Hell's Kitchen and looking for work in the theater. We were young and broke but it didn't matter. The experience strengthened us both. The past fifty years, like all good times, have gone by like the blink of an eye. Through professional and personal trials and triumphs, we hung in. And, believe us, it was worth it."

—LYDIA AND CHARLTON HESTON

He's the One:
The Real Truth About Marriage

L ET'S START WITH THE
basics, three of the most important truths I know about marriage. Take
a deep breath, and read on:

❖ **There is no such thing as equality in marriage.** We, the
women of the world, are nurturers by nature, and if we want our
marriages to succeed, we must be prepared to nurture our husbands.
And then nurture them some more.

❖ **Sustaining your marriage is your emotional job.** You love
the man you married; you made a choice to marry him; and your
choice is to remain with this man. That's the real and only true reason you're there. And because you've chosen to share your life with

this wonderful man and create something special between the two of you, something so unique that no one else in the world can share it, you've got a lot of work to do.

❖ **You realize and accept the fact that you have to do more of the work.** I'm not saying that your husband is *more* important than you are, or that his needs are more important than your own . . . but simply that more of the responsibility for keeping your marriage healthy rests on your shoulders. This means learning how to satisfy your husband's needs and your needs in different ways.

Have I scared you, even just a little bit, with the core of my philosophy about marriage? Please don't be. Let me reassure you by describing how I reached these conclusions.

When we were first fixed up in March 1972, Ernie was not interested in marriage. He was in the middle of an incredibly bitter and messy divorce from his fourth wife, and he was not thinking of women in a particularly favorable way. In other words, he was fed up with us altogether!

Nor, frankly, was I thinking about marriage. I just told myself, "Tova, it's enough to know that for one evening of your life, you're having dinner with a real movie star." But once Ernie and I met and started talking, I realized how really charming he was. I liked him, and he made me feel very comfortable—he had no "star attitude" whatsoever. Later, he drove me back to my hotel and was about to shake my hand good-bye. As we stood there and the poor elevator lady kept asking, "What floor, please?" female instinct took over. I pressed my foot against the elevator operator's foot so she couldn't shut the door.

Lady, I was thinking, *if you move this elevator, your life is over!*

Eventually, Ernie said he'd call me, let go of my hand (which he'd been shaking), and kissed me on the cheek—we were so proper in those days! I moved my foot off the befuddled elevator lady's and she took me upstairs in silence. As I walked in a daze of happiness down the hall to my room, I knew something wonderful had happened. And when I started gazing at his photo every morning, I *really* knew Ernie was the one. I had asked him for an autographed picture, and I'd had it framed. Lovestruck me used to carry it all over the house!

On our third date, Ernie and I went to the premiere of *Cabaret*. I had never had seen such a spectacle—the flashbulbs of the paparazzi erupting in our faces, the fans screaming. I thought I was literally going to die! I was holding on to Ernie for dear life—and from that moment on, nothing separated us. We were head over heels in love. I respected and admired Ernie, but was never intimidated by him. He was so easy to talk to. We had connected in a profound way, but neither of us quite believed it yet, that we had gotten serious about each other so quickly.

As soon as Ernie finished filming *The Poseidon Adventure* in Los Angeles, we went to Oregon for his next film, *The Emperor of the North*. We had a wonderful time there together, although I was still incredibly naive and easily shocked. One day Ernie came home in full makeup, after a fight scene where he'd been bloodied by Lee Marvin, and I almost passed out from the terror I felt. I can still see him standing there, laughing at my reaction.

We felt as if we didn't have a care in the world, we were so happy together. (The topic of marriage never came up, though, and any conversation in which his former wife was mentioned was like waving a red flag before a bull!)

Next, we went to Toronto for yet another film shoot. It was getting close to the holidays, so I asked Ernie if he wanted me to do his Christmas cards. He told me that would be great, and then said, "Have them printed with Mr. and Mrs. Ernest Borgnine." Now, we had been together for eight months and were blissfully content, but not once had we discussed getting married. Frankly, it really wasn't an issue for me; I knew how he'd been hurt the last time, and, besides, things were great the way they were. So I told Ernie I couldn't do that because we weren't married, and that I knew how against marriage he was. I added that I was secure enough with him to continue the way we were.

The next day, after shooting all morning, Ernie told me he wanted us to go to Niagara Falls. It was a bit cold for sightseeing, so I asked him why. "I think we should get married," he said. I had no time to think! Not about a wedding dress or a wedding bouquet, not even my wedding makeup (*that* was a real horror!).

Nevertheless, we went to Niagara Falls on November 24, with our driver and the justice of the peace serving as our witnesses. Ernie said he didn't want anyone to know (he didn't want the inevitable press attention at such a private time), and that was fine with me. Now, of course, we could send out Christmas cards signed Tova and Ernest Borgnine! Once we did, the people who knew and loved Ernie were very upset that we hadn't had a "proper" wedding. Ernie's response? "They'll get over it!"

Back then, we had no time for a honeymoon—but we've been living our honeymoon ever since.

I KNEW HE WAS THE ONE

How do you know he's the one—your one forever love? When relationships go from friendship to something more, there's always an indefinable something called chemistry. Sometimes it's a voice that whispers inside, saying, "Oh, boy, I'm attracted to this person," or, "Oh, boy, I want to kiss him right now," or, "Oh, boy, isn't he attractive?" You'll look at his face and decide he has a cleft in his chin that makes him resemble Kirk Douglas. Often it happens without warning, where you might never have thought him particularly cute or exciting or romantic, and then suddenly everything changes, and you're waltzing around the house kissing his photo as I did with Ernie's.

Nearly every woman I talked to told me she'd experienced this kind of moment, the one in which you know that he's the man you could love all your life.

◆ **Valerie:** I liked him as a person. On our first date, I thought: I could marry him; I trust him; he's a good soul. I recognized right away that he was a man who could think and act like an adult, someone who wasn't into stupid little power or money games like so many of the men I'd been dating.

Once you experience the feeling, you just can't get enough of him. Of course, there is so much more to love than just physical attraction, a connection that is beyond measure and defies description. It's a harmony you can't put into words. For me, knowing he's the one—the *right* one to marry—is beyond understanding.

It's what I call a Heart Feeling. I knew that with Ernie at a deep, deep level; we shared it in and out of the bedroom, wherever we went and whatever we did together.

Ask any woman in love with her husband (not just me!) and she'll invariably say, "I *knew*. I knew in my gut." She experienced a Heart Feeling, a sense of being bonded to the man she's given her heart to. This kind of feeling doesn't mean you have to be as alike as peas in a pod, but that you complement each other, that you make compatible partners. It also means that you envision a future together.

What's most crucial to a good marriage is a loving, trusting friendship. Can you answer "yes" to every one of these five statements?

Tova's *Strategy* 1:

Use my "Five Ways to Be Sure He's the One"

- He is my best friend.
- I trust him and respect him completely.
- He lets me know how much he loves me, in the best way he knows how.
- Even though he snores, I still want to sleep with my arms around him.
- Although he often drives me crazy, I can't imagine my life without him.

Answered "yes" to each one? Good for you!

◆ **Kathy:** You should love him as your best friend, and more. I mean, you're going to be waking up next to him every day, so you better be sleeping with your best friend, or else! And, not to sound melodramatic, but you should be able to trust him with your life. I know Ed would die for me. If a bullet were heading toward us and it had to hit him or me, he would take it.

If your relationship is built on a loving, trusting friendship, you already have a strong foundation. Because of it, you and your partner will be able to face anything together and feel safe in each other's love. And when you feel safe, the level of trust between two people automatically deepens.

WHAT DO WE WANT FROM MARRIAGE?

"I always married because I wanted to have a home, to have children, and to come back each night to a safe and sound and wonderful place," Ernie says. "If I had a wife waiting for me with a meal on the table, it wouldn't hurt, either," he adds with a laugh. "With Tova, I got everything but . . . but I wouldn't have it any other way."

(Ernie's "but" is referring to my cooking, or lack thereof! You can't give the man *everything* he wants, now, can you?)

He never got married to get divorced, mind you. He came from an Italian family, in an era where he was told that if you kissed a woman (and kissed her a lot!), you married her. He got married for the first time at the ripe old age of thirty—ancient for his generation—because he was in the Navy until he was twenty-eight. But after he won the Best Actor Oscar for his amazing performance in *Marty,* he began to have problems in his marriage. His wife put on dark sunglasses wherever they went so that people would think she was famous, and in other ways handled his new success badly. This did not sit well with Ernie, a man who can smell phonies a mile away. (Of his three other marriages, I'll tell you more later, but the one to Ethel Merman lasted only thirty-two days. When she wrote her autobiography, her chapter about Ernie was one blank page!)

It may be hard to believe, but I didn't know any of this when Ernie and I were introduced. In fact, I didn't learn that Ernie had been married four times until we'd been dating for several months. I wasn't shocked or dismayed, and it wasn't that we didn't talk about such things. I simply didn't think or care much about his past. I really didn't, because I knew him as he was with me, and that was all that counted.

All of us who have had more than one marriage have learned that it does not diminish the love we feel for one man because we've found a different kind of love with another. Even if a relationship ended badly, you hope that time will heal the anger and the bitterness so that you will be able to remember the good things that made you love that man in the first place. Believe me, I speak from experience.

You've probably figured out that one of the reasons Ernie and I clicked was because neither of us was looking for a relationship when we met. When you're not looking, you're more receptive to allowing the person you meet to be who he is. You don't have a rigid mental checklist of how much money this man should be earning, or what kind of background and family he comes from. You don't worry whether he'll be a good father, or whether he even wants children, for example. You're not *on guard,* protecting yourself from potential pain and rejection; you harbor no illusions, no unrealistic expectations or fantasies about him. When you date with no expectations, meeting as Ernie and I did, all you want is a pleasant evening with what you hope will be an interesting man.

When Marty and Frenchie fixed me up, I never dreamed that I would meet the love of my life. Now I can look back and say that it was the first time I actually trusted my womanly intuition. It was quite a stretch for timid, emotionally scarred me to trust *myself.* It was a great happy coincidence, our meeting, with no pressure and no strings. It just happened. Because we both were so surprised at how well we clicked, neither of us thought about what we were *supposed* to be doing. Ernie was working very hard, filming in Los Angeles, and I was working during the week back in Vegas. So we just let things happen.

I knew what I wanted, though. I'd had plenty of time to think about what I needed.

Tova's *Strategy* 2:

Figure out the elements that make a good marriage work.

Here are some good reasons to get married:

- A shared desire to make a lifetime commitment
- Respect and honesty
- Implicit trust
- Intimacy
- Constant communication
- A good sense of humor
- The ability to dream and plan both together and apart
- A good heart
- A desire to please and support your spouse in whatever he chooses to do, and his willingness to return the favor

How about some of the wrong reasons people get married? Are any of these true for you? (Come on now, be honest with yourself . . . and me.)

- Financial security
- Escape from family shackles or a previous relationship
- Fear of being alone
- Because you're pregnant
- Inability to live alone

It's an eye-opener, isn't it, to consider these elements, and add any more that apply to your marriage. Before you're married, putting them down on paper is a good way to focus on what you want and value, which makes it much more likely that you'll get what you need. If you're already married, recalling what drew you together is a good reminder of what you wanted when you said "I do"—and might help push you to make it true.

But don't worry—even if you know in your heart of hearts that you married for one of the "wrong" reasons, that doesn't mean you can't ever have a wonderful marriage. You might just have to be willing to work a lot harder. In different cultures, for example, many marriages are still arranged between two virtual strangers, who often grow to love and cherish each other deeply. The point is, if you marry for financial reasons or because you're scared of being single and want a man to take care of you, there will always be some payment extracted. And the person most likely to be paying it will be you. For some people, having a lot of money is more important than finding emotional and sexual compatibility. But agreeing to live without true intimacy and affection, choosing to be with a man who has little capacity to share or be giving, is not something I could do. A palatial home with no love in it is just a big empty house with no heart.

Why do I bring this up? I want to tell you about getting married for the wrong reasons—and staying married for the right ones.

MARRYING WRONG AND MARRYING RIGHT: WHAT I LEARNED

When Lou and I got married, I wanted to be saved. I was Snow White, waiting for my prince to awaken me with a kiss. I thought of Lou as my white knight in shining armor, who would sweep me off my feet into my fantasies of happily-ever-after.

I soon learned that it is possible to have passion without love, without the real communication a marriage needs to thrive and grow. Many of our problems stemmed from the fact that we were linked *only* by passion, not compatibility.

It also is possible to have commitment without intimacy. The mere fact that you have committed yourself, that you are married to your partner, doesn't necessarily mean you know how to be truly intimate. You may have exchanged rings and furnished a home, but have you taken that leap of faith into the wonderful, emotional openness that makes a really good relationship work? So many times people say the word *love* without understanding what it really means. Saying "I love you" means little without the emotional work you have to do to back it up. (In fact, I think true love is the "reward" you get *after* you do the work.)

Lou and I also had to struggle beneath the shadow of a terrible trauma, which hovered like a ghost that neither of us could acknowledge. My pregnancy and David's birth were utterly taboo topics. Can you believe that in all the eleven years we were together, Lou and I never once discussed our son?

It's often said that we marry our parents. Without realizing it, we choose a partner who may closely resemble the personality or the behavior of one or both of our parents. Looking back now, I can see that Lou was a kind of substitute for the father I never knew. Twenty years my senior, he was definitely what I'd been searching for all my life. Loving him gave me the chance to bond with the father who'd forever left a hole in my heart. And in me, Lou found a youthful playmate, an innocent girl who could make him feel virile and worldly.

Lou didn't really have a sense of what he wanted from marriage. He knew only what he didn't want—and that was someone who resembled his first wife. He'd gone right from his traumatic experiences in World War II to being married with four children. Because he didn't like to be by himself, maybe he figured marrying me meant he'd never have to be alone. But we were both deluding ourselves. I was marrying a dream and expecting a fairy tale. How could our marriage not fail?

When I look back at my life with Lou, I feel a certain amount of regret, but I cherish the fact that together we created a wonderful child named David. But my marriage to Lou never really had a chance, because it never focused on the elements listed above.

For years, I kept saying to myself, "I deserve more than this" and "I want more than this." I found what I wanted with Ernie. We fell in love in a quiet, more grown-up way. It wasn't like the flush and thrill of a first love. Not that we didn't have a wonderful sex life—because we did and still do—but I was calmer about passion. We moved in together quite soon after we met. It's not something I would necessarily recommend, but for us, it just felt right. I did move in with Lou once we were engaged, but I wouldn't have under other circumstances. (I believe each couple must work out what's best for them, regardless of what anyone else—like your parents—might say or think. This is a time for you to decide how to live *your* life, and not someone else's.)

Ernie had a much more strongly developed sense of self than Lou did. He knew who he was, and he was comfortable with himself, despite his four failed marriages. Loving him, at the time in his life when we met, helped me realize that there are many different kinds of relationships, and many different kinds of love. Not only that, but the person you love changes all the time—and so do you!

Once you get married, you have to be willing to love change, not just accept it. You have to love the give-and-take. You have to love the process when *you* step aside and put yourself in your partner's shoes. Slipping inside your lover's soul—that's empathy.

All animals need to make connections from the day they're born. Take a look at a little puppy, his tail wagging in delight at the sight of your face. Dogs love to be loved, to be petted and held and stroked. Well, human beings are not so very different. We also need to be touched, and not just in a sexual sense. It's the emotional bonding, the feeling and caring that's so important. And part of making those connections and bonding emotionally means learning to give the person you love the space to make changes—the ones that they feel they need to make for themselves, not just the ones you think they can or should make.

All this Ernie and I learned together. And I also learned that I wanted "us" to work more than anything. I began to try to understand *myself* a whole lot better, and to embrace my own fallibility. No one ever said I had to be perfect, so I certainly couldn't expect my husband to be, either. Which brings me to . . .

BEING HONEST ABOUT THE MAN YOU'RE WITH

Let's be frank. Of course you want to be happy, and be happily married, but what's really important to you?

One of the hardest and scariest things you can do is be honest with yourself. This may be painful, especially if you're the sort of person who tells little lies to herself in order to feel okay about the man she's chosen. You can't get away with this forever, you know—because eventually that little voice inside you will get louder and force you to face the truth about the man you've married. It's time now for some introspection, time to bring all those doubts out in the open. Like most fears, they're less scary when they're examined in daylight.

Tova's *Strategy* 3:

List what you believe is absolutely essential for you to have in a committed relationship.

Some topics to consider:

◆ *The importance of family.* If you plan to have children, do you want them sooner or later? Who will be the primary caretaker? Where will the money come from? Where do you want to live? What about religious beliefs?

◆ *The importance of maintaining this relationship.* How will each of you take care of the other? What are the demands on your time and on his?

◆ *The importance of shared goals and a vision for the future.* What are your dreams and hopes for yourself, and for the two of you as a couple?

◆ *How the two of you share these visions.* Do your hopes and dreams mesh or conflict?

Once you've thought about these subjects, take a moment to consider how you learned about love and family, marriage and relationships. How would you describe your parents' and grandparents' marriages? Ask yourself:

◆ Were my parents happy together—with each other and as individuals?

◆ Did they communicate with each other openly?

◆ Was their love tangible or critical?

◆ What did they fight about?

◆ Did they encourage me to seek out my own goals (or fulfill *their* dreams)?

◆ What did my mother give up? What did my father give up?

◆ How did my grandparents treat my parents?

Try to forget for a few minutes about being their child and answer these questions as someone on the outside looking in at their relationship might.

Your relationship with your parents will certainly influence your choice of partner. Talk to your siblings, if you have them, and add to your understanding of your family's dynamics. (Do remember, though, that memories and recollections are funny things. Siblings often remember certain incidents in completely different ways!)

Asking yourself these questions might seem like such a simple thing, but the most simple tasks often produce amazingly helpful insights.

Last but not least, ask yourself these questions about your partner:

- Do I love him? Really love him? (Or is it infatuation, lust, dependency, neediness?)
- Do I like him?
- Is he honest with me and with himself?
- Is he caring and thoughtful?
- Does he communicate well?
- Is he friendly and well mannered, or rude and impatient?
- Is he passionate and considerate in the bedroom?
- Does he enjoy his career and have good relationships with his colleagues?
- How does he get along with and treat his parents and his siblings? His pets?

This last one can provide real revelations about a person. How well a man gets along with his family will give you a tremendous amount of information. Listen to him carefully. Pay special attention to how he talks about his mother. She is his role model for adult female relationships; his feelings toward her are a strong predictor of how he will eventually think of you.

Looking at your honest responses (and try to skip nit-picking about little things, such as never asking for directions or leaving his socks on the floor!) should give you a good idea of who your man is. Review my "Five Ways to Be Sure He's the One" earlier in this chapter (page 7) and test yourself again. If you can put a "not" in front of any item—He is *not* my best friend. . . . I do *not* respect him—it's time to reconsider your relationship.

Do you find yourself continually making excuses for him when he lets you down? Do you wonder if you really love him or just enjoy the illusion of having a man around? Do you worry about his character? Do you feel safe around him?

If you answered "yes" to any of these questions, you're bound to experience many more problems as time goes by. So many women fall in love with a man's "potential"—and then they get angry because he can't possibly live up to their expectations. Often we see what a man might become more clearly than he does himself . . . and then we decide to mold him into our fantasy image. But after a year or two passes, reality sinks in and we tell ourselves that we don't know this person anymore. But in fact he was being true to himself all along.

How many times have you fallen in love with love, grabbed for the illusion of love instead of the real thing? Deciding you can change a man's vision of himself into what you're looking for is denying what's right before your eyes . . . and can only bring you unhappiness. So take off those fantasy-tinted glasses and see your husband as he really is!

I was very fortunate when I met Ernie because I had outgrown my need to have a relationship live up to my fantasy. I'd stopped expecting things to go the way I *wanted* or the way I *expected*. For one thing, Ernie was usually working on location, so I had either to adapt to his schedule or live without seeing him. This was something new for me to get used to, but I found it exciting. In a true sense, I was enjoying the moment, cherishing our time together. I was living in the present with him, without looking back at yesterday or worrying about tomorrow. We both were. It was a revelation, because I'd never really lived that way before. We enjoyed each other's company, and we talked.

Tova's Secret 4:
Trust each other enough to talk about everything.

And talk and talk and talk. It is crucial for you and your partner to understand what each person is feeling and where each wants the relationship to go.

Sometimes a woman can be so blindly in love that she'll ignore the nice big clues her lover is trying to give her. "Oh, I don't have to worry," she'll tell herself, "he's not going to be like that with me once we're married. He doesn't mean what he says. I know he'll change."

Believe me, this is one area where you cannot be shy about saying what you think and feel. I know it's all too typical, but it still astonishes me how few couples sit down and talk about their ideas and philosophy before they get married. If you can't talk openly and freely to each other *before* the wedding, what makes you think you'll be able to talk about it afterward? If you're not sure about *anything* your partner says or does, take all the time you need to be sure. And *talk!*

• 2 •

How His Mind Works:
Understanding the Man You've Chosen

I WAS TEMPTED TO CALL
this chapter "Getting to Know You," just like that song from *The King and I*. There is so much to learn about yourself and about the man you loved enough to marry! Sometimes it's hard to believe that men and women are members of the same species. Well, get used to it!

Here's my take on the differences between women and men—in just eight easy lessons. They're short and sweet, but oh so true.

1. ◆ Women are raised to be nurturers. We want to take care of the people we love.
   ◆ Men, on the other hand, grow up having things done for them. They're typically taught that anyone female is there to bring them their dinner, look after them, kiss their scraped

knees all better and tidy up the mess in their rooms. Simply put, they learn to expect to get nurtured.

(See how this works?)

2. ◆ Relationships are paramount to women. They fill our deepest emotional needs.

  ◆ Relationships are important to men, too—they just have a harder time admitting it! They'd rather say that a great job and financial security (not to mention a red Corvette) are paramount to them.

3. ◆ Women need to understand how they get from Step A to Step B in their relationships. This means we like to talk about and understand our feelings. We cherish emotion and intuition.

  ◆ Men just want to get there—and they want the journey to be easy . . . and once they're there, great, let's eat. They'd rather forgo novocaine at the dentist's office than be forced to talk about their feelings if they don't want to. (Since I'm a Scandinavian by birth, I think I can be objective about American men. They're brought up not to cry, not to show their feelings, to be stoic in the face of adversity.)

4. ◆ Women usually rely more on common sense. We want to finish what we start—like childbirth.

  ◆ Men are often immovable objects. Don't expect them to be sensible once they get an idea into their stubborn little heads. (A perfect example of this: An acquaintance of mine had been living with a man for nine years, and she wanted to get married. So she not only proposed to her boyfriend, but she set up the wedding and planned the whole thing. He was always going to marry her, but he was the kind of guy who didn't want to deal with the family or the details. She knew that he was an immovable object, and that he wouldn't change. He'll always have a hard time making certain decisions. So she made this decision for him, and now they're both happy.)

5. ◆ Women can juggle seventeen different tasks at once. (More on that shortly!) And we can operate on these seventeen different levels at once and still wonder why the bulb in the lamp on the end table is flickering. Whereas . . .

   ◆ . . . your husband doesn't even know there's a lamp in the room. If you give a man a list of things to do, chances are he'll remember only the last item on the list.

6. ◆ Women like to feel secure.

   ◆ Men like a challenge.

   (Of course the world might be a better place if all men would opt for challenges that helped them toward their own goals, instead of conquering other women, but I'm afraid that's another book altogether!)

7. ◆ What women *do* is what other people *need*. But because women expect to deal with other people's needs, we often have a hard time believing that we even deserve to have needs. (Because my stepfather was an exceptionally critical man, at least where I was concerned, I still have a hard time accepting compliments whenever I get my share of them today. Somehow, I can't get used to the fact that I quite deserve them.)

   ◆ Men, on the other hand, don't mince words about what they *want*. They say what they *mean*. If your husband tells you he needs to watch football every Sunday with his buddies, he's not saying it because you're a bad wife or to make you feel unloved. He's saying it because it's exactly what he *needs*. If this bothers you, you're going to have to tell yourself, "Well, I wish he weren't so obsessed with that football team, but it's part of who he is, and he's not going to change this obsession just because it bothers me." Can you do this for the man you love? I know you can.

   Men have simply been raised to be more true to their needs than women. Have you ever heard yourself saying, "Oh, I don't mind, let's eat there . . . or see that movie" (you get the idea) when in fact you really *do* mind? (Much more on this topic to come!) Men don't sit there and try to figure out why you said what you said. They just say, "Okay, let's do it!"

But—and this is a Big But—men often don't know what their *hearts* need. They may know what their physical or recreational needs are, but rarely their *emotional* needs. They often have as much difficulty expressing what their hearts and souls need as women do getting their needs fulfilled.

8. ◆ Women are better at listening to their intuition than men are.
   ◆ Men are not the mind readers we think they are.

In every aspect of their breathing, living, waking, sleeping . . . they can be amazingly dense. I speak from experience! I don't think it dawned on Ernie for about a year after we were first married that he had actually gone through with it again. *Ohmigod, number five—what have I done!* Ernie told himself. Not that he came out and actually *said* anything to me, but he kept watching, wondering just what my angle was. He couldn't figure mine out.

It took him four years to realize I didn't have one!

He'd seen them all and, believe me, he tested me on them all . . . without sharing what he was doing with me. Then one day he blurted out that he really loved me deeply and that he was so sorry for testing me.

Men! Don't they just drive you crazy? Oh, well—we still love them anyway!

KEYS TO UNDERSTANDING HIM BETTER

Because we are skilled at nurturing, we women often can seem wise beyond our years . . . whereas the men we love often seem no older than blubbering babies.

How old *is* your husband? I don't mean in literal years, I mean in emotional years. I know men who've celebrated their fiftieth birthdays, but are about eighteen emotionally! I have a girlfriend who jokes that man-years are like dog-years in reverse. You know, if a dog is one, it's really seven; at ten, a dog is seventy, and so on. Well, she says that a man who's forty-nine is really more like seven—get it? When she told me this I laughed and laughed, but sometimes it's not so funny. Especially when it's your husband who is acting like a child.

Tova's Secret 5:

Age is a state of mind.

Ernie and I talked about our age difference at first, and I know he was more worried about it than I was. But I told him, "What does age matter? We love each other, and that's what counts." We're still like kids together. Like five-year-olds in a candy shop—and the candy we can't get enough of is loving each other!

But love isn't all you need to help you understand how a man's mind works. Remember how I said that women can do and think about at least seventeen different things at a time? I've found it to be true again and again. But men are very different.

Tova's Secret 6:

Men can think about only one thing at a time.

If a man can do more than one, he's a pretty unusual guy.

I mean, if you ask him to please pick up a loaf of bread and say hello to the dog, you're asking a lot. (He'll get the bread but forget about the dog. Or he'll take the dog out for a walk and forget to pick up the bread. Or he'll pick up the bread and decide to buy a lovely salami and a jar of mayonnaise to make a sandwich while he's at it, conveniently forgetting that the doctor just told him never to eat mayonnaise again because his cholesterol is sky-high . . . to say nothing of slathering that mayo on salami!)

Instead of becoming frustrated about your husband's inability to think about more than one thing, why not do what one friend of mine did—and make it part of your plans? I call this wonderful anecdote "Joanna and the Fan."

Joanna was redecorating her house. She asked her husband what he would like to have in the bedroom. What she was really asking him was, What *one* thing did he want in the room that would make it feel like his? Naturally, he chose the one object she'd always considered tackiness supreme: a big wooden-and-wicker ceiling fan with a dimmer and lots of curlicued light shades. His choice altered the effect she was trying for in decorating their bedroom, but Joanna is a wise woman. She shrugged her shoulders, kept her mouth shut, and ordered the fan her husband particularly wanted. Then she proceeded to redecorate the bedroom— and the rest of the house—exactly as she wanted to. Her husband barely paid attention to anything else she did, because she'd already asked him what he wanted and given it to him.

Give-and-take is what makes a marriage work. In this case, Joanna had a stern conversation with herself: *Okay,* she said, *this bedroom is where my husband and I are going to be sharing the most intimate moments of our life together, and I want my darling to be happy in this room. If a fan makes him happy, then it's a small thing to give in on to ensure his happiness.*

Tova's *Compromise* 1:
**Give your husband the one thing he wants,
then make yourself happy, too.**

Joanna satisfied her husband's needs as well as her own. She took a potential conflict and turned it into a win-win situation. And all because her husband could think of only one thing at a time!

WHAT DOES YOUR HUSBAND REALLY NEED TO BE HAPPY?

Have you ever wished you knew exactly what your husband needed to be happy instead of trying to read his mind or figure out the clues he sends you in his words and actions? Of course you have—we all have! Here's what I believe are the most important needs every husband has:

Your husband needs to feel important. There's not much difference between the words *important* and *impotent,* is there? You're the only one who can make your husband feel *important*—and keep him from ever feeling *impotent.*

You can do this by bragging about him to your friends, who are sure to mention it to their husbands, who will make certain your loving words get back to him. (This is what psychologists call "positive reinforcement.")

You can do this by making him feel good sexually. Tell him: "Oh, you make me feel so sexy. Do you know how sexy you are? You're the sexiest man in the world." Frankly, you might not always be in the mood to say such things to your husband, or you may sometimes feel you're telling tiny little white lies, but saying them to your husband is quite all right if he is in real need of reassurance. Which—trust me!—he usually is.

Your husband needs to feel pride in himself. Whatever your husband does, you can help him feel good about himself by reaffirming his positive attributes. I'm not suggesting you lie by pretending he's good at something he's not. But you can make sure he knows that, no matter what, you have always been and always will be proud of him.

This way, even if he's screwed up big time on a project at work, or he hasn't made a success of something that is important to him, or if his boss yells at him or if a deal falls through, you will manage to find something positive in the situation. You can tell him simply, "I don't care what anyone else says, you do excellent work, and this was great. You should be proud that you did it the way you did." He'll have the courage to tackle whatever anyone throws at him because he'll remember what you said and tell himself, "Well, at least she believes in me. She thinks I'm the most important person in the world."

Wouldn't you like your opinion always to be the most important in his life? When you do this often, it will become the opinion he most wants to hear. Just do it, as the ads say. Tell your husband *all the time* how proud you are of him. Train yourself to say "I'm proud of you" as often as you say "I love you."

Your husband needs to take pride in you on his arm. Yes, I'm talking about *your* appearance and *your* attitude. You should always dress as if you are proud to be seen with your husband. It doesn't matter whether you're going to an important business dinner with his boss, or picking him up from work, or heading out for a quiet evening at the local pizza parlor—try to look your best. Showing your husband that you care about the way you look to the world sends him a clear message that you care about the man you're seen with.

(If, however, your husband is the one who's gained fifty pounds and let himself go, why not try to start him on a weight-loss and/or exercise program that you'll do together as a couple? Make it a date. Tell him firmly, "We're going to go to the gym together every Thursday night and Saturday afternoon." Or you could try to enlist one of his best friends, especially one who likes to work out or who shares a love for your husband's favorite sport. When it feels right, be honest with him. Say, "You know, my husband's been putting on a few pounds. I need you to help me out with this. Maybe you could ask him to play tennis with you?" Then encourage him to say go when the time comes!)

Be your husband's own private cheerleader in everything he does. Let him know you're with him every step of the way.

Your husband needs his own time and space. It's wonderful to spend time together as a couple, but it's important to let your husband be who he is. He needs his own time to be left alone to do what he wants. He certainly doesn't need you to jump on him the minute he walks in the door. Say hello, greet him with a kiss, but then let him unwind, change his clothes, read the mail, follow whatever routine he has, before he comes back to you.

Your husband also needs his own space. This can be a corner of the den, or a workshop in the garage, or a favorite chair that's his and his alone.

Your husband needs to establish and maintain trust and respect. I told you that Ernie gave me a hard time after we were first married. It wasn't exactly a communication problem, but more an unconscious fear on his part. That uncertainty was once triggered by something as innocent as a meal.

Mr. Borgnine, you see, can finish a meal in less than half an hour, so he just can't figure out why it would take anybody else in the world longer than half an hour to eat a meal. Well, before I started my company, I sometimes went out to lunch with my girlfriends. We would be happily chatting away over a couple of glasses of wine, so our lunches might sometimes take several blissful hours. The time would fly by.

Well, Mr. Borgnine could not for the life of him figure out what his wife and her girlfriends were up to for all those hours, because he couldn't believe we'd still be sitting in the same restaurant. Instead, he told himself that I was either preparing to leave him or lying—because he was terrified I really might be. And because he was so terrified, he drove himself crazy about my three-hour lunches. I didn't know how to convince him that I truly loved him, that I'd never betray his trust.

Let Ernie explain it: "I was pretty rough on Tova for the first few years of our marriage because I wouldn't take anything from her. What I mean is, I wouldn't let her give anything to me. What I tended to do, whenever she said anything, was jump all over her: 'What do you mean, I can't do this?' Or: 'What do you mean, this is the way it is. I want *this* to be the way it is.' Or: 'What do you mean, you want to spend the afternoon talking to a friend?'

"I knew what I was doing was wrong, but I had been hurt so many times before. So I had to take it out on somebody—and unknowingly, I took it out on Tova. I didn't mean to, but that's the way it came out, and for that I was truly sorry. I'm still sorry about it, but I think it was a test for both of us too. To test her out and to test me out. I think we both came through with flying colors. She stood by me; her love was that strong. And I learned a lot from how she acted, and I've toned down tremendously."

LEARNING TO TRUST IN EACH OTHER'S LOVE

You have to give trust in order to have trust. But we don't come into the world ready to trust, do we? What—leave my nice safe womb for all these lights and people screaming and blood and noises? Forget it! Yet babies must trust their mothers and the other adults around them for their basic needs, or they will fail to thrive. Trust is a tricky thing to learn, and if you're lucky, you learn it early in life. But if a parent promises a child something and doesn't follow through, that child learns not to trust the parent . . . and also learns how not to be a trustworthy person. Such behavior seems acceptable when we see it in our parents.

Even if you didn't grow up in a house filled with trust, once you become an adult, you soon realize that only when you trust yourself and extend trust to others will you be trusted. I think people respond subliminally to your ability to trust. People who are not trusting will push you away if they sense that you are grounded and secure and trustworthy; they seem to realize almost immediately that you will not fall for their games. A trusting person is just too threatening to someone unable to trust.

I realized this after my marriage to Lou fell apart. I hadn't had much success trusting the men in my life—neither my father nor my stepfather came through for me, and certainly not the man who disappeared when I told him I was pregnant.

I could have stayed bitter and resentful, but instead I chose to deal with this issue, although I found it extremely hard. What did I have to learn about trusting myself so that I could trust others in my life? I asked. Once I figured that out, I was ready to meet a man as wonderful and as open as Ernie. Because I was so unsure about who I was, it took me a long time to find my answer, and my voice. When I felt so insecure I could barely trust myself, how could I learn how to trust someone else? But learning how to trust was an important key to making my marriage to Ernie last.

For any marriage to work, there must be mutual trust and respect. They go together like the couple on the top of a wedding cake. How you trust and respect each other is a true measure of your love, your commitment to intimacy, and your togetherness. If you respect your husband, you trust him; if you lose respect for your husband, you can't trust him anymore.

So how do you build and maintain a profound level of trust in your marriage? It has to start early on in the relationship, and it has to be put into words, loud and clear and often.

Tova's *Secret* 7:

**You have to tell your husband
how much you love him.**

Tell him how much you adore being wed to him, how secure you feel in your relationship because it is based on trust and respect. Put it into words. Tell him often that you trust his love and that his respect for you is responsible for your happiness.

This is what I say to Ernie every day:

- I love you.
- You are my Prince Charming.
- I'm glad I married you.

I say these words without fail, and he says what he wants to me. It's a simple way to show him I love him, and it's effective. He knows I mean what I say.

No matter how much two people feel for each other, no matter what they've shared or lived through, no matter how many places they've been together, and no matter how many years they've been in love, building trust is a process that never ends.

Trust requires being there for each other, and doing it over and over and over again. Don't think for a minute that you can go out and fall in love and get married and come back from the honeymoon and all of a sudden trust is there. Oh no, it doesn't work that way.

Trust has to be earned, like the money in your paycheck.

Let me share two stories that illustrate just what I mean.

TRUST SCENARIO 1:

Mandy is seven months pregnant, feeling fat and unwieldy, even though she is glowing and looking forward to having her baby. But she certainly is not in the mood for sex. Her hormones are going crazy, and she has started obsessing that her husband is going to run off and have an affair just for physical release. She trusts her husband, but she's starting to panic. What should she do?

She should talk to her husband about all of her fears! He'll reassure her, and with any luck they'll have a good laugh together.

This sounds so simple, but it's not always easy to open up, especially when you're feeling vulnerable. Remember how Ernie didn't trust me just because I was having long lunches? He was scared. *Don't let your fears get in the way of your trust.*

(Do realize, though, that some men simply cannot be teased about trust. They see it as a real insult to their integrity, especially if they were raised in rigid homes with high moral values. You should know your husband well enough to be able to gauge his response to your teasing.)

♥ ♥ ♥   𝒯RUST 𝒮CENARIO 2:   ♥ ♥ ♥

Sally and Eric dated for nearly a year, and have been married for three years. They are very happy together, they're planning to have children soon, and Sally feels as if she can tell Eric everything. So when her old boyfriend Tony—the one she'd split up with six months before meeting Eric, the one who'd been an alcoholic and irresponsible in every way that Eric wasn't—called her out of the blue one day, she of course told her husband, then thought no more about it. But a few weeks later, Eric started losing his temper about little things that had never bothered him before. He began making veiled sarcastic comments about some of Sally's friends. When she asked him what was wrong, he told her, "Nothing." But the very next day he picked another fight over something inconsequential. Sally didn't understand what was going on until, in the heat of an argument, he shouted, "You haven't been yourself lately. Not since that Tony called you. I know you are still carrying a torch for him."

"What on earth are you talking about?" Sally cried. "I haven't thought about him in years, and never would have, either, if he hadn't called me. Do you think if I felt one iota of anything about him I would have told you he called?"

Eventually, after a lot of tears on Sally's part, Eric calmed down and was mollified. Sally paid an unfortunate price in learning about her beloved husband's insecurities. Eric is clearly not by nature a trusting man. Did he ask her if she still cared about Tony? No, he chose to brood about it. Should Sally have told him about the call? In retrospect, probably not. Should she have guessed he'd react as he had? She couldn't have, because his trust of her had never been tested before.

The lesson Sally learned was that, even though you are married, there are some things you don't have to share with your husband. Once you get to know the man you married even better, you'll know what subjects he's especially sensitive about, and you can try to avoid bringing them up. Stories about men you were involved with before you met him usually top the list of these subjects. (Like I said, sometimes your husband can act younger than your children!)

Just because you trust someone implicitly doesn't mean you have to tell him everything, or confess all of your secrets. Your secrets are your own to keep. There are those you choose to share and those you choose to keep in your secret heart.

Trust and blind faith are completely different things. Trusting someone takes time and involves a period of trial and error. Blind faith means giving up your power; it's about escaping from reality, expecting some prince sweeping in on his charger to rescue you or save you from yourself. It's not a big step from having blind faith in a man to believing you are not capable of being your own person.

One last point about trust and respect: You need to focus on what your husband *does* do for you and your marriage as opposed to what he *does not* do. If you truly love and trust each other, you understand that your expectations need to be realistic. Just as some days you're glowing and healthy and some days you have a cold and feel awful, some days your marriage will be so great you'll be in raptures, and some days you'll wake up wondering just who that man is lying next to you in bed.

Isn't marriage wonderful?

· 3 ·

Start as You Want to Go On—
And Learn the Rules of Marriage

T HE BEST KIND OF MAR-
riage is a relationship with open communication. But to ensure this
kind of "open" marriage, you need to open your eyes to who your
husband really is. You need to open your ears to what he's really saying.
Seeing clearly and listening closely are two of the best ways to start a
marriage off right.

Here's the challenge, though. Men and women listen differently,
and see each other with different eyes. I've already suggested that it's up
to us to teach men how to be emotionally open and physically close,
how to be empathetic and there for us. But they have something to teach
us about saying what we mean and asking for what we want. Men are
very simple and clear about what they want—if only we *listen* to them!

Part of this learning and listening process is understanding that marriage doesn't turn him into your mirror image, nor does it turn you into his. I like to look at marriage this way: Consider two circles, one for a man and one for a woman. Place these two circles next to each other, just barely touching but not overlapping. Your marriage should be represented by the parts of the two circles that are touching. That's where the bond is.

But once you start to overlap, one of you partially disappears, and two unique individuals become something less than two. Don't get me wrong: Two people in love need to connect, but they also need to support each other's uniqueness. You know how just the barest touch of your husband's hand on your elbow as you move through a crowd of people together can make you feel loved and cared for? That's why the two circles need only to touch to make a loving connection that lasts.

Will these circles ever overlap? Will you ever feel suffocated or invaded? Will the circles ever slip apart, leaving you with a feeling of disconnection? Of course. You're both human, and sometimes you may lose that perfect balance, that point of loving touch. But you can get it back, once you start looking at your marriage as an ongoing, lifelong process. It's fluid, like the weather, or like waves on the beach. You know the tide will come in and go out again, but no matter how high or low it rises and falls, it continues in motion. Your marriage, too, will ebb and flow, but it will be sustained by your commitment to each other. Your marriage will change and evolve over time, but by always trying to remain *open* to the possibility of your love changing, your marriage will enrich you in ways you cannot even imagine. You can do this best if you regard yourself as both independent *and* joined.

START AS YOU WANT TO GO ON

◆ **Jennifer:** When I expressed my fears about not knowing if he was the "love of my life," and wondered about unintentionally meeting someone in the supermarket while buying cauliflower and falling hopelessly in love with him instead, my future husband calmed all my anxieties. He said he trusted my intuition and my intelligence, and that if I decided to walk away from our relationship and our very special love, then he would know it was the right decision and he would abide by it. By giving me complete freedom, he bound me to him forever.

What did Jennifer and her husband do for each other? They started off right.

Start as you want to go on.

In other words, how you and your husband treat each other early in your relationship—when you're passionately in love, when you're courteous and careful with each other's needs and feelings, when you're thrilled to be there for each other—should become the blueprint for your ensuing years together. Of course, you also want to maintain your sense of self, and not lose this sense of self simply because you have a husband in your life.

Bear in mind that getting adjusted to each other takes time. Did you ever go with your husband to a department store to buy a new bed? Did you test it out in public, feeling silly and maybe a bit embarrassed, yet exhilarated and enraptured all at once, knowing this was going to be your very own marital bed? The early days of any marriage can be equally embarrassing and exhilarating. I know a woman who refused to go to bed with the lights on and her makeup off for three years—she couldn't quite bear for her husband to see her that naked!

Marriage is about a meeting of souls, about going to a place deeper than your external self. But it doesn't start out that way—it takes time and work and caring to create that wonderful intimacy. It's a different bond than you will have with any other person. But if you can be patient and learn to enjoy your journey of discovery together, you will become connected to your husband in a way that's extraordinary and unique.

DEEPENING YOUR COMMITMENT
THROUGH GIVE-AND-TAKE

Ernie and I are constantly reinventing our relationship. We've had plenty of ups and downs, but we've always gotten through them because our commitment to each other is unwavering. Because I didn't expect my marriage to fulfill a fantasy, or Ernie to be some kind of man other than the one he is, I gave this marriage a chance to become all it could be.

Like every living thing, your marriage must continue to grow and see its roots deepen, or else it will wither and die. All marriages go through these stages of growth and change: the courtship, the wedding, the honeymoon, settling in and getting used to each other . . . that's when the real work starts. That's when you may feel but find it hard to say, "I'm not quite comfortable with you yet." Or your husband may be experiencing what I call the "I want to embrace everything about you, but sometimes I get scared and want to run away" phase.

Every healthy marriage is fluid and constantly shifting. Things that you thought were excruciatingly important during the first year of your marriage often are forgotten by your fifth year together. And things you never noticed about the man you adore will come to drive you crazy later on!

You can survive these changes and be the stronger and happier for them. But above all else, you must love the man—and live in the moment. It's not going to be an easy job, dealing with your husband's feelings and vulnerabilities and desires (not to mention your own!). You won't be able to measure success in this job the way you can calculate sales figures in your office. You may even come to wonder how people like you and your husband who are so successful in your work relationships can sometimes have a hard time adjusting to and being successful at their relationships with each other. How many times have you wanted to say to your husband, "If only you put one-hundredth of the energy into *us* that you put into your office, we'd have a really great marriage!" STOP. Don't go to that place—trust me, it's not where you want to be.

But if you can accept that marriage is going to be hard . . . that it takes energy and determination . . . and it's not always going to go your way, then you will have a terrific chance to make your marriage very special.

Remember: You're going to make mistakes. Lots of them! Admit when you're wrong and try to laugh about it. I always say, if you and your husband can laugh together, then you can get through just about anything.

CHANGING WHAT YOU CAN

Someone used to say, there are only two things you can be sure of in this world: death and taxes. I want to add a third: *change.* Change is constant, and change is the way we grow. But here's an undeniable truth:

Tova's *Secret* 8:
The only person you can change is yourself.

It's true. You aren't going to change your husband. Give me a moment to explain what I mean. Setting out to change your husband's behavior is an uphill, near-impossible battle—and usually one you can't win. But what you *can* do (and you know I like to focus on that!) is change the way you respond to his behavior. Remember how I described him as the immovable object? But just because he can't be moved doesn't mean he can't change. It's just that *you* can't change him, and it's important to understand that from the very beginning. Your marriage will thrive and be healthy *if* and *only if* you accept your husband as he is.

So let's start at ground zero with this thought: whatever happens to you and your husband, you're in it forever. When I married Ernie, divorce was not going to be an option. I felt very sure of that. And while

nothing terribly hideous (in an emotional sense) has ever happened between Ernie and me, there have certainly been times when the idea of
a wonderful little apartment off on my own and without anybody else
in it has crossed my mind! But only fleetingly. I'm wedded to the man
forever.

There's a great satisfaction in saying that—and meaning it, too. Ernie
and I are bound together for life, for better and for worse. We have in-
dependently chosen to be with each other at a very deep level of loving and caring, and we respect and trust each other. Don't think for a
minute that this bond happened overnight! It came from hard work and
determination, from practicing everything I talk about in this book.
Most of all, it took time.

When people look at me and say, "Oh, Tova, you're so lucky. You've
got a great husband and a great career," I want to answer that luck had
nothing to do with it. Luck isn't nearly as powerful as perseverance and
persistence. My great marriage requires a fierce commitment and a constant give-and-take; my great career has taken twenty years of driving
myself hard to create. I've built my life through years of effort and struggle, combined with the buckets of discipline needed for me to get up
each day, go to my office, or head for the airport because I must be constantly on the road (which takes me away from my husband). Now,
what were you saying about luck?

It takes courage, passion, persistence, and patience to establish a loving and generous marriage. But who ever said it was going to be easy?

Okay, so it's going to take some work. But you're not alone. Let me
share with you a couple of strategies and one special secret to get you
off to a great start.

Tova's Secret 9:
Small steps can take you further than you think.

There's an ancient Chinese proverb I love: The man who removes a mountain begins by carrying away small stones.

A successful marriage is made up of the little things you do for each other. You'll soon discover that it *is* the small steps that count. For instance, because I travel so much, Ernie and I are constantly on the phone to each other. I end every phone call to my husband with "I love you." It's as natural to me now as breathing. And when I close my shows on QVC, I always say "I love you, Ernie," and "I love you, Mama." Saying those three magic little words is like getting a hug, even if it is from afar.

Whenever I say "I love you" during every phone call, I'm not just saying good-bye. Instead, Ernie and I are taking the time to express what we feel for each other. It takes so little to do it, and it gives us so much back.

"You can't just say, 'Bye, honey, I'll talk to you later,' and hang up," Ernie says. "You can't! By always saying 'I love you,' you keep your marriage good. Those three words don't mean you'll set the world on fire. They mean I love you, period."

Have you noticed how often people say, "Oh no, you shouldn't be demonstrative in public, you shouldn't do this, you should play it cool." Well, I don't care what people think. If you feel love, you should always demonstrate that love, and acknowledge it to the world. Smiling is contagious, laughter is contagious, yawning is contagious—and seeing people who are visibly affectionate should lift your spirits and fill you with happiness. (Unless, of course, they're necking in front of you in a movie theater!)

Here's another small step you can do that reaps huge rewards: Acknowledge the little things people do *for* you, and show your gratitude. I always write thank-you notes after I receive a gift, or when someone takes me out to dinner or thinks of me. It takes only a few seconds to write a card and address it and put a stamp on it, and it means so much to the recipient. Once you get into the habit of acknowledging what's good and lovely in your life, you'll find yourself acknowledging what's wonderful about your husband more often than you used to.

Another way to cherish the man you love is to pay attention to how you address each other. It's more than just having pet names. It means recognizing that a few well-chosen words can be more powerful than the most passionate embrace.

Tova's *Strategy* 4:
Practice the vocabulary of love and marriage.

Even if you've never been all that comfortable expressing your feelings in so many words, practice saying these key phrases to your husband. You'll quickly see how words of caring and love can help sustain a happy marriage forever:

♡ *I love you.* You can never say "I love you" often enough to your husband. Say it in words. Say it when he least expects it—in the airport, across the breakfast table, when he steps out of the shower. Put it on little cards or notes and place them in his pockets. Tuck them in his lunch bag. If you keep telling your husband you love him, in words and in notes and in deeds, it will become as natural for you as breathing—and just as necessary. Better still, he'll come to believe it in every cell of his body!

♡ *You are so special.* Not just a little bit special, either. Your husband needs to be *more* special to you than any other man you know, even your father. And for maximum impact, try saying it this way: "You are *so-o-o-o-o* special!"

♡ *You're so sexy, you make me feel sexy.* Not only are you confirming that your husband excites you, but you're also telling him that only he makes you feel your sexiest! Saying this to your husband provides a potent double whammy of reinforcement for both his ego and his (often self-doubting) opinion about his sexual abilities.

♡ *You make me happy, and I want to make you happy.* The male ego is a terribly fragile thing, as I'm sure you already know. Your husband spends a lot more time than you'll ever suspect wondering if you're happy. But what he *really* needs to know is that *he's* making you happy—and that you know it. By making sure he knows that you know that he's the reason you're so happy, you reassure your husband, soothe his fears, and strengthen the commitment between you and him.

♡ *Talk to me—I have something to tell you.* So many of us are always moaning, "He just doesn't talk to me." At the same time, our husbands are busy telling their buddies, "She always wants to talk when I want to read the newspaper. Why does she need this constant reassurance?" There's a lesson in the two sides of this coin: Talk to him when you have something to tell him, but don't overwhelm him by chattering about personal anxieties just so you can tell yourself, "Well, at least we're talking."

♡ *Darling, I need to talk to you.* Save these words for important occasions. And remember: Talking is not nagging. Or pleading or wheedling or whining. Timing is crucial; there is a time and a place for every conversation.

♡ *I want to hug you—and I need you to hug me.* When is it hug time? *All the time.* For your husband, a hug is a moment of reassurance that says, in essence, "I'm here for you." When you need affection, or you feel lonely, or you ache for a physical expression of your loving relationship without making love, hugs can work wonders.

Telling your husband you want to give him a hug is also like saying "I want to make you happy." Sometimes a loving physical gesture can be far more effective than words.

♡

These words of love and connection will make your husband feel like he's the most important person in your life. Isn't he? So how can he not respond in the most wonderful way to you when you make this loving vocabulary an integral part of your daily lives together?

I've got another little list I'd like you to consider. Then, once you've read it carefully, put it away FOREVER. These are words and phrases that can destroy a loving marriage, and you never want to say or hear them:

- I told you so.
- You should have . . .
- You don't respect me.
- My mother told me you'd be . . .
- I hate when you do that.
- You don't really love me.
- You never tell me you love me.
- You're not going to make me.
  And the worst one of all:
- I wish I'd never married you.

- If only you had . . .
- You promised me that . . .
- You never tell me . . .
- My mother warned me about you.
- I'll tell you what kind of man I think you are.
- Have you gained weight?
- I wish I'd never met you.
- I hate your _____. (anything)

Look at them, then do your best to set them aside. Trust me on this: saying these words can only hurt you *and* the man you love.

Having tools to help you build a loving, lasting marriage is a comfort, isn't it? I've been adding to my marriage tool chest for years now, and I've done my best to write down the things that work in the simplest way I know. People who know me know that I'm a romantic at heart, but I'm also very practical. And for me, the most practical advice I know is to work at what *works*.

Since this chapter is about starting your marriage in the best way you can, I think it makes sense to set down here what I call the "Rules of Marriage." They're one of my most important life strategies—and I think you'll agree they make good common sense.

Tova's *Strategy* 5:

**Learn the Rules of Marriage and do
all you can to follow them.**

These rules are designed to help strengthen the very foundation of a marriage. I like to think of these rules as your covenant, as sacred as the vows you made during your wedding ceremony itself.

I suggest that you write these rules down, or photocopy them from this book and carefully put them away in a drawer of your desk or dresser. They are *not* for anyone else to see—not your mother, not your children, not your friends. These rules are a private, special link between a man and woman who have pledged to share their lives.

Without Communication, There Is No Marriage

I warned you earlier that your husband isn't a mind reader. It's unfair to expect your husband to understand what you're feeling if you don't tell him. So talk, and then talk some more . . . but communicate in a nurturing way. Choose your words carefully, and try to explain what you want him to know in an organized way, instead of talking for the sake of hearing your own voice. (This is guaranteed to drive men crazy.)

And if you don't understand something your husband said or did, calmly and gently ask him to explain it. If you're so upset you can't get the words out, compose yourself first, then go to him.

Compromise Is a Must

At the heart of every healthy marriage is a woman who can bend and be flexible, who is open to seeing her husband's point of view. Besides a willingness to do for him because you love him, you should try to find ways to make both of you happy.

Take Responsibility for Your Own Behavior

Be a grown-up, not a child. Don't expect your husband to do everything for you. That's not what marriage is all about. Nor is there any room for blame in your marriage. Arguing about whose fault some problem is never solves anything; it only fills your home with tension and anger. Try to practice self-acceptance; make peace with who you are and what you do.

Keep Your Promises

Your word is your bond, so don't make promises you can't keep. If you say you are going to do something, then try your utmost to do it. If you don't think you can deliver, *say so.* Each promise you make begins building trust. And every time you break a promise, a bit of that trust crumbles away.

I think people quietly keep tabs on where their relationships are going. They keep these personal mental logs, and in them they note each offense. For example: "This is the third time he's canceled a weekend getaway with me. I'm sick of his excuses. I can't take it anymore." Enough of these negative mental notes, and something snaps.

I'll say it again. Don't make promises you can't keep.

Never Assume Anything

No matter how well you know your husband or he knows you, it's impossible to be certain exactly what someone is thinking. Jumping to conclusions or inventing the ending of a particular situation before you know all the facts is guaranteed to cause problems in your marriage. Here's an easy way to remember this rule: Never assume, because it makes an ASS of U and ME. Sort of sums it up, doesn't it?

If, for example, your husband comes home unexpectedly late from work one night, it's only natural for you to have assumed the worst; we all have fears that something might happen to the man we love (was it an accident or infidelity?). If you feel that fear, address it head-on. But don't start yelling at your husband the minute he walks in the door. Before you make assumptions, before you voice any accusations, *ask first*—as calmly as you can! Chances are, the explanation is a simple one, and you'll be more than glad you held your tongue.

Respect Each Other's Need for Privacy

No matter how much you love your husband, you need your own space and time away from him, as he does from you. (And I don't mean space in terms of square footage!) You need this time and space so you can just be you; you need time for your friends as well as time to be alone.

Sometimes this means that, no matter how much I love Ernie, I want to be by myself, and so I sleep in the guest room. He never gets offended when I do; he knows it has nothing to do with him. It's about my respecting my own needs.

Respecting your husband's privacy can be as simple as leaving him alone in the bathroom, even though this may drive you nuts, or you think he's fallen down the drain, he's been in there so long! If your husband chooses to be alone in the bathroom with his thoughts (or whatever else he's doing—I shudder to think!), you *must* respect his wishes. And vice versa. Be sure not to break this rule, unless it's a real emergency.

Let's say you are newly married and money is tight, so you're living (blissfully) in a tiny apartment. What you can do is change spaces. You might say to your husband: "You know, honey, I really need some time alone. Why don't you go out every Thursday night with your friends, and that will give me an evening to myself?" On that Thursday night you can curl up with a nice book or rent a trashy movie or order some Chinese takeout that your husband doesn't like to eat. Or you can swap nights: You might choose Monday as your night to go out with the girls, while your husband's night to go out with the boys is Thursday; this way, you each have your "free" evening and your "friend" evening.

Once you choose your private time, it must be respected by your spouse. If you buy tickets for you and your husband to see a concert on a Thursday night when you know that Thursday night is your husband's poker night, be prepared for fireworks! Respect your husband enough to check with him before making a decision that infringes on his personal time. Simply say: "I know how much your Thursdays mean to you, but there's a concert next Thursday I'd really like to go to with you. For next week only, would it be possible for you to switch your poker night to Wednesday? I'd be very grateful if you could." If he can and does, make sure he knows you're grateful. And if he can't, don't pout or whine that he never wants to go out and do anything with you. Respect his choice and his time. Go to the concert with a friend and enjoy yourself.

Be Conscious of Each Other's Needs, Moods, and Interests

Never forget there are two of you in your marriage, two individuals whose feelings need to be considered by the other. Always talk before you make decisions. Don't just think that because your husband loves you, he'll do anything for you! (I'm not saying he won't, but ask first.) Don't take advantage of his love. And certainly don't take him for granted.

Try to put yourself in your husband's shoes. You certainly wouldn't like it if your husband showed up one evening with three colleagues from work and said, "Hi, honey, look who's here—what's for dinner!" Nor do you want to dump on him the moment he walks in the door, especially if you can tell that he's in a bad mood.

Cherish your husband just as he is. Let him have his hobbies and his friends. (Wait till you read about Ernie and his bus!) Encourage your husband to pursue whatever interests him; creativity is a unique gift that should never be stifled.

Share Decision Making on Major Issues

Maybe you can't always be sure how your husband will feel about something, but early on in your relationship, you need to clarify what you each consider major and minor issues. To one person, going food shopping is a minor issue; to another, it might present a hassle of epic proportions (especially if your husband is the kind of man who has never heard of simple comparison shopping).

I mention shopping here because the act of buying almost anything can quickly turn from a minor issue into a major one (although this depends on what you're buying). You should make a point of sharing decisions on important purchases such as the family car. It's obviously much more important to agree on whether a two-seat sports car or a minivan is more appropriate for your family than it is to squabble over what brand of tissue you need to blow your nose.

How Was Your Day?

You might not think this would qualify as a rule, but it's surprisingly important. Ask your husband about his day when he comes home—or as soon as he's ready to unwind. Show him that you care, that you're vitally interested in everything that's happened to him. Some men have a hard time initiating conversations, especially when they're feeling blue, but they open up when you sympathetically question them. Is this the time to also tell him about your day? Possibly, but it also may not be. Your husband walks in; he's exhausted. He just wants to sit down, put his feet up, relax for a couple of minutes, read the mail, get the office out of his system before dinner. This is not the time for you to jump in with "I have some good news and some bad news." No matter how good the good news is, all your husband will think about is the bad news.

Here's the payoff: If you sweetly ask your husband about his routine every day, he will soon get in the habit of talking to you and being with you instead of plopping down in front of the television. Treat your husband with the same enthusiasm as your young children do. Is there any sound more delightful than hearing your children shout, "Daddy's home!" when he walks through the door?

A man I know confided to me that his wife never turns her head away from her computer to greet him when he gets home. Can you believe this? She can't be bothered to say hello to her own husband. She changes her tune only a few weeks before they're set to go off on vacation together, because she's afraid he won't go away with her if she remains so cold and uncommunicative. As you can imagine, I didn't know what to say to this man. He already knows his marriage is troubled.

What I'm suggesting is that you and your husband treat each other with courtesy, that you always take the care and the time to acknowledge the other person's presence. You might be reading this now and thinking how silly I am even to bring it up . . . that you would never forget to greet your own husband when he walked in the door! But it is all too easy to forget about another person when we're wrapped up in our own needs.

Don't Go to Sleep Angry

If you go to bed mad at each other, your anger will not magically dissipate while you're asleep. Instead, it will disrupt your rest and invade your dreams . . . and then you'll wake up with an angry, unfinished-business hangover. You'll have spent all night stewing; your husband will get up and go to work; the issue that made you angry will still be unresolved; then new anger will feed upon the old anger . . . and what began as a disagreement can escalate into a war.

Ernie can offer some help here. "If there's one piece of advice I've given to young people about to get married, it's this: I told Tova that no matter how mad we get at each other, we always have to turn around and kiss each other at night before going to bed," he says. "Don't go to bed with a heavy heart or with rancor on your mind. Try to tell yourself: 'My husband's not such a bad guy after all. We'll get through this.' "

These rules are meant not only for the early days of your marriage. They're designed to last a lifetime. Share them with your husband, along with my suggestions about the vocabulary of love, and incorporate them into your regular routine. The only thing I ask you *not* to do with these rules is this: When you and your husband are having a fight, *don't* pull out your list and shout, "Rule Number Three says . . . whatever . . . so you better stick to it or else!" Be patient with yourself and with your husband. Take your marriage one day at a time. Try to implement these rules slowly, in stages, one by one.

Then, once you've made the rules your own, you can even renew them regularly (or renew them when you renew your vows—see chapter 9). Perhaps you and your husband can plan a special Rules Weekend once a year, to go over your list and laugh about things that you do or don't do together. You can adapt the list to fit your unique relationship, and with its help, you and your husband will be able to tackle just about any problem or situation that comes your way.

❖ 4 ❖

♡

His Needs and Yours:
Is Everybody Satisfied?

WOULD IT MAKE YOU
laugh if I told you your husband has definite needs, like any man? (You
knew that already, right?) Not only that, but he constantly makes these
needs known to you, like most men. (Right again.) So what do you do
about it? How do you satisfy his needs while satisfying your own?

You see, men are trained to voice their needs: I need to go to work.
I need to see my friends. I need to paint the garage. I need to buy that
new snowmobile or computer. Women, on the other hand, often ignore
their needs and put their energy into fulfilling everyone else's. That's no
way to build a healthy marriage.

Would you like to know a simple way to evaluate how you feel
about what he says he needs? Think about the difference between *desire*

and *obligation*. Of course I can't tell you what you should or shouldn't do about satisfying your husband's specific needs. Only you can decide that. But what keeps the arrangement fair and healthy is that you choose—*choose* being the operative word here—to fulfill these needs. Whatever you do is fine, even if your friends don't agree, as long as what you're doing for him feels okay with *you*.

Being married no longer means you automatically become a man's property. Those days are long gone, but not every man understands that! There's a tremendous difference between wanting to do things for someone because it gives you pleasure—and doing something out of a misguided sense of obligation.

Here's a good exercise: Make a list with two columns. In one column, list "What I think my husband needs." In the other, list: "What I *want* to give him to satisfy these needs." (Not what I *can* give him, but what I am willing and happy to do!)

Beware of overdoing it, though. Some women want to make themselves so needed by their husbands that they turn them into unhappily dependent men. He doesn't know where his socks are, because his wife is so eager to hear him say "Honey, where are my socks?" that she's never told him where the laundry basket is kept.

Is this what you want from your relationship? I don't think so. Eventually you're going to lash out at this childish man—and he's not going to understand why you're so angry. The way to avoid this situation is to remind a man that you're not his mother. Laugh about it, joke about it, but don't let him remain ignorant about those socks! Go ahead and massage his pride (and any other parts if you're so inclined). But don't get trapped into being a permanently on-call housekeeper, laundress, and cook!

So many women seem unable to resist telling themselves and their husbands: "I will take care of the kids, the dog, the canary, the house, the in-laws, my crazy younger brother, the laundry, the cooking, and the shopping. At the same time I will be the perfect hostess, chauffeur, and maid, as well as a goddess in the bedroom. And tomorrow I will take on something more. Go ahead and ask me to do anything—I'm here for you!"

Ask yourself, Are you taking all this on because you really want to? Or because you have a relentless need to feel and say, "Look at what I'm doing for you. . . . If you only knew . . . !" You might be turning your home into martyr central!

Taking on too many responsibilities is usually the result of a woman's fear that she's dispensable; her husband isn't actually saying that she must do this, this, and this by Thursday—but she is saying it to herself. This way she *knows* that at least until Thursday, he can't manage without her! You're better off thinking carefully about a few things you can do for your husband with *all* your love, rather than trying to do everything for him.

Sometimes, I've discovered, the little bit of energy I put into doing something that Ernie needs comes back to me in a million positive ways. I don't do anything to satisfy his needs that compromises any of my own, mind you. At the Borgnines', Ernie is up with the sun, and usually brings me a cup of coffee in the morning, bless him. Maybe in your house, getting up to make your husband breakfast would send him out the door on a happy note. It's for you to decide if doing that for him is worth it. (It might be!) Or it could be something as simple as picking up a can of black olives when you go shopping (even though you hate the smell of them), because your husband loves them. He'll see that can and tell himself, "Isn't she wonderful? Look, she picked up my favorite olives. I know she was thinking of me."

With such a simple gesture, you are making yourself into someone absolutely indispensable, without giving up anything crucial of yourself (or working twenty-four hours a day to do so!). You do want to be needed and appreciated by your husband. But often the best way to do this is willingly giving something of yourself that your husband really needs and likes.

If you are really good with figures, for instance, and you enjoy balancing the checkbook, then do so because it makes you feel good. If you enjoy paying the bills because it gives you a sense of satisfaction, don't stop now. Chances are, your husband will be boasting about your math skills, and joking that the household books would be a shambles if you weren't taking care of them.

This is a terrific example of a woman satisfying the marriage's needs (bill paying) and her own (regular feeling of accomplishment) at the same time.

Let's take a look at someone else's needs for a moment: yours. It is not such a difficult thing to make certain your husband knows that you have needs, goals, and desires, and that you will continue to have them throughout your life and in your marriage. But here's something even the wisest, most happily married women know:

Tova's Secret 10:

If you don't take care of yourself and your needs, nobody else is going to do it for you.

It's time for another checklist. This time, I want you to list all your own needs. List everything you need to make you feel good about yourself. Don't be surprised if it takes you a while to do this, because it may very well be the first time you put such thoughts down on paper.

Hold on to this list and reread it often, so that you don't lose sight of what you need and want—and so that you begin to work at finding ways to fulfill those needs every day of your marriage. If it seems completely unlikely that most of them will ever be met, you may be caught in a caretaking rut, with all your energy put into making your husband happy, keeping the children satisfied, doing what your parents and in-laws expect of you.

How can you get out of this rut you find yourself in? Well, you might try warning yourself that if you don't change, your husband may begin to find you awfully boring after a while. You don't want him saying to himself, "You know, there was something about her when we were dating, she was so exciting . . . but she's not exciting anymore. What happened?"

Think back to what you were doing when you first met your husband. I'll bet you were busy and independent, in charge of your own life. How much of that life did you oh-so-willingly give up once your relationship got serious? Do you really want your husband to feel that your life is about taking care of him . . . in a way that reminds him of his mother? (What if he's always resented his mother?) Once you take over the "mommy" role, that energetic and independent woman your husband was so attracted to in the first place disappears. Take it from me, don't be so willing to give up that piece of yourself because you think your husband expects that of you. A man who expects you to give up everything for him is not the kind of man you want to have in your life.

Instead, you need to work at keeping up your own identity. You must say to yourself, what was I doing when he fell madly and passionately in love with me? It doesn't matter if you were a waitress, a teacher, a lawyer, a chef. *You were working.* Perhaps you were working twenty hours a day just to make ends meet. The point is, you weren't sitting around waiting for him to come home and make you feel glorious. You were taking responsibility for your own life. You brought something of your own to the table.

You can still do that—take responsibility for your own life and pursue what you love—*and* be happily married. Let's consider two scenarios that illustrate what I mean:

♥ ♥ ♥ *N*EEDS *S*CENARIO 1: ♥ ♥ ♥

Ned is the breadwinner in his family, working as a police officer, while his wife, Samantha, has happily stayed home to take care of their two young children. But now that the kids are old enough to be in school much of the day, Samantha doesn't know what to do with herself. At first it was great, because Samantha was able to catch up on some projects, go for long walks with the dog to feel fit and strong, and see her friends for lunch . . . but after a short while she started feeling resentful and bored. As soon as Ned would walk in the door, Samantha would pounce on him. "What did you do today?" she'd say. "Who did you talk to on the phone, what kind of cases did you have?" and so on. Mind you, she had already called his office half a dozen times for some reason or other. All because she was bored; her day became what his day was. She was living *through* Ned, not *for* him and *with* him. She was feeling neglected in every way, and unattended to. And when people feel unattended to, they tend to look *outside* themselves to satisfy their needs—instead of looking *at* themselves. Samantha desperately needed to start tending to her own needs.

None of this was anybody's "fault," of course. Both Ned and Samantha knew this situation couldn't go on, something had to change. So Samantha sat down and wrote a checklist noting what she thought *she* needed now that the kids no longer needed her as much. Using her list, she tried to figure out what she could do that would start to make her feel productive, help her feel good about herself. She remembered how much she'd always liked taking pictures, so she enrolled in a local photography course. The class immediately gave her a new set of interests and goals, and she could keep flexible hours so that she'd still be available for her kids after school. Because she was absorbed in her photography projects, she no longer called Ned so obsessively at work. And because her new interests made her feel better about herself, the more appealing Ned found her.

Clearly Ned and Samantha had to get to a near-crisis point before Samantha began to express her needs and make changes in her life.

♥ ♥ ♥ *M*EEDS *S*CENARIO 2: ♥ ♥ ♥

Morgan has been married to Jason for a year, and she's been struggling with how to express her needs in a way that her husband can understand. She and Jason are both in their thirties, extremely successful professionals, and a bit set in their ways. Naturally, they are in the process of adjusting to married life together.

"The hardest thing for me has been learning how to live my life with Jason without losing my identity," Morgan says. "I've had to adjust my way of thinking, my activities, and my decision-making process into what is best for us as a couple instead of what is best for me. Something that is important to me—an exceptional opportunity at work, for instance, which means more business travel—might not be the same thing my husband thinks is important. This has led to some pretty unbelievable disagreements!

"But I've learned that the most important thing for *us* is for me to communicate my needs to Jason in a way that works for *him*. What I have to do is talk to Jason in his language, otherwise he doesn't quite understand what I'm trying to say, and we both get frustrated. Jason is very cerebral and analytical. He analyzes everything with completely detached logic, while I am much more emotional.

"For example, I can't just say to him, 'I really want to go to this party,' without telling him *why* I want to go. He just doesn't get it! So instead I've learned to say, 'I really want to go to this party, and here are the reasons why: One is because of this, and two is because of that, and three is the most important of all because I would really enjoy . . . whatever.' Then Jason quickly understands what I'm talking about, and we move on from there.

"It's getting easier. I used to feel angry at Jason for not getting it . . . when the truth was, I wasn't giving him enough information so that he *could* get it."

Once you begin to understand and express your needs, you will also learn that it is okay to say "no" sometimes. (Men are much better at this than we are; I think our NO button came off in the genetic wash!) You might have a hard time saying no to your partner, for fear of letting him down. It might also be hard to say no if he's been counting on something in particular. So start with a small no as opposed to a large one. Imagine a man in bed with the flu; he thinks the world is going to stop turning because he feels so awful. You, on the other hand, may think the world is going to stop turning if you dare put your foot down!

Getting that very first no out is the hardest. But all you're saying is *no.* Don't get your lips so twisted that they suddenly turn into *yes.* (This usually happens after wheedling and pleading from your husband and/or children. You start out saying, No, I can't go to dinner tonight. *Please, oh, please, I need you . . . it would mean so much to me.* No, I really can't. *Please, honey, please, just this once.* Oh, all right. . . . Good-bye, no; hello, resentment!

Well, if you've nearly managed to say no and stick to it but find yourself eventually saying yes, don't beat yourself up. So you didn't make it this time. Next time you will. After all, we're not talking about brain surgery here. We're talking about a simple yes or no. But also don't blow a situation all out of proportion so it becomes the equivalent of the apocalypse if you say no. Saying no to a certain question doesn't mean anything more than, "No, I cannot do it *this time."* Be sure to make that clear to your husband!

If this is difficult for you, try this: Once every day for a week, I want you to look in the mirror and say "I have needs."

Say: "I deserve to make these needs known."

Say: "Stating my needs will make my marriage better."

Say: "It's okay to say no sometimes."

Say: "I can please my husband and please myself, too."

You know what they say about practice making perfect. . . .

COPING WITH A MAN'S MOODS
(AND YOUR OWN)

There's a great expression Ernie uses: You're having a "pity party." Doesn't it sound exactly like what it is? It certainly describes me when I'm in a bad mood. Poor, poor, pitiful me!

It's awfully hard to keep your moodiness to yourself. Ernie can smell my moods a mile away. (I start getting edgy and sniping at people—I don't mean to, and I know it's certainly one of my less attractive traits!) He always knows when I'm getting overloaded because he'll hear me say, "I'm sorry, I didn't mean to do what I did, but I can't help it." Once he hears that, he'll laugh and try to snap me out of it.

No matter how much I was struggling with my business or what headaches I'd experienced during the day, I've always tried—and sometimes failed—to keep my work moods out of our house. That doesn't mean I don't find the proper time to talk to Ernie about what's upsetting me.

What's important is that I don't look to my husband to make me feel better when I've had a bad day. It's my responsibility to make myself feel better. Ernie can do whatever he wants to do to ease my tension, but that's his *choice,* not his *responsibility.* There's a big difference there.

At least I can trust my husband not to make my mood worse!

I think women understand moodiness better than men because our hormones kick in at puberty and give us all sorts of wonderful mood-makers like PMS. But men also can get very moody; they just don't often signal their moodiness to us. In fact, men often have problems acknowledging that they are, *in fact,* in a really bad mood. They suffer from what I call TMT—Terrible Mood Time.

The first thing you need to do is identify your husband's TMTs and his TMT patterns. After you've been together for a while, you'll have a pretty good idea of what sets him off. Is he often in a terrible mood as soon as he gets up in the morning, or after he calls his mother or his flaky younger brother? Does he get into a bad mood before meetings,

or after them? Does he have bad moods before he goes on vacation, because leaving what's familiar is difficult for him and he doesn't want to
admit it? Or perhaps his TMT hits about a half hour after he gets home
from work . . . maybe after he's had time to dump his briefcase and
change his clothes and have a soda or a beer. At that point he realizes that
he hates his boss and he's hated his day. And he decides to be in a *really*
bad mood because he knows he's got a captive, receptive audience.

How should you deal with his TMT? In one of two ways:

Tova's *Compromise* 2:

**Ignore your husband's moods and let him work it out
for himself, or else try to help him—it's your choice.**

◆ **Judith:** If I leave him alone for a few minutes, he usually tries to
snap out of it. But if it goes on too long, I tell him to grow up and
stop acting like our five-year-old. Then we can usually laugh about
what's bothering him. I know I'm transferring my role from that of
wife to mother, but I've learned that a little bit of mothering defuses
the situation.

If ignoring him for a while to let him work it out doesn't work, you
could try to help him. Fasten your seat belt and prepare to battle the
storm at his side!

◆ **Cindy:** It's hard to give positive support to your husband at the
same time you want to pop him one for being so self-absorbed. I
don't panic when he's in a state. I know I can coax, charm, or bully
him out of his moody state of mind. Sometimes all he needs is a reminder that this is not the way he really wants to handle the situation.

◆ **Cathy:** I used to say, "What the hell is wrong with you?" and get angry because his bad mood would put *me* in a bad mood. But now what I do is try and bring him out of it. I might say, "Oh, Eddie, you know you look so tired, why don't we just sit down and have our dinner?" Then I add, "What's going on? You seem pretty down about something—is it work?" I'll question him, but lightly. If I see that he's still stuck in it, I'll try and be more teasing, lighten things up.

What about when you're the one in a bad mood? I usually try to deal with the situation that caused my bad mood in the first place. But that's not always possible, because bad moods are so often related to something out of your control. (Which is part of the reason they're *so* infuriating!) If I can't tackle the situation directly, here's what I do instead:

Tova's *Secret* 11:

The best way to click yourself out of a mood is to do the opposite of what you usually do.

Something physical usually helps: How about taking a new class at the gym that forces you to concentrate? Or attacking the grime and dirt in a bout of spring cleaning? Gardening is good—the act of yanking up weeds is savagely satisfying (and burns lots of calories). One of my girl-friends told me she tunes the radio to a disco station, cranks up the volume, then starts dancing and screaming along to really obnoxious songs that would drive her husband absolutely bonkers if he heard them. Asking the kids to join you for a boogie might well clear the air entirely (and give them something to laugh about). Music is a great way to fill your head with something more pleasant than the thoughts that are driving you crazy.

Take a break from your routine and celebrate a little bit. Go do something fun you might never have done before. That could mean anything from playing a round of miniature golf to having a pedicure. A little bit of pampering can do wonders for TMT!

WHAT NOT TO DO WHEN HE'S IN A TERRIBLE MOOD

Remember when I said that what women do is what women need? Well, when women are in a bad mood, they often want to be near someone—usually their husbands. They want someone to nurture them the way they nurture everyone else. It's only natural, therefore, for a woman to feel that because she needs company and solace when she's in TMT, her husband does as well. You see him suffering and of course you want to ease his pain.

Sometimes, though, you just can't. If your husband is the kind who needs to be left alone until his mood lifts, then leave him alone! ! Try not to suffocate him.

Do *not* say, "Oh, don't be in a bad mood . . . you shouldn't be in a bad mood on this beautiful day . . . why are you doing this to me?"

Do *not* say, "Snap out of it."

Your husband is not experiencing TMT on purpose. So he's not going to be able to snap out of anything, and for you to suggest it is only going to get him angrier. Trying to control his mood is like trying to control a horse that's bolting. If you give the horse the reins, all the horse can do is run until he wears himself out. Then he slows down to a trot and goes back to the stables because he's hungry. He wants his oats and his carrots and to be left alone.

In other words, *his* mood is not *your* mood. You are a completely separate entity from your husband, and his moodiness usually has nothing to do with you. He went to work okay, but he came home not okay. Did anything happen between the two of you during the day to cause this? Of course not. A woman who feels confident and trusting in herself will know enough to back off. But a woman who has no real confidence and trust will frequently blame herself. She'll tell herself that she must have done something wrong. Or that she is responsible for fixing it, for making it all better. But she can't fix it because it had nothing to do with her!

Think about that for a moment: She didn't break it, so she can't fix it . . . and the more she tries to fix it, the more her husband will think that she really doesn't understand what he's going through. Instead of being glad she cares about him, he'll convince himself his wife is such a nag.

It's the start of a vicious cycle. The conversation will go something like this:

> *Husband:* I can't stand it when you nag me. I wish you would just leave me alone!
> *Wife:* I was just trying to make you feel better. What's the matter, don't I help you enough?

Now you're both stuck on the bad-mood treadmill and you can't get off. The husband will transfer all of his anger to his wife because she's allowed herself to become the focus of his negative mood. But if she had stayed away from trying to ease that mood, she never would have been caught in that downward spiral in the first place.

I know how hard it is to stay away. I know you only want your husband to feel better, and you believe that you're the best person to help him. Maybe you are. And if you really know your husband, you'll sense whether it's the time to offer assistance or not. Think of his TMT as a tornado. You don't want to be anywhere near a tornado when it's about to touch the ground. You want to be safely protected in your storm cellar.

That's another reason why you must have a strong sense of self. Say you just curl up on the sofa with a book and start reading when he's in a bad mood. If your husband's not used to seeing you do that—remember, he's in TMT and not himself!—imagine what he might say: "I come home upset and look at you, you're sitting there reading. As if you don't even care!"

If he says something like that, stay calm. Don't start fighting, which is what he wants. Acknowledge that he's upset by saying, "Honey, I can see you've had a bad day. I'm going to finish making dinner." Or "Honey, I can see you've had a bad day. Would you like me to do anything?"

Then see what happens.

What if he responds like a big baby? What if he says: "I didn't have a bad day, just leave me alone!"

Say, "Okay, honey." Then leave the room. Don't feed into his TMT. Or you can try saying, "You know what, I'll talk to you later. This is not the conversation I want to have right now. I know you will either talk to me about it or you won't, but remember, it's not about me."

One of the hardest things to do is depersonalize a husband's TMTs. After all, you were raised to be a nurturer—and here is someone you love needing a whole lot of nurturing, help, and concern. Unless you try to help him, you feel as if you're not doing your job . . . and then you feel incompetent. When this happens, your husband's TMT stops being just about his problems, and forces the two of you into a marital struggle that had nothing to do with the mood in the first place.

This is an extremely important point. Teaching yourself to stop taking his TMTs so personally is an excellent exercise to practice. You may be there with him, sharing the same space, but his TMT is not about you.

Too often, when your man gets moody, it taps into your fears. You see your husband turning into a man you don't particularly like, a man you don't feel comfortable with; you see him turning into a man who is selfish and not loving. Your instinct when you're feeling so vulnerable is to blame yourself. But the truth is, you haven't done anything wrong—*he's just in a terrible mood!*

◆ **Corinne:** Get strong! If my husband's in a bad mood, I realize that the blame might be three thousand miles away. When I'm in a bad mood, does he walk around pinning the blame on himself and wondering if he's done something to upset me? Hardly! When six lines are ringing at home and someone is screaming and the dogs are barking, and he calls and says, "How are you, darling?" he doesn't blame himself when I start screaming: "I'M SO BUSY RIGHT NOW! What are you bothering me for? What do you want?" He knows to hang up and talk to me later.

What about lovemaking when your husband's in TMT? It is almost never a good idea to make love with your husband to cheer him up when he is in a bad mood. Because what you're teaching him is that it's okay to have sex when you're angry. But anger and lovemaking never belong together.

That's not to say that perhaps two or three hours later, when he comes to you and apologizes for the foul state he was in when he came home, you can happily accept his apology. You can ask him if he'd like to talk about what was bothering him. You can say, "Would you like to talk about it now, or would you prefer not to talk about it at all?" Give him that option. But don't get insistent and demand that he tell you about everything. That could jolt him right back to the bad mood, and he'll just think you're nagging him, even when you aren't.

Don't expect that he'll always be the same when he's dealing with a bad mood. Some days your husband will feel more like talking, and others he'll simply refuse to say a word.

Just listen, listen, listen, and try to keep any snap judgments out of it.

A last word on dealing with moods: Timing is *so* important. If your husband walks in from work and you can tell he's had a horrible day, that is not the time to tell him you found the perfect little black dress and you want him to go shopping with you to see it. Nor do you want to tell him right then how bad *your* day was—even if it was indescribably horrendous. By being conscious of the situation, you can respond appropriately. Don't let a simple bad mood escalate into a battle royal because you timed your reaction badly.

LET THE KING SIT UPON HIS THRONE, BEING QUEEN IS GOOD ENOUGH FOR ME

I am a great admirer of Queen Margarethe of Denmark. She had just gotten married when her father suddenly died and she was crowned queen. The press immediately jumped all over her: "What are you going to do now that you are queen?" they asked. "Are you going to have your husband, who will never be king, bow to you?"

Her reply? "I have been raised since I was a baby knowing that I was someday to be queen, to carry on the responsibilities for my country," she said. "But at home, my husband comes first. I have no problem being second in my household."

I firmly believe that your husband must always be the king of the castle. And of course there can only be one king. As a wife, it's your responsibility to make certain your husband feels he is the king of his own household.

But—and this is yet another Big But!—letting your husband be king does not mean giving up your power as a woman, or your self-respect. It means recognizing that you have your own role as his queen and wife.

If you don't feel comfortable with the concept of a king and queen, maybe you'd like to think of yourself as the prime minister. The king may be the ruler of his kingdom and he may have all the trappings of power, but the prime minister is really the one making all the important decisions of state. The king is in charge in a symbolic way, just as a male lion is perceived to be the head of the pride, while in reality the lionesses are out there doing all the hunting and rearing of their young.

President Harry Truman had that famous plaque on his desk: The Buck Stops Here. I know that I'm in charge like that when I'm at work. But after a long day I love coming home, where I know Ernie is the king. I don't want to have to be responsible for *everything* in my life!

That's one of *my* needs, and by satisfying it I make my husband happy, too. I like doing for Ernie. I do for him because it gives me great pleasure. It's not about obligation or to be self-serving, but instead because he's my husband and I want to.

It's my choice. It's your choice, too. So often I hear from women: "My husband won't let me be me."

My answer is simple: "You won't let *yourself* be you."

It is perfectly okay to do whatever you like for your husband if it gives you pleasure to do so. I've said it before, and this is a good time to say it again: Your relationship is your own. If your friends and family are critical of what you do, tell them, politely but firmly, to butt out. Ignore their comments and follow your heart. Because when you really love someone, you'll find yourself doing things for and with him that you wouldn't have dreamed of doing when you were single. . . .

❖ 5 ❖

Husband Worship:
Loving Actively and Deeply

I CAME HOME FROM ONE
of my business trips to find that my darling husband had decided to build
a huge wooden deck behind our house, about three thousand square
feet, with planters and lighting—the whole shebang. I told him I
thought it was a great idea and then I stayed out of his way because it
was his project. What do I know about decks?

All Ernie asked me to do was choose some lamps, which I did.
Then I went off on another business trip, and when I came back, I
went out to see how Ernie's pet project was progressing. Imagine my
surprise when I saw these enormous lamps festooned with the most
god-awful gargoyles imaginable.

I must admit that my initial reaction was to say to myself, "I don't
believe it—how could Ernie do this to me? Is he mad to have chosen

those hideous things? They're not what I'd choose in a million years . . . how could he have such horrible taste!" And so on and so forth. But I stopped myself, thought about the situation, and figured out what to do. I plastered a huge sweet smile on my face, walked downstairs to find my husband, and said to him, "Honey, when I was a child, I was frightened of gargoyles, and I've been frightened by them ever since."

Ernie started laughing. He knew I was pulling his leg, but I'd said it with such sweetness that he couldn't argue with me. "But, darling," said he, "the gargoyles were such a great deal!"

"Well, honey," I replied, "if it's a question of money, I'll split the cost with you, because I really don't want gargoyles on our deck."

You can imagine his reply: "But they were such a great deal!" Believe me, hearing that the first time was bad enough. . . .

To make a long story short, Ernie then found some even more hideous gray-white cement chickens that had been terrifying children on a decrepit merry-go-round. Their features had been rubbed off after years of use, and they were altogether so revolting that they almost made the gargoyles look pretty.

"Don't worry, honey, we'll get someone to paint the chickens," announced my husband when he saw the look of sheer amazement on my face.

"Here's the deal," I said, "I'll pay for half the lamps, but the chickens have got to go."

Naturally, Ernie remembers this a little differently: "Tova saw the chickens and she said, 'What do you mean to do with those chickens?' I told her I was going to put the chickens in the back, that they were nice little white chickens. But Tova wouldn't have those chickens for anything. So I offered the chickens to my contractor's little boy. 'Come on,' I said to him, 'don't you want to get up on the chicken?' And the little boy said, no, he didn't, that he would fall off. Then his father looked at me and said, 'What the hell am I going to do with that chicken?' "

That was the end of our patio plaster gargoyles and cement chickens. I hadn't really insulted Ernie's taste or his judgment (although both were rather lacking). Instead of getting mad, I'd disarmed the situation

with humor and good spirits. There were no recriminations, no shouting, no arguing about what could have been a problem. To tell you the
truth, I found Ernie's taste to be, well, *endearing.*

We could have had a huge argument, of course. Whenever husbands or wives make a big decision without consulting their partners,
confusion, anger, and resentment are sure to follow. This time, I chose
to be nice about a chicken, and peace was restored to the Borgnine deck.

And to make up for our banished chickens, I bought Ernie a lovely
hand-painted plate with lots of roosters on it.

Maybe another woman would have been upset about the gargoyles
and the chickens because she thought her neighbors might have
laughed. So this might be a good time to mention how easy it can be
to lose sight of your husband's good qualities because you're lost in
Keeping Up with the Joneses Syndrome. How much time do you waste
in making comparisons to what others have? Do you tell yourself, "Oh,
my girlfriend has all the luck—her husband just bought her a big new
car and makes tons of money, while I can't even balance my checkbook
without worrying."

As soon as you begin to take responsibility for your own life, neighbor envy will diminish. There is no perfect life on this planet, no Utopia
or heaven in some secret place. So vow to make no comparisons and sus-
pend all judgments. On the surface, your girlfriends' lives might seem
better than yours, and maybe they are in some ways. But the reality of
what goes on behind closed doors might easily be a lot less wonderful
than you think. And, besides, you're the lucky one—you're married to
the most wonderful man!

Tova's *Secret* 12:

Focus your attention on your husband.

Instead of obsessing about what other women have, turn your attention to your husband instead. Have you ever noticed a woman really

looking at her man, with all her attention fixed on him with delight? It doesn't matter if she's been married to him for thirty years or thirty minutes; the only person in that room who matters to her is *him*. The minute she enters a room where he has been waiting for her, she locks eyes with him and makes him feel that he is capable of walking on water.

That's what I mean by husband worship: Love him with all your heart—and make sure he knows it! Whenever you go out with him, show him how desirable he is. With words, with glances, with anything you've got, practice a little seduction on your husband. It's not all that difficult. Even if he's talking about something that you find deeply uninteresting, stay by his side and, if you're a good conversationalist, you might quietly steer him around to whatever you want to talk about, but keep your attention focused on him.

This is not manipulation—it's determination. (And it's fun!)

I've met so many women who tell me, "Oh, but that's playing games. I thought women didn't have to do that anymore. Why should we have to use our feminine wiles around men?"

But we *are* feminine—and we know the power of well-chosen words when it comes to our men. I want to be considered both intelligent and feminine, because both those qualities are part of who I am. If you deny your femininity and take your husband's masculinity away from him, you are stripping him of his male ego, his male pride, his *mane*. He's the lion; he's the head of the pride, king of the jungle. Let him be the leader of your pack.

Furthermore, if we have to deny our natural aura of femininity to be loved, how can our relationships with men be fulfilled or fulfilling? I don't want to be a man—I'm proud to be the woman I am. I certainly don't want to drive my husband off by needing to be in charge all the time. (Equality in the workplace is a separate issue. What I'm talking about is capitalizing on your feminine strengths.)

◆ **Cathy:** There was a woman who worked with me who was a ball-buster, a real toughie. She would go after the men, pick fights so if they said something was blue, she would say it was pink, just to get them. And she would look at me with a smirk on her face (as if I was crazy) when I would say to one of our assistants, "Oh, John, do you think you could just help me with this . . . because I thought if we did this and that, it would look really great. I really need your input." Naturally, John would run in circles to do this task for me, and it would get done exactly as I wanted it to be. I got results because I was nice to him and I respected his abilities. Whereas the other woman kept screaming her head off: "John, you better get your ass in gear and do this and this and this or else!" John decided he wasn't going to do anything to help that @$%&! For her, nothing got accomplished.

Not every moment of husband worship is delightful, but sometimes it's about simply being there or going out with him, even when you don't want to. Problems can arise if your husband has a lot of business functions to attend (perhaps with boring colleagues) and he needs you to go with him. This is one of those times when you have to grit your teeth and remember that "for better or worse" sometimes means that "worse" is what you get! You may feel there's nothing more boring than having to socialize with people you'd never choose as your friends, but keep in mind you're doing this for your husband and you'll get through it fine. And he'll appreciate you all the more!

Too many women in this situation build it up in their minds, getting all wound up even before they've left the house. They'd never confess their anxieties or their displeasure to their husbands, of course, but some almost make themselves ill so that they won't have to participate.

If you let your resentment build up, or if you begin to tell yourself your husband's doing this to you on purpose, you've got a real problem. Try to look at it this way: How important are these few hours out of a lifetime, especially when you're doing something to please your husband? Why not try turning it into a game where you laugh together in bed about the people you met and the horrible rubber-chicken dinner?

Whatever you do, don't make yourself into a victim, busy telling yourself that you never get your own way. Don't let this responsibility turn you into a spoiled little girl, pouting and digging in your feet as you cry, *"I don't want to go play there, I don't I don't I don't. You're not going to make me, I'll show you!"* The point is not that you have to go to a boring dinner, but rather that you'll gladly do what your commitment to your husband and your marriage requires of you!

◆ **Frieda:** I think women are making a very big mistake when they choose not to accompany their husbands to business-related functions. Sure, those evenings are often dull as dishwater and may be the last thing you want to do after a long day at your own job, but to me that's not an acceptable excuse. I know far too many women, especially Hollywood wives, who feel that their husbands owe them a living but they owe nothing in return. I feel that if a man is bringing his salary home and sharing it with his wife (who is eagerly spending it), she should be giving something back to him. Especially if it means helping him in his job. What I've heard so often from divorced businessmen is that their marriages ended because they felt they never got any support from their wives. "I was bringing home the paycheck, but she didn't want to work," one told me. "She wanted to spend that money, look nice, have lovely houses everywhere . . . but she wasn't prepared even to come to one dinner a month with me."

Believe me, your husband doesn't always want to go to these functions, either, but he usually has no choice. Your commitment to the man you married means you should go—especially if he asks for your company.

Ironically, these days, I'm the one who usually goes to functions by myself. I like social events much more than Ernie does. It took me years to understand that Ernie really didn't want to go to black-tie charity functions; he doesn't enjoy them the way I do. Ernie prefers to eat in

Italian restaurants where he can wear a pair of slacks and a casual shirt. Years ago, if he had gotten crabby and asked why I *insisted* that he accompany me, I would have been devastated, because I didn't want to do anything to upset him. But I realized that Ernie's displeasure had nothing to do with me. It didn't mean he didn't love me. It just meant he didn't want to go. Now, of course, if the event is truly important to me for my work, I explain this to Ernie; sometimes he grumbles and moans, but eventually he gets all dolled up . . . and usually has a swell time.

MAKING THE LITTLE THINGS COUNT

Husband worship isn't something you save for a special occasion. It isn't about making him feel adored only on special days such as Valentine's Day or your anniversary. You can slip little notes into his briefcase telling him how much you really love him, or one that says, "Thank you for being such a wonderful man." You can write him silly messages in lipstick on the bathroom mirror. You can cook his favorite dinner, or order in that special something he loves to eat—for no other reason than to please him.

You also can surprise him with the unexpected. Let's say you had an argument in the morning; when your husband walks in the door after work that evening, he's probably bracing himself for the argument to continue. Instead, meet him at the door with a big smile and a hug. Tell him how sorry you were that you lost your temper (only if you were in the wrong, of course!) and that tonight you're going to take such good care of him.

Even if he started the fight, ask yourself if your anger or frustration is really worth it. Try to let it go. Making a point of doing nice things for each other and being attentive to each other's needs tend to lessen the number of arguments between a husband and wife. Your lives are so intertwined. By constantly talking about how much you love each other, you'll be reminded of all the things you share, not about your differences.

Why not start a project or hobby together? You can walk for health together, ski together, collect stamps together. These shared activities will add to your marriage's uniqueness—and make you feel even closer to each other.

Isn't it sweet how couples often take on each other's habits, usually without realizing it? Sometimes when Ernie is really tired, he goes, "Uhhsss"—this very melodramatic sigh. Now, whenever I'm in a super-stressful situation, I hear myself going "Uhhsss," just like Ernie. It's extremely attractive, let me tell you!

Many couples find that they develop a special shorthand only they share. Ernie's favorite is saying to me, "Let's go to bed, darling. These people want to go home." The first time he said this when we were having a party in our house, I nearly died of mortification!

❖ **Trudie:** My husband and I have certain eye signals. If we're out with other couples or at an event and one of us gets bored or wants to leave, we connect with our eyes. Then my husband makes his beeper go off—when no one's watching! He announces there's an emergency and we're so sorry but we have to leave. The sense of co-conspiracy makes us laugh.

❖ **Sarah:** We like to let others in on our shorthand. I love making members of our inner circle privy to our own language. It's like having passwords and nicknames as adults and it's really fun.

❖ **John:** My wife and I have our own language. A silly one. For example, I'll say to her: "You wanna do that thing?" "Uh-huh," she'll reply. That means we're going to order Chinese takeout for dinner!

Tova's *Strategy* 6:

Write down the best things about your husband and refer to them often.

Remind yourself regularly what you love most about your husband. Keep a list of these qualities in your wallet, in your top drawer at work, or taped to the bottom of your jar of favorite moisturizer (mine, I hope!). That way, even if you've just had a disagreement, or he is driving you crazy doing one of those silly things he always does that drives you crazy (for me, it's Ernie playing with the loose change in his pocket), look at the list.

Another idea I love is taking a picture of your husband and writing all the things you love best about him on the back. This will become a tangible affirmation of the bond that exists only between the two of you. In addition, why not carry a picture around of how he looked when you first met, next to another one of how he looks now? It's fun to see the progression of your relationship.

Or try writing down one key word about your husband—the quality you love the most. Put this key card in your purse or on your bulletin board at the office. Whenever you look at it, it will reaffirm what attracted you to your husband in the first place. And it will remind you why he's the one!

Ernie has taught me so much about love. I want to share my love with him at every possible moment. Don't you want to do the same for your husband?

Part
Two

Communicating with the Man You Love

"We both used to think that marriage bound two people into one indistinguishable unit. But in our forty-three years together—years that have seen many challenges that have brought us even closer as a couple than when we were first married—we've found that it's still important not to lose our own identities, but to discover them within the marriage."

—ANNE AND KIRK DOUGLAS

♦ 6 ♦

The Inner Makeover:
Why Changing Your Actions
Will Change His Reactions

H AS YOUR HUSBAND EVER
done something that drove you in a mad flurry from the house? Have
you ever found yourself wondering why things haven't gone the way
you thought they would? Have you struggled with disappointment because your fantasies about love and marriage haven't been fulfilled?

You're due for an inner makeover!

When I moved in with Ernie in Los Angeles and gave up my business in Las Vegas, what I call my Brain Thinking clicked into overdrive.
This is what it said: "Oh, Tova, what kind of fool are you this time? . . .
If you give up your career, what are you going to do? . . . You are now
totally dependent on a man. . . . What if you break up? . . . Where
will that leave you? . . . What if you have to start all over again, what
then? . . . What if . . . What if . . ."

So what did I do to shut off this chattering voice in my brain? Did I let this "voice of reason" influence me? You know the answer, of course. I let go of my Brain Thinking, and instead I trusted the feeling in my heart. My Heart Feeling told me that Ernest Borgnine was the best thing that had ever happened to me. And that I must allow whatever was going to happen . . . to happen!

Isn't that what love is all about?

Relationships are all about feeling. You don't get love from thinking about it, you discover love from feeling deeply about someone. You don't develop anger from thinking, you churn with anger from intense feelings about something. What I want you to try to do is shift away from letting your Brain Thinking make your decisions for you . . . and begin giving your instincts, your female intuition, and your inner core—your Heart Feeling—a larger voice.

In other words, I'm telling you to trust your heart.

You see, the minute something happens—maybe your husband says, "Let's go to my brother's house for Thanksgiving this year"—your brain takes off in eighteen different directions simultaneously. All these pictures start forming in your brain . . . and then all of a sudden you are throwing eighteen different pillows at your husband, and he's completely flabbergasted! That's because he's still busy thinking about going to his brother's house, while you've already been there, had a bad time, gotten indigestion, and come home again. Why is it always so much easier to focus on the negative when things don't seem to be the way you want them to be?

Because you're letting your Brain Thinking run away with you! It's what I call Attachment to Outcome. That means you are letting your thinking about potential (and potentially important) outcomes make your decisions for you. Read on, and you'll soon see that there is no room for Attachment to Outcome in a healthy, happy marriage!

I recently read an amazing letter in an advice column from a little girl who didn't realize what an undemonstrative mother she had until she went for a sleep-over at her girlfriend's house. Her friend's mommy tucked both little girls snugly into bed and kissed them both good night. Well, to this little girl, whose own mother was extremely reserved and restrained, such behavior was a revelation. Her own mother had never done such a thing.

Let me tell you how this little girl reacted. Was she hostile and pouting and angry at her mother for "failing" her? Did she "blame" her mother for not being like her girlfriend's? *No.* She said to herself, "Well, if my mommy isn't going to kiss me good night and hug me and tell me she loves me, I'm going to do it to her anyway." And so she did, every day, no matter how hostile her mother's response was. She hugged and kissed her mother in the morning, and when she got home from school, and every night before she went up to bed. Before long, her mother blossomed. How could she not in the face of such generosity and unconditional love from her child (which clearly this mother had not been taught or given by her own parents)?

This little girl used her instinctive Heart Feeling (her instinct and capacity for love), not her Brain Thinking (anger, blame, resentment, jealousy) to woo her own mother. It worked like a charm.

Isn't this a marvelous story? By changing herself and her own actions toward her mother, this wise child transformed herself and her entire family. And she helped her mother realize what an impact a change in her own behavior would have on everyone around her.

When you work with your brain as opposed to your heart, you're apt to take things too personally. You're likely to obsess, to need to reason things out, to try and understand everything someone does. Women are masters at coming up with excuses about why things *aren't* happening. (I think we've been that way ever since the boy we liked in the seventh grade said he'd call us and then didn't!) You're especially likely to do this when you're going through a rough patch and everything is magnified out of proportion. Or when you're feeling vulnerable and your husband says some little thing that upsets you. You perceive it as a personal attack when it's far more likely he was only making conversation about something that had nothing to do with you.

Trusting your Heart Feeling will help you learn how to let go.

I recently saw an interview with Christopher Reeve, who was explaining that before his horrific accident he felt he was too responsible as an actor. He took great pains to have all his lines and marks memorized, and everyone else's, too; his performances became self-conscious as a result. He was constantly watching himself from the outside, *thinking* that someone said he should behave in a particular way, as opposed to simply *being* himself. Well, one of Christopher's drama coaches told him that he needed to be a little more irresponsible. In other words, he wanted Chris to become more at ease with himself. What he needed was Heart Feeling in his acting instead of the Brain Thinking he relied on.

The first thing Ernie tells young people who want to be actors is: "Think with your head and feel with your heart simultaneously. Otherwise it won't work. Then try not to bump into the furniture!"

I want to tell you my favorite story about Ernie changing his focus from Brain Thinking to Heart Feeling: In 1951, Ernie was married to his first wife and living in New York. They had just had an adorable little baby, Nancee. But there were no acting jobs in sight for Ernie, money was scarce, and he was worried and depressed. On a bitterly cold day, he was walking down Seventh Avenue on his way to the post office to see if he could get a job delivering Christmas mail. He had just read this book called *From Here to Eternity* and gone to see his agent to discuss how desperately he wanted to be in the film version. As he walked, he was muttering to himself that, if there was a God in heaven, would he please let him play the role of Fatso Johnson? Ernie just had the feeling it would be the breakthrough role he'd been dreaming of. But so far no one was committing to anything.

Freezing cold, Ernie was bemoaning his fate and wondering how he was going to be able to feed his family. Yes, he was feeling very sorry for himself. Then all of a sudden he smelled something delicious—roasting chestnuts. Ah, how the scent of them immediately recalled images of his mother, standing in her kitchen and humming as she worked. As Ernie kept walking down Seventh Avenue, the scent of the chestnuts was getting richer and stronger, until finally he spotted the vendor with his cart, roasting his chestnuts. Then he saw a sign on the side of the cart that read I DON'T WANT TO SET THE WORLD ON FIRE, I JUST WANT TO KEEP MY NUTS WARM.

That phrase became the philosophy of Ernie's life. He got the part in *From Here to Eternity,* and so many good things followed!

Heart Feeling means letting the moments of your marriage happen spontaneously; if you rely on your brain and create expectations about what these moments are going to be—if you Attach yourself to the Outcome—you will always be disappointed. In a duel between your brain and your heart, your heart usually loses; logic overpowers intuition. But you can change that in yourself. Stop thinking so much about what *might* happen and enjoy the wondrous journey of discovering all about your husband instead.

Tova's *Secret* 13:

Trust your intuition.

We don't trust our instincts enough. Your gut nearly always tries to tell you the right thing to do—if you let it. (But too often we don't let it, because the thought that our gut may be right is too scary!) Instead of analyzing a situation (Brain Thinking), you'll find your body's instinctive response to it (Heart Feeling) is usually going to be most valid.

Going with your gut is not like believing an old wives' tale. If your body is telling you to do something, I think you should at least try to listen to it. Your body is responding for you, because it knows that your brain is getting in the way! After all, there *is* such a thing as muscle memory—what do you think helps you ride a bicycle if you haven't been on one since you were little?

I also think our society has always put too much emphasis on what research studies tell us is true. Intuition is a powerful process of deciphering information, but it is perceived as being "female" as opposed to scientific thinking ("male"). And because intuition can't be measured or manipulated, it can't be absolutely proven to exist. So many people don't believe in it.

Yet your brain can't "think" a stomachache; you can only *feel* it. Your bum knee can *feel* a storm coming, but what if the weather report on the radio says it's going to be a sunny day and you leave your umbrella at home . . . and then get caught in a downpour after work?

Trust your instincts. Remember how it was when you were out there dating, before you met your husband? If your gut was telling you that a man might not be everything he said he was, your gut was usually right . . . wasn't it?

Here's another way your instincts can actually help transform your husband's behavior. Yes, I know I said you can't change him, but you can help him to change!

Tova's *Secret* 14:

Changing your actions will change his reactions.

That marvelous anecdote about Ernie and the chestnuts is not just about trusting your Heart Feeling. It's also about how changing one action brings about a completely different reaction. When Ernie changed his action from moping to patient optimism, he got the reaction he hoped for: the job he wanted more than anything in the world!

As his wife, you have the power to alter your husband's behavior by changing the way you act toward him. When you change yourself and your response to something he does, you set a chain of events in motion.

Let me show you what I mean.

John comes home from work. His wife, Mary, says, "Hi, hon. How are you? How was your day?"

But John's in a terrible mood. He throws his briefcase down and starts yelling because he's so crabby. "You won't believe what a horrible day I've had," he yells.

Mary waits a minute, then says, calmly, "Would you like a drink? Or a cup of tea?" She is not going to feed into John's bad mood. Instead, she does something that takes his mind off his awful day. (But just because she's offering him a drink doesn't mean that she's become John's servant or that she doesn't plan to talk to him about *her* awful day at some point.) John soon calms down and apologizes, and all is well.

What does Mary *want* to do when her husband walks in like that? She wants to scream back at him and tell him what a selfish jerk he is! He's completely unaware and uninterested that she might be in a bad mood, too.

Mary *used* to scream at John like that. Their fights sometimes went on for days, because they kept fueling each other's frustrations. Until Mary decided to change. She realized that as long as she reacted the way she usually did, she became the bad guy. All of John's angst from work immediately got transferred to her—away from his real source of anger (namely, his boss).

By changing her action, Mary immediately changed John's reaction, and peace was restored to the household.

Here's a different situation: There's something you need to talk about with your husband. Let's say that it's about going on vacation. If you have something you're dying to say, instead of letting it well up inside you until you get really angry and annoyed and think you're about to burst into a million pieces of frustration . . . then say it!

But what if you're afraid to have this conversation because you're so busy telling yourself (Brain Thinking) that your husband won't want to go to Aruba (Attachment to Outcome) that you don't know where to start?

When you really need to talk, and the time is right, say so. Just say: "Honey, I really need to talk to you. Could you sit down with me for a few minutes? I'm asking you for some time."

If you need to have this conversation but the time isn't right—your husband might be too tired, for example, to make an important decision—say, "I would really like to talk to you about our vacation, but I see that now isn't a good time. Can we make a date to have a conversation about this?" Then see what happens.

If you want to talk and your husband snaps, "I can't talk to you now—can't you see I'm busy?" don't react to him with anger. Say calmly, "Okay, then please tell me exactly what time you'll be available to talk. Do you think you could talk with me after dinner? Or fifteen minutes from now? You tell me what's a good time for you." Your action will change his reaction. By answering him this way, you're allowing him to feel that he's in control of the conversation, so he won't be intimidated or afraid of what you might want to talk about. It's a very helpful way for you both to get what you want.

Tova's *Compromise* 3:

When you give your husband freedom of choice, he won't feel that you are trying to tell him what to do.

Giving him this "freedom" is a little bit of a trick. It's how you deal with unruly children. By offering a child a choice, he has to pick something—either/or—instead of whining about what he doesn't want to do. So when you offer your husband a choice, he too will have to take his pick. But he will feel that he has the power—which is all he really wants—even if the decision he has to make is as simple as scheduling time to talk about where you're going on vacation!

What you are also saying when you present him with this choice is: This situation will not go away just because you don't want to deal with it now. We are a couple, and we need to be able to communicate and make joint decisions.

MAKING CHANGES TAKES WORK

It's much easier to blame everybody else around you for the problems in your life than admitting it's up to you to make changes. Ouch!
It can really hurt, looking at yourself truthfully and objectively. The first
step, obviously, is to recognize that you *need* to change. Then you take
tiny steps in a new direction and try to do things differently . . . very, very
slowly. You'll have better luck sticking with your new behavior if you
accept that this is not a process that takes place overnight.

◆ **Rosie:** Writing it down on paper was what helped me figure out
what to do. I wrote probably a hundred pages of things about myself and situations in my life, and then I tried to look at my part in
all these situations. I realized, my God, I had played a much bigger
part in my arguments with my husband than I'd ever thought. I was
so busy saying, "Well, he was the cause of *this* problem, and he did
this, and if *that* hadn't happened *I* wouldn't have responded the way
I did." I sure didn't like admitting that I was responsible for so much
of what happened.

That was a tough place to go to. But I got over it. Oh, sure, I got
depressed and cried a lot, but soon I felt better. I realized I wasn't
such a bad person and I wasn't going to make the same mistakes anymore.

Once Rosie confronted herself, she began to look at her husband in
a different light. She didn't want the same problems to happen again, and
she was determined not to let them. Because she made changes in herself, she and her husband both felt happier about their marriage.

Are you willing to change as Rosie did? Do you wonder just how
you can start to break your own patterns? Ask your husband to help you!
Say to him, "You know, honey, I realized that when I do
_____, it really bothers you, but I don't mean to do it. So what
I'd like you to do is help me break this habit. Every time you catch me

doing _____, give me a secret little sign, or come over to me and whisper in my ear. Or just remind me in some quiet, subtle way what we've agreed upon, that I am doing _____ now."

He can hold up a finger or give you a crooked smile or tug his earlobe, something adorable and private. But whatever you decide to do together, it must be done with love. It can't be done in anger. Your husband screaming "How many times have I told you not to interrupt me?" will not stop you from interrupting him again. Make that clear to him from the start.

MANAGING YOUR EXPECTATIONS

(I was going to call this section "A Farewell to Girlish Fantasies, or How to Deal with Change and Face Reality Instead." Kind of a mouthful, I decided, but that *is* what we're going to work on now.)

This is one of my favorite jokes: John goes to church every day for twenty years, praying to God to help him win the lottery. He never wins, and finally gets fed up with the whole thing. Instead of praying, he starts shouting at God, cursing him for abandoning his faithful believer.

"Well, John," a voice suddenly blares out from above, "it would help if you bought a ticket."

Fantasy versus reality—it's the conflict that most of us face every day. We dream of how we'd like our lives to unfold, but no matter how lovely the fantasy, it's life's realities we need to cope with and accept.

We all use fantasies—to help us deal with or avoid the truth, or in order to cope with changes. It's only human nature! We cling to these fantasies because the truth is often too painful, or we don't want to face ourselves. It's easier to focus on a fantasy scenario: *If I get married to him, then everything will be perfect. And once I am married, I'll have that fancy car and a pool and a big house and then I'll be happy. And once I get his big house redecorated and have two perfect children and a golden retriever and a minivan, I'll get a full-time nanny and then I'll be happy. . . .*

Stop, stop! Is it any wonder that some women find their marriage a bitter disappointment? Women can be masters of delusion. They fall in love and blithely say "I do," thinking, "Well, now that I'm married, all my problems will be solved." What kind of an attitude is that? Marriage doesn't solve problems, it often creates new ones.

- ◆ "I won't have to worry about money because he'll take care of me, and he'll pay all the bills," you promise yourself. (So then your finances will become a shambles.)
- ◆ "I won't have to worry about my figure because he'll love me no matter what I look like." (So you'll let yourself go and become unhealthy and unattractive.)
- ◆ "I won't have to treat him with the same loving-kindness I did when we were courting because he married me, didn't he?" (Wrong, wrong, wrong.)

Or the scenario shifts a little bit: "He's fine, he's wonderful—well, as soon as we're married, you'll see, he's going to change," a woman declares. "He'll change because he loves me." In the next breath, this same woman adds, "And if he doesn't, I'm going to make him."

You've already learned that the only person you can ever change is yourself. If you come into marriage with the attitude that you can somehow mold your husband into the man you've always dreamed of, you are not going to have a healthy marriage. If you start out wanting your husband to change his behavior and he doesn't do it, it's all too tempting to ignore the way he's really behaving. You tell yourself it doesn't exist and isn't true . . . because *you* don't want to admit the truth.

At that stage, it's only natural that you are confused and fed up. You'll look at your husband with anger and frustration instead of love, and you'll turn to your fantasies for solace. You'll dream of how wonderful your life would be if only he emerged from his cocoon as the remarkable butterfly you know he can be. Or else you might even dream of what your life would be without him. If only he would change—or disappear! What's wrong with him, anyway? If he changed, then your life would be everything you've ever dreamed of.

Since our marriage, I know that I've changed a lot more than Ernie. The one way Ernie has changed is that he's mellowed. I, on the other hand, have been broadened, emotionally and intellectually, in just about every sense of the word—except in my waistline, thank goodness! I've come to realize that you must *act* to experience life fully; you'll never know all life has to offer if you choose to do things passively, or just sit at home watching television. I've learned to choose from the many options in my life, and that it's my responsibility—and no one else's—to do the choosing.

How else have I changed? I was finally able to look back at my marriage to Lou and understand how I'd let my fantasies make decisions for me. Not unreasonable, given the circumstances of my life, don't you think? But until I was able to let go of some unrealistic ideas about marriage, I couldn't grow up.

HOW WOMEN FANTASIZE ABOUT MEN

There are three basic fantasies women have about men. These fantasies tend to end with a perfect kiss and long before unfortunate reality sets in. Fairy tales almost always end at the "happily ever after." They never show Cinderella and Prince Charming arguing about whose job it is to take out the garbage or put gas in the car. They wouldn't dare describe a night when the Prince doesn't want to make love to Sleeping Beauty. How can they? Then they wouldn't be fantasies!

The Fantasy That Your Husband Will Change

Fantasy: He'll get another job. He'll stop calling his mother twice a day. He'll stop eating like a pig and lose weight. He'll get more stylish and throw out those disgusting old shoes. Our sex life will get better, and he'll be more generous in bed. He won't yell at me so much. He'll be more frugal with his money and stop his impulse buying. He'll love me the way I want to be loved.

Unfortunate Reality: Your husband is not going to change just because you want him to. Your husband will change only when he wants to or is ready to.

The Fantasy That Marriage Changes Everything

Fantasy: As soon as I walk down the aisle, as soon as I pull back my veil and say my vows, my husband is going to become everything I ever dreamed. He's going to be there for me in all the ways I want . . . which I haven't quite told him yet . . . but I know he can figure it out because he loves me so much. He'll know. Now that we're married, he'll love me the way I want to be loved.

And then we'll be able to move into a much bigger house in a much nicer neighborhood after we get back from the honeymoon, because he knows I really don't want to live *here* anymore. He'll borrow the money from his parents—they've got enough, so what's it to them? He'll give up his bowling league because he loves me so much he'll want to be home with me every night.

Unfortunate Reality: Adjusting to life with your husband can be, well, *difficult.* All of a sudden it dawns on you that the wedding itself might have been wonderful, but now you're bound to another person. Another human being is living with you and you have to do things his way as well as your way. No one ever told you it was going to be like this! What have you gotten yourself into? Why haven't all your problems disappeared?

Probably because you have . . .

The Fantasy That You'll Be Taken Care Of

Fantasy: We all dream about some rich man who will sweep us off our feet into happily-ever-after. Or maybe you'll win the lottery—get handed a check for doing absolutely nothing except picking the right numbers. Hallelujah! You're free! No more work, no more commute, no more rushed lunches at your desk, no more idiot co-workers . . . and time to do whatever you want!

Unfortunate Reality: What exactly will you do during all those hours you previously filled with work? If you've been working more than forty hours a week for the past fifteen years, what will replace those forty hours of focused activity? Are you going to go to lunch or shopping with your girlfriends every day? (Oh, wait a minute, they'll get sick of you. Besides, they all still have their jobs.) Will that make you feel okay? Will you take courses? Will you have a baby? How will you expand your mind and make yourself an appealing human being (without losing your sense of self) if you don't *do* anything all day long? How can you retain your power as a woman if you have no economic power, if you're no longer productive?

Women who harbor this fantasy need to be particularly careful not to do what therapists call "merging." We've all known teenage couples who are desperately in love. They're inseparable. They've built an unhealthy cocoon around themselves. Everyone else is an outsider. It feels exciting for a while, but this state can't last, and often leads to disaster.

Don't merge your identity so closely with your husband's that you lose your self in him. Don't stop doing whatever productive "thing" that gives you this sense of identity. At first he may love you even more because you're such an appealing reflection of *him*. But then he'll get bored—because being with you is like looking in a mirror.

MAKING PEACE WITH YOUR FANTASIES

How can you deal with these fantasies? First, by choosing to live in the present, in *reality*. Then ask yourself why it is so important to you to hang on to this illusion. If it *is* so important, try to figure out how to get it yourself.

In other words, you can fulfill your fantasies in two ways: *changing your fantasies to fit your reality,* or *making your fantasies real yourself.* You need to stop expecting your husband to fulfill your fantasies, and face the fact that your fantasies are your responsibility.

Instead of dwelling in fantasyland after your marriage, tell yourself:

- ◆ I know my husband is not going to change after the wedding.
- ◆ I am beginning a new journey with the man I love. I realize there is going to be a period of adjustment, no matter how much we love each other.
- ◆ I am willing to try to evolve and grow, and to change things I don't like about myself. Then my husband and I will learn how to evolve together.
- ◆ I will do my utmost to communicate with him, and compromise when necessary, because I am willing to do whatever I have to do to make our marriage work.
- ◆ This marriage will take more than love. Love is only a fraction of what makes a true marriage.

Being grown up enough to let go of your fantasies is the mark of a healthy adult. Yes, I do believe that fantasies can be useful. Dreaming and imagining about what might be help us move forward, and can be tremendously satisfying (and fun!). Who doesn't want to dream of escaping to a tropical paradise when there's a blizzard howling outside? Nor am I saying that you must give up *all* your fantasies, either; or all of them at once. Fantasies are fine as long as they do not keep you from dealing with the reality of your life. It's when your fantasies get in the way of your marriage that problems ensue.

I've found that being able to let go of an unrealistic fantasy is deeply satisfying—and often *more* satisfying than the fantasy was for me in the first place! That's because the letting-go is a *real thing,* an *accomplishment,* something you have actually done for yourself. Whereas the fantasy didn't ever really exist.

Whenever you accomplish something difficult—letting go of fantasies certainly qualifies!—it gives you a tremendous sense of completion. You are no longer waiting for your husband or anyone else to give to you—you are giving to yourself. You are no longer going to feel as if you can't function without . . . whatever your fantasy was. And you no longer accept the excuse that if your husband couldn't do it for you, there was no reason to go on being married. Once you give up that old fantasy, you'll be able to look at your husband as a true *partner* in your marriage, and not as your caretaker or savior.

Letting go of fantasies can be truly liberating; it can completely change the dynamic of your relationship for the better.

◆ **Lucinda:** When I got married, it was with the fantasy that everything my husband and I did with the house and the children would be split fifty-fifty. But after my husband got a big promotion, he had to put in a lot more hours at work, even go in to the office on weekends. (I was at a stage at my job where I had to work less, for once!) That's when our problems really started. We had many, many weeks where I kept feeling that something wasn't right.

And then my husband finally confessed. He told me, "You love spending all day with the kids, taking them to birthday parties and play dates and shopping; and you know how much I love our children and that I'm willing to do my part and whatever I have to do . . . but I must tell you that this is not my idea of fun."

What my husband was saying, truly, was, "I love my children, but honestly I can take only so much of them."

It's not that he doesn't deeply love our children; he was simply having a hard time admitting that "fathering" them was incredibly difficult. His confession was a big revelation for me. Instantly, I became so much nicer to my husband, not only because he had told me the truth about his feelings (and communicated something that was incredibly difficult for him to come out and say). But because he was right. For us, child care was not something that should be split fifty-fifty. Thinking it should be was *my* fantasy. Not only did I have the time to be with the kids more than my husband did, since my workload was lighter than usual, but I enjoyed the day-to-day work of raising the children more than he did.

Now my husband is so appreciative. It's as if some huge weight had been lifted off his heart. He goes to work on weekend afternoons if he has to, and I no longer give him a hard time about it. And we're all fine. I'm actually easier with the kids as a result, because I don't begrudge either him or them the time we spend together. Even better, my husband now spends as much time with the kids as he can, because he's not feeling any pressure. We're all happier.

Lucinda learned to let go. She'd fantasized that she and her husband would share all the chores—good and bad—of raising their children. But she was wise enough to take a good hard look at her situation and ask herself some tough questions. The reality of her marriage and her husband's needs was so different from her original dreams and hopes. But she let her husband communicate his needs to her and was able to listen objectively to what he had to tell her. Instead of letting her fantasy poison her reality, she let her fantasy go—and it was replaced by something far more fulfilling. Why? Because now she and her husband know they can talk anything through and deal with whatever the future may bring.

Isn't that a great description of a good marriage, one that celebrates trust, communication, compromise, and acceptance? I think so.

Can you imagine what could have happened if Lucinda and her husband didn't trust each other enough to communicate when this kind of serious problem arose? What if Lucinda didn't hear "I love my children" (her husband's Heart Feeling) because she was too busy focusing on his having said "I can take only so much of them" (her Brain Thinking)? If she'd let her Brain Thinking click in, she would have been convinced only of how selfish her husband was, how unfeeling, what a terrible father—a man who didn't want to be there for his own children!

Instead, they experienced a true breakthrough of understanding, after twelve years together. Breakthroughs like this will happen throughout your marriage, you know. Breakthroughs like this *should* happen—if you let them.

❖ **Adriane:** All of my expectations and fantasies about marriage and my husband were superficial, like the ads in glossy magazines: that we'd both have glamorous, high-powered careers, go to lovely cocktail parties with all our fabulous friends, throw barbecues at our summer estate. Most of these will obviously never be realized! In fact, my career was ultimately sacrificed when we had kids. And though I was angry for years, I realize now that we would have grown apart if I'd kept working at that career. This relationship is more rewarding than my job ever was. I never knew love like this was possible, so it was worth it.

There's one more fantasy that many women hang on to for dear life, and it's perhaps the hardest one to give up. Maybe that's why I saved it for the end of this chapter. It's the "C" word—*control*. It can be the most important part of your inner makeover, and the one that will change your relationship with your husband the most. Confronting your feelings about control and powerlessness can be painful, but getting to the heart of your need for control is the key to needing it less.

CONTROL—OUR GUILTY SECRET

Every married couple struggles with control issues, but it's usually the wives who comfort themselves with fantasies of seizing control from dominating husbands. I think it's also because many women feel powerless to control their fates in what is still mostly a man's world.

But control is also an issue for men. If you know that you have no power over a certain situation—an unpleasant boss at work, for example—exerting control at home can make you feel better. It's only natural to want to have some measure of control over the way you live your life. And a take-charge attitude is often a force for good: it's what gets our taxes done, our houses painted, and those thank-you notes written.

But when you try to exert control over your marriage and your husband, the message you're sending is not a loving one. You're saying to your husband, "I will love you as long as I can control you and have my own way." That's setting up a battle nobody wins; it makes love conditional.

Fights about control skew the balance of a marriage. It might start when one of you insists on choosing the movie or the restaurant, without consulting your spouse. Defeated on that, he or she raises the stakes, trying to exert control on larger issues such as your choice of friends or the way you spend your free time.

Some women's control fantasies focus on changing their husbands (yes, that old problem again!). But beware: your husband will react the same way he does to your desire to change him. And he'll run as fast as he can in the opposite direction.

So here's my rather paradoxical suggestion:

> ### Tova's *Compromise* 4:
> **Letting go of your need for control
> will give you more.**

(Bear with me here—I'm not loopy!) Once you relinquish your need to control your husband, it's like magic—it'll come back to you. That's because you're changing your actions, so your husband will automatically change his reactions. When there is no pressure from you to do things your way, he can relax. And a relaxed husband will be a happier and more loving man.

❖ **Roberta:** When I got married to my second husband, I was so grateful to have this other person in my life helping me, especially with my kids. Yet it scared the hell out of me because all of a sudden I didn't have total control over my life. To me, control meant having things the way I wanted them to be. It also meant I was unwilling to admit I'd ever been wrong about *anything*. If I were wrong about X, you see, then maybe I was wrong about Y, and maybe I'd have to concede to someone else's way of doing things.

Then, when I fell in love with my husband, I realized that I had to alter some of my behavior. I noticed that I was very impatient. This sounds so silly, but when I did the dishes, I used Comet on the counters and wiped the sink off and so on. When my husband did the dishes, there would be food stuck on the counters and crumbs on the floor. . . . I'd walk in, and he'd be so proud the dishes were done, but instead of being grateful for his help, the first thing I did was notice the dirty counters and the crumbs. I'd make some comment about the counters, and he would just look at me, his expression clearly saying, "Well, hello to you, too. Thanks for saying thank you."

I'm so lucky that he's patient with me. And thank goodness he's calm and understanding. I have to try very hard to allow him to do things his way, and ignore what bothers me about it. I'm trying to give him praise and thank him for all he does. Because he's actually very happy to do things for me. But it's so hard, almost excruciating! I still have to hold my tongue, just leave the room and remind myself not to get upset, that it's not that big a deal. Because I know that it's *not*.

I am now willing to go to any length to change my controlling behavior so that our marriage can work. My husband deserves that.

Roberta was already feeling defensive and self-protective because her first marriage had ended badly. Her need to be in control was her way of making certain that her surroundings were secure for her own needs. Learning to share her needs and trust her husband was a scary proposition. It meant admitting her own vulnerability.

Let's take a look at two more control situations.

♥ ♥ ♥ TYPICAL CONTROL SCENARIO 1: ♥ ♥ ♥

Jane, a newlywed, phones her mother, crying. "Wally won't wear his wedding ring. Why is he doing this to me?" she asks, sobbing, as her mother listens with a sympathetic ear.

Well, the real reason Wally won't wear his ring is because he's a carpenter, and he works with his hands all day long, and he doesn't like the feel of the ring on his finger. He's also worried about the ring getting caught on a piece of machinery, which could impede his work or even hurt him. Did Jane ask him about this? No—she was too caught up in her need to have her new husband do what she wanted, fulfill her "perfect husband" fantasy. Why was it so important to her that other people see a wedding ring on Wally's finger? Her need to make Wally wear the ring had nothing to do with *him* or her feelings for him, but rather her own insecurities.

♥ ♥ ♥ TYPICAL CONTROL SCENARIO 2: ♥ ♥ ♥

(This one has an Attachment to Outcome twist.) Alice and her husband, Luke, have been invited to a fancy party, and she's been looking forward to it for a long time. She bought a sexy new dress and high heels and a new lipstick. She booked appointments for her hair and nails. Alice spent hours imagining herself at this fabulous bash: "I'll be wearing my lovely new dress and shoes . . . and so-and-so will be there, and isn't she going to be jealous of how splendid I look. . . . I'll show off my new diamond ring, and my this and my that . . . oh, I just can't wait! It's going to be too wonderful for words!"

Until Luke comes home and bursts her fantasy bubble. He is absolutely shattered about a huge problem that suddenly developed at the office. "Darling," he says, "I know how much you were looking forward to tonight, and I'm really sorry, but I just can't go. I've got to go back to the office." Alice is astonished, then angry. She screams, she sulks, she pleads. She'd already lived through an entire made-up version of this fabulous party in anticipation—how dare Luke come in and ruin her fantasy?

Who is trying to control whom here? Alice had a choice: She could have chosen to be a baby and yell and make her husband feel worse than he already does (although, it might be said, he could have called her sooner to give her the bad news), or she could have chosen to be an adult.

What if she'd been mature enough to say: "Honey, I'm really sorry you can't go, and it's too bad you have this problem at work. I'm disappointed, but you know what? I've been looking forward to this party for a long time, and I'm going to go and have a good time. And when people ask where you are, I'll simply tell them that you're tied up with a project, and we're both sorry you can't be here enjoying this event with me."

Alice preferred to hang on to the fantasy in her head—the one she could control. Instead of a pleasant evening diminished only somewhat by her husband's absence, she picked a fight she couldn't win and ruined the party for herself.

Don't let yourself be like Alice. As soon as you recognize your need to control and feel it kicking in, you can start to let go of it. You can start being grateful for what you do have—like the loving man you married who's sorry he let you down.

CONTROL AND CHILDISHNESS

Being a responsible adult doesn't mean you can't hold on to a child-like sense of wonder. That's the good child in all of us, the child of fairy tales, the child of delight and innocence and learning and expectation. I think staying in touch with your "good child" brings joy into the bedroom, where a sense of play and anticipation can add so much to your lovemaking and your intimacy with your husband.

But then there's the bad child, who uses pouting and temper tantrums to get his or her way; who says "I won't do it" and "You can't make me," who's spoiled rotten and deserves a spanking. I find this kind of childish, controlling behavior in adults so unpleasant.

What else do I consider childish behavior? Abdicating all responsibilities is childish. Whining is childish. Using a baby voice to talk to your husband is childish. "Oh, honey," this adult-sized baby will whine, "I don't want to do that . . . why do we have to go there?" I imagine her husband saying to himself: "Who in the world is this creature? The woman I married is not a five-year-old brat."

Hearing that baby voice drives me particularly crazy! I see it as nothing more than a woman manipulating her husband under the guise of being a little child who wants to be taken care of. I also consider it manipulation when a woman plays to her husband's emotional side and insecurities by making him feel guilty about not giving in to her. Once this woman finds her husband's weak spot—the sight of his wife in tears, for example—she can plug right into it when it suits her, and he never knows what hit him.

This kind of childish behavior sends me screaming for the door. Indeed, the best way I've found to deal with a spouse who's acting like a child is to leave the room. If your child starts screaming and kicking his heels in the supermarket, he stops when you walk away. (There's no audience to play to.) Walking away from your husband when he's acting like a child usually does the trick, too.

Of course, if you're the one who's acting out, do try and act your age!

Don't be a little girl about decision making or getting your own way. It's not attractive. Too many marriages break up because of a childish emotionality that has never been confronted and dealt with. As any divorce lawyer will tell you, this degenerates into fighting over objects: "I want that table and that's my chair and I picked that out and you can't have it." Two supposedly sane adults are now acting like kids fighting over toys in kindergarten.

◆ **Catherine:** If I see that my husband is in one of his childish moods, this is what I do. I say to him, "I'll tell you what—I'm going to run out and do a few errands and pick up the groceries . . . and when I come back, I'm hoping I will see a smile on that face. Because if not, I will go right back out again. I don't want to sit around the house all day with you looking that miserable. Hopefully by then you'll have worked out whatever has gotten to you." I don't want his mood taking me over as well.

I think men throw tantrums as their way of being childish, while we women pout and mope. Except for me—I'm a screamer. I know I have a bad temper; mine is far worse than Ed's. I'm very quick to blow, I hate to say—so he knows that once I get started it's going to be a twenty-four-hour ordeal.

When I'm about to take off howling like a freight train, my husband will say: "Now, Cat, let's sit down, I'm going to go through it all with you. Let's talk about why you're so upset." Whatever the problem is, he'll work it out that way with me.

With his help, I've been able to stop acting like such a child when I'm angry, and I'm better able to control my temper. Instead of screaming and yelling, I've learned to take a few deep breaths and say, "Hey, Ed, you know what, let's sit down right now and have a cup of coffee and talk this out."

And then we do.

Good communication is at the heart of every strong marriage. But learning how to communicate what you're feeling—love, anger, desire, frustration—is the real challenge.

· 7 ·

Communication:
Expressing Yourself with Love,
Dealing with Anger,
Finding the Humor in It All

COMMUNICATION. YOU
hear the word all the time, but let's talk about what it really means.

It's a subject of particular sensitivity for me. When I moved to America as a child, able to speak only three words of English, I lost my ability to communicate—and because of that I withdrew into my own little world. It took me years to find my voice, years during which I felt isolated and lonely. Even now, whenever I am feeling emotionally overwhelmed or insecure about something, my natural reaction is to clam up and keep it all inside.

Imagine how difficult it is to sustain a relationship when one or both partners struggle to put emotions and needs into words! If a wife and husband can't talk to each other, how can they ever reach a true level of intimacy in their marriage?

When I was married to Lou, we communicated well only when it involved something that *he* wanted to do or that he was very happy about. Then, because he was in a good mood about what had been decided, we could discuss whatever was on our minds.

Not exactly the ideal marital communication, was it? Neither is it when a couple is gushy and lovey-dovey to each other only after they've made love. That post-coital intimacy doesn't last long.

Good communication is not something you can turn on and off like a faucet. When I was married to Lou, I don't think I ever dared say what I truly needed and wanted. I was too immature, too afraid. And because my needs weren't being met (since I couldn't communicate them to Lou), anger began festering inside me. That kind of frustrated fury eventually explodes—and you tend to blame it for all the bad things that have ever happened to you. My inability to communicate with Lou was like exercising on a Stair-Master. You climb one step and then another, over and over, but in the long run, you're not going anyplace.

With Ernie, I've learned to communicate what I want and need. But it takes practice to get it right.

"The most important thing about Tova and me is that we try to talk about our troubles," Ernie says. "We try to talk to each other as much as possible. She claims we don't sometimes—'Oh, you never listen to me, you never do this,' she'll say, that sort of thing—but I'm way ahead of her. She knows I'm right there with her and I'll do anything I can to help her."

He's right. I am thankful every day of my life for a man like Ernie.

Why is communication such a struggle, even when you've known someone a long time, and you love him? Partly, it's that we often fantasize about the way a conversation will play out. We Attach ourselves to the Outcome. When we do, we've already got the ending worked out before a word is spoken. And then often what happens is, since you've already decided how the conversation is going to go and how it is going to end, you don't bother talking at all.

That's when communication can go from so-so to not-at-all.

Here's what I call a "nothing" scenario: You're going out to dinner on Thursday night, and as your husband is getting ready, he senses that something is not quite right. "What's the matter?" he asks you.

"Nothing," you reply.

He knows it's not nothing. He tries again. "Well, would you like to tell me . . ."

"No, don't worry about me."

"Well, honey, there must be something wrong."

"Oh, it's nothing."

At which point his eyes glaze over at your refusal to discuss it. He walks out of the room, refusing to react to your pouting and infantile behavior.

He's frustrated, and so are you. Not only that, but you're still expecting (or rather, fantasizing) that your husband's going to come running back into the room, sweep you into his arms, beg your forgiveness for not being able to read your mind, and make everything all better again.

But that's not what's going to happen. "Oh, it's nothing" will escalate into "Oh, it's really something," and the fighting will start in earnest. All because you couldn't tell your husband what was bothering you when he asked.

You've got to communicate with your husband! What are you waiting for? If you don't talk to your husband and tell him what you think and feel and want, how is he ever going to know?

Whether you like it or not, you are responsible for initiating conversations with your husband. They don't have to be lengthy or full of your opinions about the news. Just tell him how much he means to you. Tell him what you're feeling after a hard day. Tell him what you want for a birthday present.

Talking to him regularly and encouraging him to respond is a vital part of being married. The better you do it, the better your life together can be. And most of the responsibility for good communication in marriage rests on the wife's shoulders.

Remember when we talked about how great men are at making their needs known? For many, that's the extent of their ability to communicate. Few real-life men connect as well as those super-delightful heroes we remember so well from the movies. Do you know any man who can figure out exactly what you want and need even as he's wining and dining you and dangling diamonds in your martini—not to mention hurrying off to save the world after stupendous sex and changing the baby's diapers? He's a screenwriter's fantasy.

But there are some terrific techniques we all can use to make your very real marriage smoother through better communication. Psychotherapist Joan Child gave me a terrific formula using an "I, not you" model. This will automatically improve your communication skills and can be adjusted to fit any topic. (Try practicing it with a girlfriend or with people at work, if you like, before using it with your husband.)

- ◆ I notice that _____.
  I notice that you've been preoccupied for the last few days.
- ◆ I'm wondering if _____.
  I'm wondering if something's going on at work that I might not be aware of.
- ◆ I'm feeling _____.
  I'm feeling worried about you.
- ◆ I need for us to _____.
  I need for us to talk and share. I love you and care about you.

By using "I," and not "you," this conversation technique automatically shifts away from any hint of blame (as in "You never talk to me") or accusations ("What is your problem?"). The key, of course, is not to make judgments, but to open the door to communication. As soon as your husband thinks he's being blamed or attacked, he will not want to talk to you. But when a conversation occurs in a non-judgmental, non-threatening, and loving manner, your husband will be able to open up to you *without* worrying about being attacked when he's feeling vulnerable.

You don't need me to tell you that men often have an excruciatingly difficult time expressing their feelings. Be sensitive to this; encourage his first tentative steps with warmth. Search between the lines of his conversation and hunt for the matter that is genuinely troubling him. Don't rush in and put words in his mouth. Don't be too hasty with advice. And of course, don't slam the door in his face. He needs to know he can trust you. If you shut him out, or criticize him, or say something sarcastic, or act judgmental when he's expressing himself, then you become untrustworthy in his eyes. You're suddenly someone he has to defend himself against instead of the most devoted ally in his life.

Another therapist friend of mine told me about a couple she was counseling. The wife would come in for a session and say, "No, no, we really love each other. In fact, the relationship is getting better all the time." And then the woman's husband would come in and sit down and say, "You know, I really don't love my wife at all. I haven't loved her for at least the last six months. I don't know why she thinks that I love her."

Then the therapist asks him if he's told his wife this. "Oh, no," he'll say, "no, I didn't, because she didn't ask. I didn't want to hurt her feelings."

Those two could stay unhappily married for years at this rate!

HOW TO DEAL WITH THE STRONG, SILENT TYPE—AND WITH HIS OPPOSITE

If your husband is not a big talker, how do you get him to open up?

First, try positive reinforcement. That's as simple as praising him when he talks. Every time he says something that you know is difficult for him to say but revealing about himself, tell him:

- ❖ It makes me feel so good when you share that with me.
- ❖ I feel so wonderful knowing that. Thank you for telling me.
- ❖ Hearing you say that just makes my day. In fact, that is just about the best thing you could have said to me right now.

❖ That makes me feel so special. I'm so glad I married you. You make me so happy. I wish everyone knew how incredible you are.

Was that so difficult?

On the other hand, what if your husband is one of those talkative types, the central storyteller in any gathering? Getting him to talk isn't the problem—in fact, sometimes you wish he'd just shut up once in a while! But just because he likes to talk doesn't mean he's communicating from his heart. And sometimes he's only telling stories, not communicating with you at all. At those times, the only way you can find out what's bothering him is to *ask*.

When you sense he isn't telling you something, it's easy to start feeling nervous or worried about it, and that makes you even more vulnerable. You click right into the mental overdrive of Brain Thinking, fantasize and obsess about what might be wrong (Attachment to Outcome), or look everywhere for answers. The conversation in your head might go something like this: "He isn't his usual self tonight, therefore he must be having an affair. Or maybe he's upset about something I've done. Or he just doesn't love me anymore."

Why are you doing this to yourself? Maybe he's so burdened with a problem at work that he literally doesn't have the energy or desire to talk about it at home. Or maybe he doesn't want to burden *you* with it. How will you ever know if you don't ask?

There's more to it. Communication is not just about *how* you communicate, but *when*.

"Everywhere Tova goes, she calls me," Ernie says. "She'll say, 'I'm fine, everything is wonderful, and I love you.' Then I know she's safe and sound and everything is okay and I don't worry about her. But there are times when I don't hear from her and, boy, I start to fret. I get itchy until we find each other. And when we do, after that everything is fine."

Although you want to be able to talk to your husband about anything, you know that it's not always possible to do so. Sometimes you need to postpone a conversation to make sure you'll both be ready to give it your best.

Tova's *Secret* 15:

Never talk about money after ten P.M.

Late at night is just not the time to bring up problems. All this does is get your adrenaline pumping, which means you're not going to get a good night's sleep.

In fact, when you talk at night, try not to talk about:

- Children
- Food
- Medical issues
- Money
- Parents, yours and his
- Problems in general
- Sex (good, bad, or lack thereof)
- What he didn't do that day that he was supposed to

So—what *can* you talk about?

- Good friends
- How much you love each other
- Nice things that happened that day

Try doing this—I bet you'll both feel so much more rested and ready to deal with anything the next morning.

Of course, the success of this advice requires that no other "negative energy" has invaded your bedroom. That requires an entirely different strategy. For instance, what should you do if your husband is so mad after a fight that he thumps into bed, turns his back, and refuses to talk?

Try tapping him gently and say: "We don't have to resolve this now, but could we at least talk for the next few minutes so I can have some closure before I go to sleep?"

But what if your darling says no or falls asleep? Try (if you are feeling brave) to wake him up. (Believe me, he will hate to be awakened, and that can trigger a whole new fight.) Don't engage in sniping, but at the very least, say, "Okay, tomorrow morning, when we wake up—could we deal with it then?"

By giving him the option (that old trick again) of discussing things now or in the morning, your husband has to choose: Either he deals with it now and gets it over with, or starts a whole new day with this same old fight. You hope he'll decide that he'd rather get it over with. If he doesn't, don't let him slip out of the house earlier than usual the next morning so that he can avoid talking about it.

(Although I must confess that diligence in the morning has never been one of my strengths!)

DELEGATING AND SHARING

One of the most important communication tasks you face as a couple is to figure out who's good at what chore, or who's willing and able to do it anyway. As the years go by, experts say, all the new "to do" list items end up on the wife's side. Psychologist Dr. Ron Taffel says that women's lists run six times longer than men's. (And that's even when both the husband and wife work.)

Don't let this happen to you! Periodically sit down with your husband and actually write down your chores. Compare notes and reapportion responsibilities as needed. (Maybe it's time he started balancing the checkbook if you've taken on all the cooking. Or vice versa!) Your marriage should be invigorating, not exhausting. If you insist upon taking on too many of its tasks, I can guarantee that your exhaustion won't be good for your relationship.

I ought to know. I am not very good at delegating at the office; I never have been. Delegating also means sharing, something else that many women find hard. Not only do they assume far too large a share of the practical work that goes into running a household, they take on all the emotional burdens as well. We wives tend to want to protect our husbands from taking on too much. I once carried this to a ridiculous extreme. . . .

After a routine mammogram in 1994, I was told that I had a lump in my breast and that it had to come out. The doctors assured me it was nothing serious, and because they did, I chose not to tell Ernie, who was out having a good time vacationing on his bus. I had the lumpectomy as an outpatient, and I wasn't worried at all . . . until the doctor called to tell me about the results. It's cancer, he told me. The dreaded word. And the sooner I had surgery, the better.

It was time to make another choice. I chose not to tell Ernie, who was still blithely driving around in the bus. I *chose* not to share this burden with him. I felt I needed to deal with it first myself.

A few days went by, and I scheduled the surgery. Ernie called me one afternoon as usual. "What's the matter?" he asked.

"What do you mean?" I replied.

"You know, the last couple of days you just haven't sounded right," he said. (He knows me better than I know myself!)

So I told him. He was instantly worried and very upset that I hadn't told him sooner. Then he started trying to figure out how he was going to get his bus from Oregon to Los Angeles in record time so that he could be with me for the surgery. It wasn't that he was angry. Rather, he was justifiably perturbed that I hadn't trusted him enough to confide in him right away. He was more concerned because he was far away and helpless to do anything to comfort me in person the way he wanted to.

Being able to share and communicate my feelings is something I must constantly work on. That *every* wife must constantly work on. If I couldn't openly share all my fears and communicate them to my husband when I became seriously ill, to whom could I turn? Especially with something as serious as breast cancer, which was attacking not only my body, but the very site of my femininity.

Well, once Ernie got home he couldn't do enough for me. He kept saying that he should have known. I said, "Ernie, please, I didn't tell you—so how could you have known?"

He said, "No, I should have known *you*. I've been with you long enough, I should have known instinctively that something was up. I felt it when you were talking to me on the phone, and I just didn't get it."

Would I do the same thing now? No, absolutely not. I wish I had told Ernie the minute I found out. It would have saved both of us a lot of grief. I was busy worrying about protecting him from my crisis, and he responded by worrying about why I couldn't trust and share with him after all this time. It was a very painful lesson to learn.

ANGER AND FIGHTING—HANDLING BOTH WITH FINESSE

Every healthy, happy couple fights. A husband and wife who don't disagree or argue should seem alarming rather than admirable. Their problems are sure to rise to the surface eventually—and then watch out! All intimate relationships must be able to tolerate conflict, but two people who are deeply committed to their relationship learn how to work their disagreements out.

First, though, it's up to you to handle and manage your own anger so that any fighting does not escalate out of control . . . and undermine your love for your husband.

Anger comes from many sources: fear, surprise, worry, jealousy, work pressures, exhaustion, stress, insecurity. We get defensive when we feel vulnerable and alone. Most fights do not start because of the issue at hand, like your husband's forgetting to file his health insurance claims, or your feeling rejected because he'd rather cut the lawn than spend Saturday afternoon sitting on the patio with you. Fighting is almost always about something that has unconsciously triggered a memory of what this person or someone else did or did not do in the past.

We have so many committees running around up there in our heads.

You know what I mean—committees of ourselves at different ages, all vying to be in control and make the decisions. The committees of the three-year-olds and the ten-year-olds are competing with the fifteen-year-olds and the twenty-one-year-olds—and the one who usually wins is the one who can scream the loudest and generate the most anger.

The problem with anger is that it is such an intense drive. When we're mad, we forget about everything outside of that madness. By its very intense nature, anger overrides and tramples anything that has happened before, during, or after a fight.

Every couple discovers that certain things they say or do guarantee a particular response, usually a painful one. And often you find that you can't keep yourself from pushing those buttons, from saying or doing these things over and over and over again. Sometimes it's a test. You're testing your husband to see how much he really loves you (and you want him to care even when you're being awful—that's the point!). So you keep pushing and pushing until you've started a fight.

Why are you doing this to your husband, and why are you doing it to yourself?

We are all the end result of what we've lived through, and that's usually what sets us off. What sends me into a rage, what gets to me every time, is feeling abandoned, that someone is leaving me. It doesn't matter where I am or who does it or how insignificant the incident, my abandonment anxiety is a powerful trigger. It happens so fast, in a millisecond. I have to work extra hard to calm myself and try not to blow up when this happens. I certainly owe Ernie a debt of gratitude for helping me learn how to manage my rage. (He's not responsible for it—so why should I take it out on him?) But I'm still susceptible to these powerful, angry reactions.

Let me tell you about the time Ernie and I nearly let anger get the best of us.

OUR BIG FIGHT

After we'd been married for about three years, Ernie and I had an argument. A big one. It got so bad that I called a cab and got into it with Ernie's blessing. I was going to my mother's, I tearfully announced to him, and I wasn't ever coming back.

The cabdriver took me to the airport. I was sobbing all the way, feeling that this was going to be my last day in the whole world and how could Ernie have done this to me? (I didn't really want to sob in front of the cabdriver, but I couldn't stop crying. Can you believe that I was more worried about what this stranger would think of me than about dealing with my own feelings? *I really was.*) We got to the airport, I opened my purse to pay the driver, and I discovered that my husband had taken my wallet out of it, my credit cards, everything.

So now, what I had been upset about before turned into pure, white-hot rage. Ernie had thought, obviously, that I'd have to turn around and come right back home. Well, I was going to show him!

I must have had enough cash in my pockets to pay the driver. Then I ran into the terminal to find a pay phone. I called Ernie and said a few choice words. *"How could you do this to me?"* was the only thing I can print here. And he said, "Come home, I'll pay for the cab."

"Are you out of your mind?" I said. "I'm on my way to my mother's."

"Well, you can't get there," said he.

And I said, "Just you watch me." And hung up.

Then I called my mother and explained to her how to get me a ticket. Survival I'm good at. I've learned it over many years of experience.

It didn't take very long for me to get the ticket and board the plane, sobbing the entire trip. I sobbed all the way to my mother's and I sobbed all night. Oh, poor, miserable me, crying until the pillow was soaked! I hated myself for having left the house like that. Part of me wanted to get down on my knees and tell Ernie how sorry I was, but at the same time, that little girl in me didn't want to apologize to him at all, ever again, because he had hurt me so much.

In the morning, I picked up the phone, trembling and bleary-eyed, and I called my husband. It seemed as if the phone were ringing forever; I'm sure it didn't but it *felt* that way. Finally there was this abrupt hello from Ernie. (Don't forget what a good actor he is.) "Now, what are you going to do?" he asked me. I told him that I really didn't know. So he told me to come home. That's what I wanted him to say.

As my mother, poor thing, was driving me back to the airport, I realized that this was the first time Ernie and I had been separated. And in such a negative way. Why, the world had stopped turning—why wasn't everyone else crying? How carried away we both were with the sheer momentum of this tragedy! Never mind what started this fight—to this day I can't remember. I only know that it was fairly innocuous when it began, but that soon we were both deeply engrossed in the colossal melodrama we'd created.

I arrived in Los Angeles, and I was very, very nervous. I got into a cab, because Ernie had said he was going to pay for it. My mother had given me some money, just in case. (I think it was about twenty dollars, which wouldn't have gotten me halfway home on the freeway, but I appreciated the gesture.)

I arrived at our house and Ernie did pay for the cab. For the first half hour he was very cold to me. He looked fine, which made me mad. I wanted him to be visibly suffering as I was. I wanted him to look as bad as I did, with my swollen eyes and red cheeks. I'd had to use some of my mother's makeup, and that was the height of calamity for me. To leave the house without my makeup—I mean, please! I do remember that I had a lipstick in my purse, but nothing more.

Well, it took about a day and a half to cool this one off. Then Ernie and I sat down, and we started talking. It was about time, too. Yes, it was hard. Yes, it had been hard to get into bed with him the night before, but it would have been tougher *not* being there with him. As we spoke, my anger slipped away. I understood that whatever Ernie's transgressions had been, the one thing he'd never intended to do was to shame and humiliate me. I was the one who brought all those negative emotions to the table. And as soon as I got upset, I got *even* more upset because I couldn't live with *my own* negative feelings.

So the next time you feel a fight coming on, step back and decide what's really happening. There is the "thing" you two disagree about. And then there are your feelings swirling around. Consider those feelings, but don't blame your husband for creating them. Examined carefully, they'll fade away. You'll be surprised at how suddenly you'll be able to see all sides to the issue. And that's the way you and your husband will begin to change the way you communicate.

I think part of what started this fight was that I was still figuring out who I was, still finding my niche not only as Ernie's wife but as my own woman. And that's a thing you can't hurry. Some people find their niche when they're young, and some people have an epiphany at eighty. Sadly, some don't ever find it at all.

For me, though, that fight and the communication that resulted from it changed our marriage. It strengthened our friendship and deepened our love because we—no, *I*—was forced to face reality and talk to my husband.

Instead of driving us apart, this fight brought us closer together.

ADMITTING MISTAKES AND LEAVING ANGER BEHIND

Anger taps into the patterns of behavior we learned as children. If there was a lot of anger and shouting in your house, either you'll be so used to it that it doesn't bother you (that's what you *say!*), or else at the first raised voice you instantly feel that you are being attacked. You might perceive a situation as *war* when your husband may just be blowing off steam about something. You'll only be able to differentiate between anger that's deep and threatening and anger that's a momentary eruption when you get to know someone really well.

Many men can go ballistic and then twenty seconds later look over and ask you what the matter is. Sometimes they really don't have a clue! Well, *he* may have gotten the anger out of his body, but it is certainly still resonating in *yours*. You can try to drive it from your mind, but being able to silence your emotions is a lot harder. Even when you know his rage is not about you.

I'm sometimes like that myself. Let Ernie explain: "It's hard to leave a room with Tova angry," he claims. "Believe me—she'll follow you! She's a hard-headed Norwegian! Finally I'll just tell her, 'Look, there's the door—don't let it hit you in the ass on the way out.' There'll be a couple of cusswords thrown in between us, but a half hour later she'll call me and say, 'Honey, how are you, is everything okay?' It's all forgotten, you see."

(Well, I never said I was perfect, did I?)

If, on the other hand, your parents did everything possible to internalize their anger—they'd act out by leaving, perhaps—you may find yourself doing everything possible to avoid a scene. You'll only feel comfortable if you can walk away.

A woman raised like this tends to panic during a fight. She just wants it to be over so that she can make nice. She also needs to know that everything is going to be okay again, which unfortunately often keeps the argument going.

When I can't calm myself down, the best thing for me to do is let go. Leave. Go away. Escape the heat of the moment and say: "You know, this is going nowhere. I'm going to go cool off. Let's talk when we both calm down."

But what if your husband persists and says, "I want to talk about it *now*"?

You reply, "Okay, fine, we'll talk, but just not right this minute. We'll continue this discussion in an hour."

If he still persists, don't give in to his bullying. Say, "Okay, we'll talk about it in exactly forty minutes, at eight-forty." Give him a specific time so that he knows you are serious about coming back to him to discuss it. Or try asking him what time he would like to have this talk. Offer him a choice, but stick to your guns. Say calmly, but with assurance, "You know what, I can't deal with this anger now, and you won't be happy if we deal with it now. So let's talk about it at eight-forty."

While you're waiting for that time, go for a walk or sit by yourself in your private space and try to relax. Take a nice warm bubble bath. Light a candle, then rub some sweet-smelling body lotion all over so that you smell delicious. Do whatever you need to do so you can calm down, gather your thoughts, and stay focused. Do not call your best friend and complain about what a monster your husband is. This will keep you in the angry place, torn by negative emotions. Your friend will eagerly support you, and that won't help you work it out. Instead, spend your time considering different ways that initial conversation might have been played out.

> ◆ **Sandra:** It took me a while to figure it out. For the first five years of our marriage I screamed and acted out when I was angry. It never got us anywhere, because all our solutions went toward easing my screaming, as opposed to dealing with the real issue behind it, which my screaming was covering up. Now I wait until I can express myself clearly and quietly say what I need. Amazing how it's changed our relationship!

Part of building a healthy marriage is owning up to mistakes. That means acknowledging them *and* taking responsibility for them.

When your husband apologizes to you, let him know how important it is for you to hear him say that. Acknowledge him. Tell him how proud you are that he did something for you that's really hard for him. If he says, "I'm really sorry," never forget to say, "I really appreciate that you apologized like that. It truly makes me feel good."

And what if, in the heat of anger, you said something you really didn't want to say? Tell your husband, "Yes, I know I said that, and I'm very sorry I did. I don't think I meant it at the time, and I certainly don't mean it now. It must have sounded terrible and hurt you so much when I said it. Please forgive me."

When you *do* apologize, you must really mean it.

It's not "Oh, I'm *so-o-o* sorry," said with sarcasm. Instead, apologize *and* promise to do better. Say, "I'm truly sorry, this is my fault. It got away from me and I apologize. I will try not to act like this again."

Of course, before you apologize, you have to be clear and certain that it really *was* your mistake. If you apologize falsely, then you're going to feel like you're betraying yourself.

Nor do I ever want you to say you're sorry to your husband when you don't even know what you did wrong! If apologizing has been drilled into you from an early age—maybe you were taught that a woman should be deferential to men or maybe your mother always took the blame for everything—you need to work on figuring out why you still do it, and how to stop.

Your husband will know when your apologies are meaningless. If you instantly say you're wrong and grab the blame, your apology is as if you were saying, "Okay, sorry, love you. Okay, sorry, love you." That's a quick-fix solution that will get you nowhere in a hurry. You'll sound more like a parrot than a loving wife, and your real apologies will lose their potency.

When you stand up for yourself in a fight, you are not being a bad wife. When you apologize, or try to understand why the fight happened the way it did, you're not giving up your power. You're not losing your identity. Your husband will know you're not capitulating simply to please him and get the fight over with. You are in essence taking responsibility for what you did do. Even better, you're going a step further: you're acknowledging the pain that you caused and the pain that your husband felt.

Touching is very important after a fight. (Not lovemaking! Anger will never be a good reason to initiate sex; if sex follows fighting, then the two will become inextricably intertwined for all the wrong reasons.) Try to go over to your husband and do whatever makes you feel comfortable—give him a hug, or a peck on the cheek, or rumple his hair, or massage the back of his neck. Snuggle up together. Give him a physical acknowledgment of how sorry you really are.

If your husband's still mad, he might try to push you away . . . but you have to keep at it. You don't want to be overwhelmingly touchy-feely, but after a fight try to touch your husband both *emotionally* and *physically.* You're trying to reestablish closeness in all the ways you can.

Sometimes, taking a break from your routine will help you get the anger out of your system. Try to get away, just you and your husband. Do whatever you can to set aside that special time to be together. Start dating each other again.

AVOIDING THE "OVERWHELMED ZONE"

Even couples who usually communicate well sometimes find themselves fighting over the silliest things. In most cases, it's because life has gotten to be a big pain in the you-know-where, and your instinct is to take it out on someone, *anyone.* Considering how stressed out our lives tend to be, it doesn't take very much at all to send you right off into what I call the Overwhelmed Zone.

At first you might get forgetful, or you might find yourself repeating things, or you might get panicky about little inconsequential whatevers that never bothered you before. In the Overwhelmed Zone, these little things are the first to go. You put the milk in the freezer and the ice in the fridge and then you can't find your keys because you left them in the freezer next to the milk. You *overreact.* Everything starts looking so black. The whole world is coming unglued. In fact, the whole world is going to come to an end if the light turns red before you go through it! Then your husband says something about your nail polish and you scream at him and slam the door.

Hold on.

Calm down.

You are in the Overwhelmed Zone. Once you're there, you tend to lose your temper with the people you love most. You focus your anger and hostility on the people you love instead of the situation that put you in the Overwhelmed Zone in the first place. They're easy targets because they're right there in front of you.

When I get stuck in the Overwhelmed Zone, it's usually because I've taken on too many projects or am unable to say no. I become my own worst enemy. Thank goodness for Ernie, who sees the warning signs that I'm about to erupt and can calm me down. He gives me the confidence to keep going. He is gentle, not judgmental, with me as I approach the point of being overwhelmed. He doesn't accuse me of being a "hysterical woman." And just as important, he doesn't take it personally.

How can you climb out of the Overwhelmed Zone? First, recognize that fatigue makes everything harder. So clear your calendar and make sleep a priority. Taking care of *you* is now your most important job. Delegate responsibilities, schedule time alone, nurturing time. Acknowledge that you *are* overwhelmed.

You may find that your times of feeling overwhelmed are hormonally related. Try charting your menstrual cycles. Watch for signs of PMS. Remind yourself that you've felt this way before and survived; that should reassure you that life will be sunny again.

What you should *not* do, even if it's what you automatically want to do, is walk away from whatever got you so overwhelmed. If you do, you'll be walking right into the Denial Zone. You'll hear yourself saying things like "This is not happening. . . . I have nothing to do with it . . . it's your problem . . . don't ask me. . . ." That's abdicating responsibility. Acting like a child. Making everything worse. Avoid the issue some more, and it becomes a monster that can damage your marriage.

Do not be ashamed of yourself when you are in the Overwhelmed Zone. It happens to everyone! Nor should you feel bad about telling your husband; in fact, it's best if you warn him about your state of mind. Say to him, "Honey, I am really overwhelmed right now, so unless you want to get into big trouble with me, I think you should keep your distance. And please realize, honey, that I love you very much, but this has nothing to do with you. I'll be better soon, as soon as I figure out what to do."

By saying something like this, you have admitted you understand what's happening to you and you've taken responsibility for your own state of mind. You're not blaming your husband for something he can't control or fix, and you have effectively communicated your needs.

Once you've taken steps to preserve your relationship, what you really need to do is focus on why you are so overwhelmed right now. Were you trying to meet a deadline? Did you take on too many things? (Well, who made you take on so many things to begin with?) Can you change anything? Can you delegate? Are you taking on too many commitments because you don't know how to say no, or because you need to be in control of everything? Be honest with yourself, and try to learn how to avoid becoming overwhelmed like this again.

Make sure you're not harboring unrealistic expectations about what you can deliver. Or if you think that you're always giving, giving, giving, and getting nothing back, ask yourself why that is. The other day I had to make a choice: keep on working when I was completely exhausted or get in a tub and collect my thoughts. So I got in the tub. But not without a struggle with myself. That was a huge step for me—to be good to myself and at the same time stop tumbling into the Overwhelmed Zone. And all by simply taking a bath!

Each person copes differently in a time of crisis. Just as when she's feeling moody, I've found that a woman in the Overwhelmed Zone tends to crave the companionship of her husband. Only he can make her feel better. So she might say: "Honey, when I feel this way, I really need you to come over and hug me."

Men, on the other hand, often push their spouses away. They might say, "Sweetheart, when I feel this way, I need to be alone. I know you understand."

Accept and honor these differences in each other. There's no right or wrong here. In fact, by recognizing that, you have taken a giant step forward. Your marriage is growing ever more intimate as you polish your communication skills.

Sure, fights and anger are inevitable. But try to learn from your anger. Use your fighting to help you communicate better, as Ernie and I do. And try your hardest to laugh about it.

WHY HUMOR HELPS

Research tells us that laughter has healing properties, and marriage counselors suggest to couples that they cultivate a sense of playfulness in their relationships. But finding the humor and the play in your life isn't easy for everyone.

As I told you earlier, I almost never played as a child. After the war, I spent all my time with adults. I turned my playtime into work time, and work became my haven and my escape. Well, if you find it hard to play, then it follows that you might very well find it hard to laugh, too. As I got older, I actually had to give myself permission to enjoy people. It took me a long time to be able to tap into and develop my sense of humor.

Ernie, on the other hand, has such a delicious, contagious belly laugh that comedians use him to try out their jokes. They beg him to come to their live shows, because he'll get everybody rolling on the floor, even when the jokes aren't funny. Bless my wonderful husband—he has really helped me learn to laugh and see the humor in any situation.

It's true what they say—the more you laugh, the better you feel. (And remember, it takes more energy to frown than it does to smile!) Taking yourself too seriously can undermine your ability to grow and change and learn. If you can't find the humor in even the most painful situations, life will be a miserable struggle.

Humor can defuse the most difficult situations faced by a married couple. When you and your husband can laugh together, you'll feel closer and able to conquer anything.

When I'm feeling down, I like to watch screwball comedies. One of my favorite scenes ever is from *My Man Godfrey,* when Carole Lombard is jumping up and down on the bed, soaking wet, shrieking as only she can: "Godfrey loves me! Godfrey loves me! He put me in the shower!" It reminds me how romance and humor go wonderfully hand in hand.

Sometimes, though, if I want a really good laugh, I remind myself of this story:

Early in our relationship, when Ernie was filming up in Oregon, I was keeping him company. I did a lot of riding to pass the time and stay fit, and I had fallen in love with a beautiful quarter horse I had named Baron Borgnine. But poor Baron was so thin his ribs were showing, and I wanted to fatten him up. He was also very dusty. As much as I would curry him, he just seemed to have more and more dust on his poor thin body.

Well, every time I went from my hotel to the stable, I would pass a veterinarian's office. One day, I decided to do something about all that dust, and I walked into the vet's office. "Excuse me," I said to the receptionist, "I would like to make an appointment for my horse." She didn't bother to look up at me from the papers she was filing, she just asked me what the matter was.

"I don't think anything's the matter," I replied. "I would just like him to be bathed and fluffed."

At this, the receptionist excused herself and went back to get the vet. He came out and said to me, "If you don't mind, please explain exactly what you'd like for your horse." So I told him all about Baron's dust.

"Are you part of that Hollywood group?" the vet asked.

"Well, I'm part of it, I guess," I said. How did he know? I wondered.

"We don't have those machines to fluff your horse that they have in *Hollywood*," he said. "But have you ever thought about a hose?"

When I repeated this conversation to Ernie, he laughed for hours.

There is a postscript to this story. A few days later, we were in a restaurant for dinner. Ernie's back was to a group at a nearby table, but they were within earshot. One man at the table started talking about some ditzy woman from Hollywood who'd just asked if she could have her horse bathed and fluffed. My God, we realized they were talking about me! Ernie waited until the man was completely finished, walked over to that table, and gave that man one of those infamous Borgnine looks. "That *woman* happens to be my wife!" said Ernie. (Even though we weren't yet married.)

That was the first time Ernie had breathed a word of anything close to a proposal. I was shocked and delighted, and I kept my mouth shut. See how important a little dust can be? (Not to mention a sense of humor!)

❖ 8 ❖

The Seductive Wife:
Discovering the Temptress in You

Ernie can now joke that whenever he went to bed with a woman, he married her. (Hence his four previous wives.) In those days, that was what you did. "My God!" Ernie would tell himself. "I've been intimate with this individual! I must do the right thing!"

Sexual intimacy is the bond that links you to your husband in a way that nothing else does. It fulfills your marriage vows and makes your relationship unique. If you open yourselves fully to each other, it brings you closer every time.

Making love is a wonderful thing. Sex relaxes you and can make you feel positively sublime. It works marvels for your skin; it helps you sleep; it allows you a physical release after a hard day; and it can provide a delectable intimacy that you'll re-create over and over again with your husband.

Sexuality is a natural part of life for every creature on this planet. But just because it's part of nature doesn't mean we instinctively know what to do when we feel sexual attraction for someone. We have only to turn on the television or flip through a magazine to be bombarded with sexual messages, which can confuse the issue even more.

When I first became sexually active, did I know what I was doing? Hardly! I'll never forget how I felt when I first made love to Lou. It was passionate and exhilarating; I was a bit ashamed yet thrilled to be a woman at last. But I had no one to share these experiences with, no one to give me advice or comfort, or share my joy. And obviously I had no one who could counsel me about birth control. For me, sex was like swimming. If you're thrown in the water, you're likely to start swimming and survive, even if all you can muster is a doggy paddle.

And like swimming, sex is something that we, as grown-ups, feel we should have mastered years ago. But maybe you didn't. Maybe no one ever made you feel comfortable or free during lovemaking. Are you feeling just a little bit bored? Maybe you'd like to add something new to your repertoire. It's okay to admit it—are you a little worried that the sexual "rut" you're in will be the place you and your husband spend the rest of your marriage?

Not likely! Not if you decide a great sex life is worth fighting for!

KEEPING BOREDOM OUT
OF THE BEDROOM

No matter what your body looks like or how "experienced" you are, it is almost impossible not to be inhibited the first time you take your clothes off and get into bed with a new man. Compound this with natural shyness (which I have in abundance . . .) and, well, it was very awkward with Ernie in the beginning. We were two people who wanted very much to be with and belong to each other, yet we didn't quite know what to say or what to do. There was something very endearing and sweet about our efforts to please each other. We soon grew more comfortable in bed together, and our lovemaking got better and more satisfying every time.

I'm lucky that Ernie is very affectionate and imaginative in the bedroom. He's also very protective, so I feel safe with him, which has always made it fun to try new things. But not all men are like Ernie. And even though we love each other passionately, there comes a time for every long-married couple when a certain sameness creeps into the bedroom. Monogamy can be tremendously satisfying from a psychological perspective—the idea of vows and bonding and a firm pledge to each other—but I've never met one married couple who didn't, from time to time, worry that their sex life had become uninspired. It happens to all of us.

But be warned: Boredom starts with you, not with what you do in your bed. If you are bored with yourself, that will not only spill over into the bedroom but put a damper on your entire marriage. So before we start blaming our husbands for lackluster performances, let's get in touch with our own sexual needs and desires.

Some women are sexually inhibited, others aren't. Some women can talk to their girlfriends about sex, some can't. Some women are comfortable reading sexually explicit books or renting sexually explicit movies to get ideas from them; some find them embarrassingly graphic or even offensive. You need to find your level of comfort, but before you decide, hear me out: Looking for sources of sexual information is not a criticism of your husband's lovemaking techniques. It's a chance for you to think about new ways to give each other pleasure. "Well, well, I haven't thought of that kind of kissing," you might say after glancing through a book on sexual play. "Let's see if that will be fun!"

I'd like you to draw up another one of my famous checklists. Choose a time you can be alone, and answer these questions:

- What do I need to enjoy an exciting sexual relationship?
- What does my husband do that I really like?
- What do I wish he would do?

Don't approach this exercise from a "me" place. Instead, try to write from an "us" point of view. After all, you've chosen to be together in bed *and* in life.

If, like so many of us, you have a hard time expressing your sexual needs and desires, don't expect to change overnight—even if you want to! Be creative—if you have trouble talking about sex, try a bookmark placed in an illustrated book to show your husband what you would enjoy, or highlight a section or story with a yellow marker. Set some time aside to read these books together in the privacy of your bedroom. Go ahead, be brave—read some of the passages out loud. Chances are, you'll be rolling off the bed, collapsing in giggles. Great! Laughter is among the best kinds of foreplay. Laughing together about sex, especially if you are inhibited or shy, is one of the best ways to relax you and get things going.

Tell your husband what you like in bed—in words *and* by the way you respond to him. Try, and keep trying, until you get your message across. It's never too late to embark on your great sexual adventure to-gether. If learning and exploring are done with love and laughter, you'll feel that you can conquer the world!

Try not to be self-conscious in bed. Many women are far too crit-ical of their bodies. If you've gained a few pounds, chances are your hus-band hasn't even noticed. (If you've gained a lot, that's a health issue you'll want to tackle separately. But when you're in bed with your hus-band, focus on how you feel about him—not on your imperfections.) Above all, don't deny yourself the pleasure of intimacy with your hus-band because you're obsessed with losing ten pounds.

Do you ever find yourself thinking during lovemaking, *I know you want me to do this for you, but I really don't feel comfortable when I'm doing it.* Or *Why do you keep asking me for that? I know I'm not gonna like it but I'll have to try and fake it because you want it so much. And I can't even get mad at you, because I haven't told you what I like . . . but why can't you just* know *what I like?*

Whew! No wonder you're not having fun yet!

Lovemaking, like so much else you'll tackle in your marriage, is often all about compromise. It can be a fluid thing: You'll give him what he really wants this time and next time it'll be all about what pleases you. But remember, compromise can't work without *communication!* Your husband needs you to show him and tell him what you're feeling.

For many women, the innate need to nurture carries over into the bedroom as well. Have you ever decided to fake an orgasm simply to give your husband pleasure and massage his ego? Did you tell yourself this was just one more way you were taking care of his needs?

You're not alone if you did. But the bedroom is where this attitude must stop. You need to be able to be honest with your partner, to be able to say (if it's how you're feeling), "Honey, this isn't okay. It's not good for me."

Let's say your husband really likes to do certain things when he's making love to you, and always has, but you're really not that crazy about them, or they don't give you pleasure. You want to please him, but of course you also want to please yourself. That calls for compromise. There's no clear-cut right or wrong, only what works for the two of you.

Even if you never have before, take responsibility for having fun in the bedroom. If you say to your husband, "Honey, let's try something new," or "Oh, that movie scene got me so excited," I'm sure he'll want to follow your lead—and thrills and chills for both of you will ensue! Maybe next time he'll even say, "That was so much fun last time, let's do it again." Or "Let's try this. . . ." All because *you* took the initiative.

If you trust your husband, then his desire to add anything new to your lovemaking should not fill you with apprehension. The best sex is all about mutual pleasure, don't forget.

But let's say that your husband, inspired by your response, takes the lead next time and says, "Okay, now let's try this." But "this" isn't something you find arousing. Don't panic! Tell your husband, "Well, that's not exactly what I had in mind." Just don't start screaming, "I can't believe you want to do that to me. What kind of man are you? That's sick!" in the middle of a clinch. Simply tell your husband that "this" is uncomfortable and you want to stop. Communicate without criticizing, and then shift into something you do enjoy.

You might simply say, "You know, some of the things we've tried lately have been really fabulous. But this, well, honey, it doesn't really thrill me the way *this does.*" And then you can show him exactly what you like. In this manner you are clearly expressing your needs and preferences without deflating your husband's vulnerable ego in bed.

Here's the thing: If you're feeling good about yourself and you make it clear, your husband will feel good, too. He'll know he's pleasing you, and just that little bit of feedback will rev him right up again! How simple it is to be kind and generous with your praise . . . and how desperately your husband needs to hear it all the time, whether you think he does or not! And how rich the rewards will be for both of you.

Of course, the opposite is true as well. If you're not feeling good about your lovemaking, this will come across loud and clear to your husband. And instead of bringing you closer together, sex may drive you apart.

But it doesn't have to! If you have trouble achieving simultaneous orgasms—like most people on this planet—you could tell your husband so, in a loving and non-threatening way. Or better yet, stop worrying about it. Some couples actually prefer to reach climax separately so each can enjoy watching the other's pleasure!

But if you want to experiment, why not switch around the pattern or the timing of your lovemaking? If you always make love on Saturday night, imagine his surprise when you wake him up on a Thursday morning eager for a little sex before work! If you usually like to be on top, let him be on top, and vice versa. Head for the kitchen and enjoy a late-night snack *in the nude.* Tackle him on the living room couch after the kids are asleep. Or if you're worried that'll wake the kids, see what you can do in the bathtub or the shower. Do the unexpected, and enjoy the fireworks you set off.

Avoiding boredom is easy if you do what I try to do, which is look at every sexual encounter with new eyes. I don't spend time thinking, *Why isn't he the same way he was last time?* I don't say, "Hmm, he did that before—why isn't he doing it again?" Stay in the present instead of focusing on what you've done another time.

It's just as important not to let your fantasies overtake your reality. Catch yourself asking why your lovemaking doesn't seem as exciting as it looks in your favorite soap opera or movie. Why can't your husband pucker up like Robert Redford or George Clooney? you may wonder.

Probably because real life is not a movie, that's why. And it's time for you to stop expecting it to be. But that doesn't mean it can't be wonderful—it can be. It's just that making it so in real life will take some effort from you.

PLAYING FOR KEEPS

One of the most wonderful aspects of lovemaking is not just the physical pleasure you can give each other but the sense of play and intimacy. You should always want to have fun in bed. And part of that fun is learning and exploring and touching your husband in all kinds of ways. Yes, I'm talking about foreplay.

(Frankly, I think foreplay should be respelled as "for play.")

Foreplay allows you to be silly and childlike with wonder; it offers a way for you to be as spontaneous as you can possibly be with each other. Foreplay is about feeling free and having as much fun as possible. It should be as adventurous as you can possibly make it.

Foreplay can go on all day, building your anticipation for lovemaking later on. But when you've been with someone for a long time, you tend to forget the windup. You go straight to the pitch. Yet foreplay often can be more satisfying, more intimate, and more generous than intercourse itself.

Foreplay can start in the morning and last until just before bed, believe it or not. Let's say it's Monday morning and you're both crabby at the thought of getting up early and going to work. Leave your husband a little note in his pocket. On it, write: "Tonight we're going to do something really wild." Then call him in the middle of the day and tell him you can't wait for him to get home. I assure you he'll do his best to arrive home early!

Or you could call him up in the middle of the day and say, "You know, I'm in my office, sweetheart, but I just thought you might want to know that I'm not wearing any underwear." (Maybe you are—you just want to tease him a little.) By planting this sexy little notion in his head, you've initiated an all-workday-long tease. If he's out of town or you are, you might enjoy a lengthy sexual interlude on the telephone where simply what you say to each other can drive you wild.

Often the most seductive ways to get his attention are when you're apart. Don't forget the power of your voice every time you speak to him, or the potency of your sexy suggestions. Leave sweet and subtle messages on your husband's voice mail (as long as you know they won't be intercepted by anyone else at work). Use special code words that only he will understand. Write him a love letter that you seal with ruby red wax. Send him long-stemmed roses in a box at work, for no reason other than you love him.

Sometimes frustration can be the most delicious foreplay, the ultimate tease. Tell your husband you're not going to "go all the way" with him tonight. All you can do is touch each other. And then tell him the next day you're going to touch each other a little bit more and give him a massage. And then the day after that . . .

You get the picture. The goal is to break out of your routine.

But remember that every marriage goes through its ups and downs, and that the sexual part of your relationship has its own ebb and flow. Sometimes, if you're under a lot of stress at work, you may not feel like making love. On the other hand, if your husband tells you he's not in the mood, don't assume he doesn't want to make love to you because he doesn't find you sexy anymore. Most likely he really is tired.

Keep in mind that humor can defuse the stickiest sexual situations.

It's important to be able to say, "I feel so silly" or "Look what I did—can you believe it!" Sometimes things happen during sex that feel awkward or embarrassing—you made a funny noise, he slid off the silk sheets you bought. But sharing the humor brings you together in a special way. And laughter in bed can be as delicious as making love.

It's okay to have a vivid fantasy life, too. It's all right to fantasize about Sean Connery, even when you're in bed with your husband—as long as these fantasies don't get in the way of reality. If your fantasies stimulate you and give you pleasure, then enjoy them with every ounce of your being. But if they become so potent that you wonder about acting them out—a flirtation with a co-worker that could escalate into an affair, for instance—ask yourself what you really want *before* you head for trouble.

And if any particular sexual act causes you problems, you may want to see a qualified therapist. Counseling can help liberate you from your discomfort, especially if you were brought up in a sexually inhibited environment. Were you taught that some things are wrong for women to enjoy in bed, or that good girls don't do things like that? (For instance, most men greatly enjoy oral sex, but some women find even the thought of it intensely uncomfortable.) Don't let your inhibitions deny you one of the greatest pleasures in this world—being truly intimate with your husband.

WHO IS THIS MAN IN BED WITH YOU?

Some men are great drivers and great dancers, purely by instinct. Others can't drive a car without driving you crazy, or they have two left feet so clumsy they'd never know the difference between a rhumba and a stalk of rhubarb. It's the same with lovemaking—some men are masters in bed (or think they are) while others have a rather limited repertoire and are not by nature what you might call world-class lovers. It's not that they don't have the ability; it's just that they never learned how.

I think it's fair to say that most men are as frightened as women are about their own sexuality. (Part of this is purely anatomical; they certainly can't fake their arousal.) But I also think they're better at hiding their fears under their male bravado.

You as his wife can go a long way toward teaching and reassuring him; by your reactions, you can make sure he knows that he's pleased and excited you, and he'll come to bed with more confidence next time, and the time after that. You can also help him by understanding how he may feel when he comes to bed. Don't forget that your stoic husband may have spent all day at work struggling to be top of the heap and head lion in his pride, so when he gets home he could be really tired from trying to slay all those dragons for you. If you expect him to be Don Juan, Casanova, and Clark Gable as Rhett Butler all rolled up into one the minute he walks in the door, you're likely to be disappointed. But if you pay attention to how he's feeling and adjust your expectations, you'll find yourself loved with everything he's got!

Some of the most intimate and satisfying moments of a marriage happen immediately after lovemaking. That's when you're lying in bed together, feeling safe and happy and satiated. Relaxed and snuggling, you feel you can talk about anything. But don't hold it against him if your husband falls asleep. (This drives so many women crazy!) He isn't doing it to spite you—he's falling asleep because his body has given up the ghost, literally! Sometimes Ernie will be talking to me in bed—in the middle of a sentence, mind you—and if I blink for half a second, he's gone. I can't get frustrated with him because he simply can't help himself. All I can do is laugh.

I speak from years of experience on this topic, because my dearest husband also falls asleep at the oddest moments outside of the bedroom. Once he gave me a birthday party in Houston while he was shooting a film there, and right in the middle of a sweet and delightful toast to me, he just sat back down and instantly fell asleep. That was the first time Ernie had ever done such a thing, and I didn't know quite what to do. Nor did anybody else. And then Ernie woke right back up, stood up again, and finished the sentence exactly where he'd left off.

When the man you love also makes you laugh, it's a winning combination both in and out of the bedroom!

MAKE A DATE WITH YOUR HUSBAND

Consider this scenario: It's just another wonderful day at your house. Your kids are screaming, your office manager just quit, the laundry isn't done, your neighbor's dog won't stop barking, and you forgot to mail the bills. . . .

Instead of hyperventilating and driving yourself nuts, recognize that you've got to get away from all this. So . . . make a date with your husband. Literally. Make a date with him. Cancel everything else. Secure the time and place.

And don't, whatever you do, *ever* cancel date night.

Dating your husband means just that—being alone with him, just the two of you together. It doesn't necessarily mean you even have to go out on a "date." You can easily date your husband in the privacy of your bedroom. Or any other room in the house, for that matter!

Once you make a commitment to dating your husband, it'll be harder to get bored or fed up with each other. You'll be proving to him how much he means to you—that he is, in fact, *the most important* person in your life and *always will be*—and how important and crucial your time together is, no matter what you're coping with in the rest of your life.

Dating your husband is a truly romantic act. If your goal is to keep the romance in your marriage forever (and who wouldn't want to?), this is a great way to start.

Whatever you do, though, don't tell your husband how hard "date night" can be to arrange! Let your husband *think* it's spur-of-the-minute, breathless romance, not the result of your amazing organizational skills. Don't spoil his fun with details or crabbiness, or expect a pat on the back for your Herculean efforts to find a decent baby-sitter.

Date time is time you've set aside just to be alone with your husband. Consider it *sacred*. This is most emphatically not the time to discuss your children, your hassles at work, your in-laws, your tax bill, the dog's hangnails, or how your cat just "marked his territory" all over the brand-new living room sofa.

Instead, try to be as lighthearted and playful as you can be on these dates. Once you've lived with someone for a long time, it can be hard to rekindle that sense of wonder, to remember what it was like when you first met. Think back to that first intoxicating rush of lust, your heart pounding madly when he came to pick you up. (Now what usually makes your heart pound is being so exhausted you don't have five minutes to yourself! Not much fun in that, is there?)

Dating your husband is like exercise. At first you don't think you have the time, but once you start doing it, the more energy and vitality you'll find you have.

Here are some "going-out" ideas for dating your husband:

- Wear what you were wearing the first time you met. Set a rendezvous point and pretend you don't know each other. Flirt madly.
- Book a lunch date and take your husband to a hotel room instead of a restaurant. Day-rate rooms at hotels and motels can make you feel terribly illicit and sexy.
- Go someplace out of the ordinary. Take a long drive to nowhere, but end up at a local hotel where (by some wonderful twist of fate) they have reserved a room for you. What a splendid coincidence!
- Tell your husband there is a mandatory family function at a hotel not too far away. Say nothing when his grumbling starts, then smile when you get there—and the two of you are the only "family" expected.
- Try the same concept with a vacation. Tell your husband you have scheduled an important business trip and ask him to join you. In reality, of course, you've planned a romantic getaway.
- Go anyplace that is new to both of you. Try seasonal spots in the off-season. You could go to a resort town like Vail or Aspen in the

summer, perhaps. The rates are usually much cheaper, and the hotels aren't so crowded.

◆ Have a contest in which the winner thinks of the most exotic
place to go on vacation, and the loser has to get you there.

Now here are some ideas for dating your husband—and staying in:

◆ Set the mood with soothing music, soft lighting, and freshly laun-
dered sheets. Wear something that makes you feel intensely sexy.
Don't wait for your husband (who may have different tastes in
lingerie than you do) to buy you a tacky, scarlet see-through
teddy for Valentine's Day because he thinks he's supposed to. Buy
something you love and feel comfortable in, something that
makes you feel slinky and turned-on.

◆ Surprise him in the shower or the bath.

◆ Have an interlude while the house is packed with company—as
long as it's your secret and you can slip away without being
caught!

◆ Save up your pennies so you can hire a professional massage therapist to come to your home to give you both massages.

◆ Take turns being selfish. For one date, he can demand his favorite way to play, and on the next date, it's your turn.

◆ Rent a favorite video (hopefully one with lots of smooching in
it), rent or improvise some silly costumes, and act out scenes from
the film. Be prepared for lots of laughter and hilarity.

◆ Have a nice cozy dinner, just the two of you, alone together and
talking. Hide the remote control and keep the television off. If
your husband is exhausted, tell him you're going to pamper him,
and all you're going to do is give him a light back rub. (This way
he won't have to worry about performance anxiety.)

◆ Eat "sexy." (A lot of diet doctors say you shouldn't eat in bed, but
food nibbles can turn into love nibbles!) Ernie and I love the
film *Tom Jones,* which has the one of the most sensual scenes ever
filmed, of a man and a woman devouring food with wild aban-

don before they fall into bed and devour each other. Whenever I eat lobster, I can't help thinking of that movie, which Ernie and I have replayed many times.

Once in Europe, I must confess, we found tubes of body chocolate, which was great fun to play with and eat. And then of course there's champagne. . . . Letting it trickle all over both of you and licking it up is too wonderful for words.

Dating your husband means never losing sight of what made you two fall in the love in the first place. It also means you will never take each other for granted.

MAKING YOUR BEDROOM YOUR OASIS

Your bedroom is your sanctuary. It should be your heart center, ground zero of your home and your marriage, the setting and scene of all your most intimate adventures together. Take charge of your bedroom, and you set the mood for all the nights to come!

When there are problems in a marriage, the bedroom can easily become a war zone, a place of brooding and anxiety that spill over into sex. When you have problems to discuss, choose a good time and a comfortable space in which to do it—as long as it is *not* your bed, or any other spot in the bedroom.

Your bed is reserved for the communion of your marriage. Your bed is for pleasure. That's why I believe your bedroom and your bed should be as comfortable as conceivably possible—a warm, inviting, sensual place where you can happily relax and unwind.

Because the bedroom is a place meant for intimacy, it should not be bright and loud and vibrant. Save that feeling and those colors for the kitchen or den or even the bathroom. Try instead to go for soft edges and soft tones and soft, relaxing colors. I'm a big fan of upholstered walls, which soften the edges of the room and keep the noise down. Your bed itself should be the best possible quality you can afford. I like mine heaped with piles of pillows to luxuriate in. The right kind of lighting is also crucial, so you can read in bed if you like (and with individual his and hers switches). Music is also very important, as is anything else that gives you a sense of comfort.

Your bedroom is your cocoon, where you can be insulated from the world. Place your treasured objects and photographs all around you so that you're reminded of all that you love.

I always sleep on Ernie's side when he's not home—it smells like him. And it comforts me like him. But I'm not offended that he doesn't sleep on my side when I'm gone—he likes his side!

When you and your husband get into bed together, turn off the ringer on the phone so that you won't be disturbed. If you have an answering machine, there's no reason for your sacred time with your husband to be disturbed. Which brings me to one of my pet peeves: having a television in the bedroom. There's no easier way to make a wife go crazy . . . because once the man of the house gets the remote trapped in his palm, she knows she can kiss any thoughts of sex good-bye. When you and your husband are together in your oasis, there should be no television—period. I'm not insisting that we move televisions out of bedrooms altogether (after all, how else can you watch movies together as I've just suggested?), but it's a good marital habit to keep it off most of the time.

I love candles. My sweet husband does not. He is concerned about fire (and has been all his life), so candles make him nervous. We've worked out a compromise: I get to burn my favorite candles for half an hour each night. If I'm lucky it goes up to forty-five minutes! This is one of our little give-and-takes, but it's quite effective.

One time, though, my candle interlude lasted a little bit longer than usual. We have a store here in Los Angeles called Trashy Lingerie— don't forget that this is a community where Frederick's of Hollywood is a living legend. Well, I wandered into Trashy Lingerie one day, and bought some silk lingerie that wasn't trashy at all. It was really lovely . . . very sexy, with garters and lace and embroidery. Of course, once I got home and put it all on, I felt very silly. I silenced my embarrassment and waited for Ernie to get home from work. Once he saw what I was wearing, Ernie forgot all about my candle burning on the side table.

As a matter of fact, I think my candle burned all night!

Tova's *Compromise* 5:

**Persuade your husband to let you burn candles
occasionally, as long as he's around
to put out the flames!**

WHEN LOVE ISN'T ENOUGH

If your husband has lately been withdrawing from you sexually, there can be many reasons. It might be simple exhaustion. He might be angry about something and using your sex life as a weapon to punish you; he might be depressed; he might be preoccupied with work; he might be comparing himself to one of his more successful friends and wondering if he's worthy; he might be feeling like a failure—and obsessing that perhaps he is a failure in the bedroom as well.

Other times, women are the ones who turn away. Have you ever withheld sex as a way of punishing your husband? Maybe you told yourself, "After what he's done to me, I'm so mad at him I just can't stand it . . . so he's not going to get any this week." Think about how ridiculous and childish this is. Besides, who are you really punishing? Withholding sex is no way to handle his problems or yours.

What you need to do is *talk*. And it is *your responsibility* to initiate this conversation, and to find the most amenable time—preferably when you are alone, relaxed, and in a good state of mind.

Try going back to the "I, not you" method I suggested earlier—and see what happens:

- ◆ I notice that . . . we've been neglecting our sex life for the last few weeks.
- ◆ I understand that . . . you're going through a difficult time.
- ◆ I'm wondering if . . . there's something you might not have told me about or that I might not be aware of.
- ◆ I'm feeling . . . hurt and rejected and scared.
- ◆ I'm really concerned . . . because I love you so much, and I want to try to understand exactly what's happening.
- ◆ I need for us to . . . talk and share. I love you and I'm here for you.

Try to keep the conversation light, even if your heart is heavy. You might say something like, "Well, honey, I know it's been a rough couple of weeks, and we haven't had a chance to spend any kind of time together, have we?" Maybe try a little teasing. Tell your husband: "Boy, we've turned into a couple of ninety-year-olds, haven't we?" or something that might produce a wry smile.

Keep accusations out of it! Do not start yelling, "You never have sex with me anymore—what's wrong with you? What kind of man do you think you are, anyway?" Nothing could make him less interested in sex than such an attack.

Whatever the cause of the problem, talking will help. It will reengage your emotional life and become something you're dealing with *together.* Your sex life may not resume right after this talk, but at least you've opened the door. Leave it open for a while, and then go back to it. Don't let weeks go by, with both of you growing more and more uncomfortable.

If the situation deteriorates, I suggest professional counseling for both of you, to get to the root of the problem. So often counseling not only tackles your immediate concerns (sexual difficulties respond to therapy with an extremely high rate of success), but it also provides a way for both of you to deepen your level of communication.

In the meantime, do what you can to remain physically close. Offer to give him a massage, maybe a face or foot massage so that it is less sexual. Make it clear that you are doing this solely to help him relax, not because you're expecting anything else. Then he *will* relax because he trusts you, and you can take it from there.

Return to what brought you two together in the first place: your friendship. As long as you continue to be friends and confidantes, if you've built a secure foundation together, you will be able to deal with this situation.

WHAT ABOUT INFIDELITY?

Paradoxically, infidelity often can save a marriage instead of destroying it. I've seen it happen many times, and that's what the experts tell me as well. That's because it can force a couple to deal with their problems instead of ignoring them. A case of infidelity also can make a husband and wife realize how very much they love each other and what the marriage means to them. Forgiveness is a gift.

I do not condone infidelity in the slightest. It makes any person feel violated and betrayed. Trust is shattered and destroyed, and the reverberations of that betrayal can last for a very long time. Remember how strongly I reacted when I found out Lou had been unfaithful to me, and in our own bed to boot? That was the end for me. No discussions . . . no forgiveness . . . no going back.

But temptation has been a part of human life ever since Adam and Eve listened to that sweet-talking serpent. What should you do if it happens to you? Recognize that you are in shock, that an earthquake has shaken your very existence. First, get to safe ground. Find a therapist; turn to friends who can be trusted to listen without judging. Don't tell too many people; don't tell your children. Do know that in six months this will make more sense; right now it doesn't.

You, your husband, and your marriage will be transformed by this experience. It's a demarcation; it presents you with a "before." If you can find a way to forgive him, there will be an "after." Understand that this new you, this new marriage, will have a different quality than the old life had, but you may find that eventually it will become a comfortable, joyous place to live in.

THE POWER OF PLEASURE

What would life be without pleasure? Pretty awful, if you ask me.

Then why do so many women deny themselves pleasure, not only sexual enjoyment but other sensual joys? Unfortunately, a lot of women don't feel entitled to pleasure, and that affects every part of their lives. If you don't think you're entitled to pleasure, maybe you don't think you're entitled to much else, either. Like money, for instance. Like a nice home, a good job, healthy relationships, and especially a wonderful marriage.

Take it from me—if you feel unworthy, you'll act unworthy. What kind of man will you attract if you act unworthy? Most likely, a man who supports your opinion of yourself and who may treat you poorly.

I want to end this chapter by asking you to keep telling yourself, over and over again until you believe it, that pleasure is part of life. It is absolutely essential for every woman to experience as much pleasure as conceivably possible, to infuse it into every aspect of her life.

Pleasure doesn't have to cost a lot of money or take a lot of time. It can be as simple as burning an aromatherapy candle that fills the air around you with a scent you love. (Unless, of course, your husband is as opposed to burning candles as mine is.) If you travel a lot, as I do, bringing a little bit of home with you is a special pleasure. (I never leave home without a tiny, heart-shaped silver frame, with pictures of Ernie and David in it.) Treating yourself to a beautiful bouquet of flowers or a brand-new best-seller or some lovely gloves or a hat is a pleasure.

There are things women have been told that they shouldn't buy for themselves, such as jewelry or silver or the kinds of things they hope to get as wedding presents but somehow never do. Well, I believe that if you want a nice ring or a lovely set of china, then go buy your own. Buy the very best you can afford, as long as you don't max out your credit cards. (Overspending and dealing with the consequences are definitely *not* pleasures. Be a grown-up about your money.) Buy on a layaway plan if you're on a tight budget. Even if you buy only one cup or one salad plate at a time, these objects will become your treasures. And you deserve to have them.

Because women are the nurturers, we have to nurture ourselves once in a while, too. Even if money is tight, you still need to take good care of yourself. If you can't afford a new winter coat . . . then buy yourself the most exquisite scarf or pair of gloves you can find. This is a trick I've learned from European women. They often buy only one or two new outfits each season, but they buy only the very finest. These outfits always look terrific, and because they're top quality they last a lot longer than something cheaper. They don't care if their colleagues see them in the same suit more than once in the same week. They care about looking their best.

Putting a special pin on a dress you've had for years can make that dress look as if it just came from a designer's showroom. If you search out a lovely little pin in an antique store, something that is unique and wonderful, it will absolutely change the look of your whole wardrobe.

If you need a touch more pleasure in your life, do something that is (unfairly) perceived as a luxury—have a manicure, a pedicure, a facial, your hair professionally cut and colored. Even just having your hair washed and blow-dried takes very little time, costs very little money, and makes you feel like a million dollars. It's just one more way to get in touch with the seductive, sensual you.

And when you feel sensual, your husband will be the first to notice!

❖ 9 ❖

Romancing Your Husband:
The Promise of Forever

YOU ALREADY KNOW WHAT
kind of clothes and furniture you like, but do you have any idea what
kind of romantic you are? Are you demonstrably romantic or quietly so?
Are you spontaneously romantic or do you prefer the pleasures of planning that weekend getaway? (Ernie and I, incurable romantics both,
wanted to have the booth at Chasen's—where we had our first date—
bronzed, but unfortunately that restaurant recently closed its doors. Too
bad!) Whatever your romantic style, keeping the romance in your marriage is the key to making it last forever.

Tova's $\mathcal{S}ecret$ 16:

As soon as the courtship stops, the magic stops.

Are you willing to do everything you can to sustain the romance of your love throughout all the years of your marriage? Most married couples are so busy and their lives are so fraught with demands that sometimes it seems that their romantic lives consist of no more than a quick peck on the cheek in the mornings or an occasional phone call to the office to catch up. As the years go by, many couples fall into a pattern of treating each other more like business partners than lovers. They talk about work and bills and taxes and the roof that needs repairing and the parent-teacher conferences and their parents' health problems. Romance is the last thing on their minds.

Making time in your life for romance isn't easy, but the effect it has on your marriage will persuade you it's some of the best time you could ever spend. I found my own romantic style by incorporating certain rituals and public affirmations of my feelings for Ernie into my daily life. I discovered it was easier than I expected to keep our romance going, because once you create a routine, it soon becomes as much a part of your day as drinking a cup of coffee in the morning. These rituals and affirmations can be small—like my saying "I love you" to Ernie whenever I end a phone call—or huge, as in planning for a special occasion.

In January 1997, I decided to give Ernie a surprise eightieth birthday party to acknowledge my love for him, as well as to honor his many years in show business. This party took the planning precision of a military campaign, but we pulled it off. Ernie was told that there was a stag event for one of the top honchos at NBC, and that he was really needed to make an appearance. We had the public relations people from NBC fax Ernie all the details, and they told him when they'd send the limo for him. He didn't have a clue. In fact, my darling husband actually apologized to me that he couldn't take me with him. And he never wondered why I was so busy and distracted, because that's normal for me!

As soon as Ernie arrived at the ballroom of the Beverly Hills Hilton, the first thing he saw was a woman dressed as a real-life mermaid—I'd planned a nautical theme in honor of Ernie's Navy days—and he thought this must be a heck of a stag party! As they opened the doors, the band started playing, and a Navy honor guard stood waiting. The lights were so bright that Ernie was temporarily blinded. He couldn't see a thing. All he could hear was this voice—my voice!—saying, "Don't move!"

The party was a wonderful success. It was so important for me to do the best I could for my husband. The energy it took to organize the evening nearly did me in, but I didn't want to trust it to a party planner. People flew in from all over the world, and the room was filled with love and laughter, tears of joy, and so much happiness. What I wanted this evening to express was not just *my* love for Ernie, but the love that all his friends have for him as well.

This party was the last thing Ernie expected that night. Why not try doing the unexpected for your husband to show *your* love for him as well? If, for example, you're going through a rocky patch, try to let go of the anger and do the unexpected—take your husband out to dinner instead of fighting with him. Maybe it will work that night, maybe it won't. But at least you tried!

Nor do you need to throw an elaborate party to keep the romance of your love alive. Making any kind of unusual effort, whenever you can, is more than enough. When it comes to romance, it really *is* the thought that counts!

Tova's *Strategy* 7:

**Create a scrapbook of your marriage
that holds your memories.**

Did you make a scrapbook when you two got engaged? Or when you had a baby? Do you remember what fun it was to record every last detail of your baby's growth and development—his first tooth, his first birthday, his first screaming tantrum in the supermarket?! Why not keep a marriage scrapbook as well?

You can start one at any time, and you don't have to spend a lot of money on it. All you need is a blank bound book. It can be covered in beautiful leather with vellum pages, or a plain school notebook—it's the thought and love and energy going into it that count. Fill this scrapbook with mementos, photos, tickets, menus, whatever—and write notes all over everything so that you can remember each event. Every couple of months, make a date with your husband to work on your scrapbook together. Laugh about your memories of the silly and wonderful things you said and did.

Making this scrapbook together is a delightful marriage ritual. It will give you something you'll always be able to look back upon and say, "We've lived this life. We've danced through this life. And wasn't it grand?"

RENEWING YOUR VOWS

I believe every couple should get married at least twice: once for their families and friends, when they do the whole big wedding thing; and the second time years later for themselves, to honor the couple they've become.

One way you can do this is by renewing your vows. After all, if your wedding day is supposed to be the happiest day of your life, does this mean that every subsequent day isn't ever going to be as happy? Of course it doesn't.

Ernie and I have been remarried four times. We try to renew our vows about every five years. I must admit that we didn't go into marriage thinking this regular renewal was going to be part of it. It evolved into our own personal adventure.

"Tova and I were on a cruise on the *Sea Goddess,* and one day, at sunset, I said to her, 'Honey, how would you like to get married on board ship?' " Ernie explains. "Oh, my God. In half an hour she had the entire ship in total turmoil. We finally had the captain radio to New York and say, 'Listen, the Borgnines want to get married, is it all right for me to perform the ceremony?' He got the okay, obviously. All the guests were there already, and of course the champagne was free and so were all the flowers!"

The last time we renewed our vows, we were on yet another cruise, with twenty-four of our friends. Well, when it was time for the rehearsal in the morning, it was about ninety-nine in the shade and about ninety-nine percent humidity. So the guys were like cranky little three-year-olds, complaining: "I don't want to stand here." "I don't want to go there." "When the hell is this going to be over?" I felt like screaming, "Boys, behave!"

But by the twilight hour they were just perfect. (Or maybe just prostrated by the heat.) There was a lovely soft breeze from the sea, and all the ladies in our long wedding gowns were escorted by officers from the ship to our waiting husbands, standing there tall in their tuxedos with their little black ties. We all felt rejuvenated, like kids again going to our very first junior high school dance. All the guys were beaming, simply thrilled to pieces. After the ceremony, we stood in a big circle, holding hands, feeling the love flow through our fingers.

Renewing our vows is now well known as a Borgnine tradition. The ceremony on board the ship was so beautiful, and the force of the love from all the couples wanting to restate their commitment helped strengthen everybody's marriage.

You don't have to go on a cruise to renew your vows, of course. You can go to Las Vegas or Chicago or your local church or synagogue to declare your love for each other.

You can also, in a slightly more informal way, renew your vows in the sanctuary of your bedroom or your house. You don't have to have any guests present. Or you can ask your children to participate—they'll be thrilled.

And what's to stop you from buying your husband a little token of your renewal vows, as long as it's one that fits your budget? The simplest gold band or cuff links, perhaps engraved with the date of your renewal, will become a treasured reminder of your love. And if your husband is looking to buy you a renewal present, do be specific if you don't want a toaster!

Look, we are here on this earth for such a very short time. When you look back at your life, why spend any time in regrets or wishing that you had done something wonderful for and with your husband when you had the opportunity?

◆ **Belinda:** We have friends who are celebrating twenty years of marriage just as we are, on the same day. At the wedding of the other couple's daughter, we jokingly decided we two couples would reaffirm our vows in a double wedding ceremony, and afterward my husband would sleep with our friend's wife and vice versa. A wonderful idea, yes?! I hope you know I'm kidding!

◆ **Wendy:** We renegotiate our marriage contract on our anniversary every year. Then we celebrate by getting away somewhere special and romantic.

I want Ernie to tell you another story, about one of our more unusual renewals. I hope it makes you laugh!

"One day Tova came home, about a week before my birthday, and I'm sitting in bed with a nasty cold. She said, 'Honey, get packed, we're going.' I said, 'Where are we going?' She said, 'I can't tell you, but we're going and I need you to start packing right now.'

"Well, something hit me and I told her I was not moving from this bed until she told me just exactly what was going on. She cried, she carried on, she begged . . . and finally she told me that we were going to Spain to get married again.

" 'What! In the middle of winter? Are you crazy?'

"She said, 'Yes, never mind, and don't worry about the weather. We're going to Marbella.' Her friend Rudy from the Marbella Club had set it up so that we could get married on my birthday.

"So we packed up and we got to Marbella. What with jet lag and such short notice, we were both completely exhausted. Plus our tiny hotel was cold and miserable. Neither of us speak a word of Spanish, and the only thing we had for company was a television set, which naturally had nothing but Spanish programs on it. We even watched it. I think we'd have watched a ghost if it had been on that set. But we stayed huddled together, you know, and kept warm. Tova said, 'Oh, isn't this nice, isn't this wonderful . . .' and I gave her such a look.

"Well, the next day did kind of dawn a little better and the sun came out, even though I still think we were the only tourists in town. We did a little shopping, and Tova bought some shoes. 'Look, Ernie,' she announced. 'Aren't these beautiful? And they're so cheap. You can get these shoes for practically nothing.' I said to myself, 'Oh, shoot, as long as I pay for them. I mean, how much did it cost for us to get here to pay for the shoes?'

"Anyway, along came that wonderful day when we were going to get married. Tova got all dolled up and looked more beautiful than ever, and her friend Rudy met us and took us in a car to this ancient church. We sat waiting in a pew, until a priest came out with a long, long white cassock with wine stains all over it. At first he didn't want to marry us, and I thought it was because we'd been married too many times before . . . but Rudy finally persuaded him. He read the marriage service as we knelt down before him, but of course we didn't understand it because it was all in Spanish. Rudy translated for us, and the priest finally beckoned for us to kiss. I gave him some money, and he was very happy.

"Then I turned to Tova, and I said, 'Honey, what do I tip our guide?' She said, 'What guide? You mean Rudy? Ernie—he's a count, and he owns this place!'

"The very funny part about it was when we were walking back up the aisle, the entire back of the church had filled up with people, saying, 'Ahhh, isn't that nice, they got married.'

"Then, to top it all off, I caught the flu on the way back. I'll never forget that one. That wedding kept me in bed for weeks!"

Ernie would probably agree that every five years is often enough for us to renew our vows. But celebrating our love for each other as often as we could has been part of our lives since the day we married.

Tova's *Strategy* 8:

Celebrate your love as often as you like with "monthaversaries."

Because, as you know, Ernie and I are both such hopeless romantics, we started another of our own traditions not long after our marriage. Instead of waiting for our one-year anniversary, we decided to celebrate our love once a month, with what we dubbed a "monthaversary." One month we would, for example, have a private little dinner (with candles, if I could convince Ernie to let me light them!). Or we'd give each other one flower. Or I'd give Ernie a silly little present or a stuffed animal, and he would find an equally cute one for me. Sometimes I would send Ernie a card, and he would write me a card.

It's little things like this that add so much magic to a relationship.

After a while, though, it got a little bit difficult to top each monthaversary present. Ernie finally said to me, "Honey, that's enough. You're breaking me, kid." That's when we decided to give each other cards instead of presents for our monthaversaries.

I like to place a card in Ernie's bathroom, a card in the kitchen, and a card on his dresser. We do this for our monthaversaries, as well as on holidays such as Christmas, Easter, and Valentine's Day. The cards are really so touching; they're thank-yous for being there and for sharing our lives. Ernie signs his cards as P.C., which is short for Prince Charming, and I sign mine as Cindy, which is short for Cinderella. Affectionate names like these are just one more way for us to feel close to each other.

Which reminds me of a girlfriend who was out food shopping with her husband in Beverly Hills. There they were in the supermarket—and neither of them is young—and her husband was looking for her in one of the aisles. "Snookums," he called out. Well, she knew it was her pet name but she didn't want the *world* to know it, so she paid absolutely no attention to him, hoping he'd shut up. In the meantime, he couldn't find her, so he kept running around, screaming, "Snookums! Snookums!" I'm not sure she ever got over it.

♡

Another great idea is to set aside a day devoted to your husband.

◆ **Elizabeth:** I decided to have Totally Benjamin days for my husband. I told him that we could do whatever he wanted, wherever he wanted it. He could choose the restaurant, or the movie, or the event to go to. He loved not having to constantly negotiate. It was liberating for both of us. I used to call up his friends and tell them that, for example, next Wednesday was going to be Totally Benjamin Day, and they should call him to send their greetings. Benjamin got such a kick out of it, and this became such a popular concept, it spread to our whole circle of friends. They all started doing it for each other.

Why wait for Valentine's Day, which comes but once a year? Every day should be Valentine's Day in your marriage. (The same with holidays—why is it the only time strangers talk to each other is when they say "happy holidays"? What's wrong with having a Happy Tuesday?) Giving pleasure is contagious. Nothing is more delightful.

◆ **Samantha:** My husband makes me Valentines out of strange materials each year, as well as different things for most of our anniversaries. In return I appreciate the hell out of them, which he quite enjoys. I consider them artworks and I proudly hang them on the wall.

Even if you've already done it one hundred times that day, never stop reinforcing the idea that you are thinking and caring about your husband. It's so easy to let him know that you're utterly delighted to announce to the world that there is something special and unique about him.

Keep the romance of your love alive forever!

Part
Three

Making Your
Marriage Work

*"Being married to the most wonderful man
in the world helps! Frank and I have been married for twenty-one years, and as he says, 'It's
like fine wine. It just gets better!'...Our time
together is the best—with lots of hugging and
kissing. We enjoy each other's company—good
conversation, great romance, and all the rest that
makes a marriage work. And, besides, Frank is
an excellent cook!"*

—BARBARA SINATRA ON TWO
DECADES OF MARRIAGE TO FRANK

· 10 ·

Love and Work, Marriage and Money: How to Keep Them from Driving You Apart

ERNIE IS OFTEN ASKED why, after four failed marriages, his marriage to me has worked so well, why it's still so wonderfully romantic and exciting after nearly twenty-five years. "Well," he replies, "one reason is that I've seen Tova for only twelve of those years."

Ernie and I are both extremely busy and happy with our work. It suits us to be apart for periods of time due to business; in fact, we're convinced that we'd be quick to annoy each other if we were constantly together. Though I wouldn't dream of implying that what suits us would necessarily work for anyone else, I think it shows that all kinds of marriages can be happy and healthy—and that you can't measure closeness by the amount of time a husband and wife spend in each other's company.

For me and for many people, of course, work is the cornerstone of my identity. The only time in my adult life that I didn't have a job was when I moved in with Ernie. Even then, though, my mind was always percolating about my professional future, because I needed and wanted a career as well as a husband.

I want to tell you how my business began. The reason why I'm going to go into such detail is because I learned so much about myself along the way—about my needs for control and creativity, and about how to run a business without harming my relationship with Ernie. As you'll see, I was forced to use my wits, improvise, and deal with each situation as it presented itself, without knowing what would happen next. There was no rule book to guide me. In fact, I discovered that the early days of my business were very much like the "getting-to-know-you" period at the start of a marriage.

HOW TO START A BUSINESS, BY TOVA

The strip in Las Vegas was still pretty wild when I arrived, heartbroken but determined, in 1969. Meeting and working with the showgirls was how I became so dedicated to developing my own skin care line. Most of the showgirls wore superthick pancake makeup, because anything else would melt under the double onslaught of hot stage lights and perspiration. Pancake makeup, though, completely clogs the pores; add to that a showgirl diet of junk food, late-night partying, and about a thousand cigarettes a day, and you have a recipe for skin disaster. These dancers' bodies were in great shape because of their strenuous routines, but when these gorgeous women took their makeup off, I was flabbergasted at how positively awful their skin looked. So I became determined to create something to help them.

I started looking around and talking to other skin care people, but it wasn't until I met Merle Oberon (who was famously discreet about her beauty regimen) that I found something that might work. Merle told me that she used a formula on her face that was distilled from cactus and said that she got it from a Mexican family. She explained to me that the Aztecs had discovered the healing properties of the cactus; her luminous skin was certainly testament to that. Since Merle would say no more, I didn't have a clue about how to start my search for this Mexican family with the formula and the raw materials, but at least I had my dream.

After we were married, I kept talking to Ernie about those healing cacti in Mexico, telling him I just knew I could develop the raw materials into a good business. My poor husband must have been a bit sick of my one-track conversations, but he was instrumental in helping me find the family I'd been searching for. It turned out that they lived in a remote village about four hundred miles outside of Mexico City. When Ernie had a break between films, we took a trip down there and I finally hooked up with the right people.

Once I had the cactus essence—I called it cactine—I began experimenting with it, and eventually created a facial masque, a toner, and two moisturizing creams that I gave to my friends to try. Ernie was my best guinea pig, and he loved to boast about how great his skin looked and felt. So when he was being interviewed for a San Francisco newspaper, Ernie started talking about my products, as usual. The journalist wrote a lovely article about Mr. Borgnine, who couldn't stop blabbing about his wife's cosmetics. He called my masque a "face-lift in a jar," and told everyone that they too could buy it for only sixty dollars—a figure he invented, because I hadn't even put a price tag on anything yet. Because there was nothing to sell!

Not long after the article came out, I went to the post office to pick up Ernie's mail. The postmaster handed me a huge sack crammed with letters. I joked to him that I knew my husband was popular, but this was ridiculous! I lugged the sack home, poured out the letters, and was astonished to realize that they were all addressed to me. There were nearly 20,000 requests for information and $56,000 worth of checks for my "face-lift in a jar"!

Did I jump in the air for joy? Are you kidding? I panicked! I had no product, no raw materials to make the product, no company, no containers, no packaging, no labels, no staff, *nothing.*

Once I calmed down, I called the postmaster for advice. He explained that the postal laws were carefully regulated and severe, and that all I had was thirty days to deliver, or else. ("Or else" meant mail fraud.) But, he added, if I thought I was going to be late delivering, I could write to everyone who'd ordered, and explain to them that since the shipment was late, they had the option of getting their money back. I asked Ernie for his advice. He encouraged me to go ahead, telling me that this was it, the opening I'd been waiting for.

I put my company together in six weeks. But it was a pretty hysterical six weeks. First I had to send out the "we'll be a little late" letters, hand-signed one and all, to the kind people who'd sent me the orders. This was all pre-computer, so everything had to be done by hand. I hired twenty typists from a temp agency, and they started pounding away in a tiny rented office, addressing labels. Then I got on a plane with an adviser and flew to Mexico City, where I met with the trade commissioner, the family with the cactine formula, and an interpreter. I said, very sweetly, that all I needed was two and a half tons of cactus essence in eleven working days, thank you very much.

They walked out on me. I started putting hundred-dollar bills on the table. Eventually, they walked back in. (This wasn't bribe money; it was start-up money.) I told them there was plenty more money in escrow for when the product arrived, and we were in business.

I phoned a graphic artist I knew and told him I needed a label design in three days. I flew back to Los Angeles and looked in the Yellow Pages for a filler company, the factory where the jars would be filled with the product. I called one of the companies, and the man told me he'd be glad to fill my order . . . but where was my packaging? (He meant the jars.) I told him I didn't have any. But before he had a chance to hang up, I said that if he wanted this huge rush order, he'd better get me the packaging. So he did. The cactine arrived, and we were cooking.

So now all we had to do was ship it out, pre–Federal Express. Along with Ernie and as many of our friends as we could muster, we set up an assembly line in our driveway. We made it an all-day affair. It took twenty-four hours and we did it in three shifts. My friends worked for nothing. Or, rather, they worked for love. I felt a little bit like Tom Sawyer getting the other kids to paint his fence, but I was forever grateful to the people who were so gracious with their time and energy to help me get through this.

We shipped all those boxes. I made my deadline, then collapsed. And that's how the Tova Corporation started!

HOW THE TOVA CORPORATION CHANGED MY LIFE

If I had known then what I do now, I wonder if I ever would have tried to start the Tova Corporation. It's an extraordinary amount of work. For each item I sell, there must be a box, the box liner, the label, the product itself, the jar containing the product, shipping, delivery, insurance—not to mention managing my employees and running the company. I am responsible for everything, and even more so because all my products carry my name.

The success or failure of my business has been inextricably intertwined with my marriage from the very beginning. For instance, while I knew I had an incredible product in my cosmetics, no one knew who I was. However, people *did* know who Ernie was. And in terms of Hollywood credibility, Ernest Borgnine has always seemed like a trustworthy member of the American family.

Yet Ernie's very credibility created a problem for me. I needed to know if it was my products or the Borgnine reputation that my customers were buying. This was extremely painful for me, because I had to answer some tough questions about my identity, about how I saw myself in terms of my husband's work and my own. I had to ask myself if I, Tova, was worth something—or if I was no more than an extension of the mythical Borgnine celebrity. Out here, couples are almost always referred to as Mr. and Mrs. As in Mr. and Mrs. Gregory Peck, or Mr. and

Mrs. Milton Berle. The wife is the "Mrs.," and usually not a whole lot more. My being Mrs. Borgnine paradoxically gave me *less* credibility in Hollywood.

PUTTING IT INTO WORDS

The most important lesson I learned in those early years was to have faith in myself, even when things looked bleak. But I needed more. I had to develop my own business philosophy and figure out what my strengths were. This is my five-point plan:

1. To have the best personal relationship with my customers I possibly can
2. To improve and enhance the quality of my customers' lives
3. Ladies and gentlemen serving ladies and gentlemen
4. To make certain that the business environment is as creative as possible
5. To encourage the quick execution of creative ideas

Looking at this list, I see just how these points also can be applied to marriage. You want:

1. To have the best personal relationship with your husband you possibly can
2. To improve and enhance the quality of your husband's life and your own
3. A lady and a gentleman serving each other (manners and courtesy!)
4. To make certain that your home environment is as creative and loving as possible
5. To encourage the quick execution of creative and loving ideas (and actions)

Think about the strengths you bring to your own career, and see if any of them can be applied toward improving your marriage. It certainly worked for me!

BALANCING WORK AND FAMILY (AND EVERYTHING ELSE)

"I'd always insisted that no wife of mine would ever have to work," Ernie says. "I saw myself as the breadwinner in this family, and that was all there was to it. Yet after a while, I could see Tova's side about starting up her career; I knew that she had been in business before. Plus, she was going crazy in that house. You can only clean so much, or walk around so much, or read so much, or shop so much. Then something's got to pop. I could see myself coming home and saying, 'Hi, hon' and there'd be a book thrown at me or something because my wife was being driven out of her mind with boredom.

"After Tova's business took off, I never said to myself—or to her— I want my housewife back. I was too busy being proud of her."

This is a good example of why it's vital to your relationship for both of you to feel energized and occupied in your own spaces. I didn't *have* to work, as most women do, to help keep the family financially afloat. I had to work because I needed it, for me. I couldn't be my own woman without work.

But don't think Ernie and I haven't had our share of difficulties trying to find our balance between work and romance. After we'd been together for about fifteen years, Ernie went through an unusually slow patch in his career. In other words, he wasn't working—and it was driving him crazy. This coincided with a very busy time with my company, so I had to be on the road a lot.

He began pouting about this but never complaining in so many words. Still, I always knew when he was sulking because he would hang up on me when I'd check in! It was a frustrating and infuriating time for both of us, because I was counting on my husband's support as my business grew.

We got through this tough time because we continued to talk, no matter what kind of mood either of us was in. Then we talked some more. As long as we kept communicating, we kept our marriage alive and well. Work, however, was more of a challenge for me.

Around this time I learned just how hard it was for me to delegate. I used to think that I had to do everything, that nobody else could do it. The more the pressure built, the less I was able to handle it. I realized I had to find a way to get each of my sticky, anxious fingers out of every piece of the Tova Corporation pie.

Finally, I realized it was all about *trust*. I already trusted the effectiveness of my products, but I had to learn to trust my employees. After all, their jobs were on the line if the company didn't thrive. I started to look at my company the way I viewed my marriage. I had to establish trust, communicate effectively, and learn to compromise. Then we could all grow together.

Part of bringing some balance into my life involved using my work as an outlet to fill one of my basic needs. Even though I rarely played as a child, I began trying to play every day at work. I savored the fact that every workday was different from the day before, and I found each day as full of wonder as a child does a new toy. Today, I still get intense pleasure from creating new products and connecting with all the people I meet on my travels.

PASSION, PERSISTENCE, AND PATIENCE

You never know when a chance encounter will send you down an entirely new path. Ernie was on location in San Francisco, so one day while he was shooting, I decided to go for a long walk. I was happily wandering around the neighborhood when I spied a cute little shop with all sorts of bottles and pipes in the window. (Only afterward, as

Ernie was roaring with laughter, did I realize this cute little store was a head shop, filled with all sorts of drug paraphernalia. Can you believe how square I was!)

Anyway, I went inside—and instantly smelled something indescribably wonderful, an amazingly delicious scent that was *me*. The man in the shop said it was one of their bath oils. I simply couldn't get my nose away from it. So I bought a few bottles, then kept calling the shop back, asking and then begging them to tell me who made that divine oil. At first they refused to divulge the name of their supplier, but after a month of my persistently nagging them on the phone—it can be done!—they gave in, and gave me the number of an essential oil house in New York called Manheimer. (Essential oils are the basis of perfume.) Naturally, I called Manheimer to make an appointment. Once I arrived, I proudly announced that I wanted to create a fragrance based upon the notes in the head shop's bath oil. They told me that they weren't in the perfume business. *"Oh yes, you are,"* I replied. I shall spare you the rest of the conversation, but they eventually caved in—and this unforgettable scent became Tova, my signature fragrance. (And now QVC's best-selling fragrance.)

I didn't know anything about the fragrance business when all this occurred. I bet that, had I gone the traditional route, I would never have made it happen. The marketing people would have asked, What is your target? Why are you planning to go *there* when everyone else is *here?* You can't work that way! What do you mean, you smelled a bath oil in San Francisco? And so on and so forth . . .

But instead I created a business by trusting my instincts and wanting to make the best perfume I could. I did not conform to anybody's preconceived notions of how I was supposed to create my product and run my company. I trusted my heart.

So many times in the early days of my business, I heard: "It can't be done." This wasn't a good idea, or this product couldn't be made, or this box couldn't be delivered, or this or that. Did I give up? No, I did not. Instead I said, "Yes, it *can* be done. Go back and just do not take no for an answer." Well, my employees would usually return with surprised looks on their faces and tell me, "You won't believe it, but they said yes; they changed their minds."

OVERWHELMED BY WORK

On the other hand, I'll be the first to admit that I made several tremendous blunders as my business grew, blunders that very nearly ruined my company. One business partner nearly bankrupted me.

When I realized my soon-to-be-ex-partner was about to flush my company down the toilet, did I sit down calmly and explore all my options? Of course not. I cried. I cried so much that every part of me ached and my eyes were nearly swollen shut. I looked like a drowned rat.

"I can't go back to that office," I announced to Ernie. "I just can't do this anymore. It hurts too much."

Ernie, bless him, gave me one of those *From Here to Eternity* looks that only he could master. (The kind of look that would make you cross the street in a hurry.) "You started it, and you wanted it," he told me sternly. "Now get out there and show them you can do it."

I started crying again. It was pouring outside, and I couldn't face the calamities waiting for me in the office.

Ernie took me by the hand and nearly dragged me to the garage. "Get in the car," he said. "You started this company. You've got to go. You're going to face it." I shook my head again, so he opened the car door and pushed me in.

"Go back there and show them what you can do," he said, and left me.

So what did I do? I sat in the car and sobbed some more. Then I wiped my eyes and drove to my office. I called my lawyers. It was one of the hardest days of my life. But I fought back, and I showed myself yet again that it can be done.

Another time, Ernie had just flown off to Czechoslovakia to shoot a film when a major catastrophe erupted in my office. (I'll spare you the details.) This time, I made myself sick, running a fever of 103. It was a living hell. But this crisis taught me more than anything else I have ever learned in business. I finally stood up for myself and decided I wasn't taking it anymore. And then, *without emotion,* I proceeded forward and resolved the situation.

As hard as it is to admit, we often learn far more from our catastrophes than from our successes. Yet it can be an almost unbearably painful trauma when you're actually living through it. During this last predicament, because Ernie was on location, I was alone. I was extraordinarily emotional, feeling very sorry for myself, which is the worst place in the world to be. I had to literally roll out of bed, I was so hot and feverish, and crawl on my hands and knees to the bathroom to pick myself up. I wanted my husband so badly, but at the time it took three days just to put a call through to his remote location. The only person who could get me out of this mess was *me.*

This turned out to be a blessing. It focused me, and I realized that most of the blessings we find are usually the ones we least expect. When you're not clear about a problem, or when there are too many options, it's easy to get into trouble. And the minute you start second-guessing yourself, or thinking that you can't do something, or when the fear sets in, it's easy to want to give away all the responsibilities. At that point, I almost did—until I realized I didn't want to anymore.

I'd gotten into trouble because I'd forgotten KISS, one of the cardinal rules of business. As in Keep It Simple, Stupid. But shortly after this crisis, the computer chip changed everything, literally overnight. All of a sudden, toll-free 800 numbers made ordering simple, and everyone started using credit cards. My struggles lessened. Mail order was no longer a place for bottom feeders and shady operators. Well, what do you know—my already well-established mail-order business was starting to make me look like a total genius!

Keeping the Office in the Office (Unless, of Course, Your Office Is in Your Home)

I don't know how Ernie does it, but he never comes home with work on his mind after a hard day's shooting. *Not me.* I find it hard to let go of the day's events, to be able to separate myself from my work. Many women have told me they have the same problem.

It took me at least ten years to understand that even though it was *my* business, my products weren't *me.* I often had to remind myself that I'd done the best I could, whether someone liked a product or not. And I had to understand the difference between professional and personal relationships.

It's a lot like marrying into your husband's family. Whether you like his relatives or not, you need to get along with them—at least during the holidays. The same is true for the office. You may not like everyone at work, and they may not like you—but you can still work together without being dear friends.

What's still hard for me to handle is how my reactions are sometimes judged by other people. Suppose I'm in a meeting and someone brings me work that I consider shoddy or unacceptable. If I react strongly, powerfully, the way a manager must, perhaps even raise my voice, some colleagues may think, *What a bitch!* Or *She should really be committed! Who does she think she is!* Yet when a man does exactly the same thing, the same people say, "What an effective manager!"

I know that many working women struggle with the problem of respect and being taken seriously. If you're going to be an effective manager, of course you can't be a screaming maniac. (The same is true at home!) But you *can* be strong and stay true to your vision.

And—learn to delegate effectively.

And—leave the office in the office.

CHILDREN VS. YOUR CAREER

It's tough enough being a wife and working woman. What about when children are added to the equation? See if this scenario sounds familiar:

Cassie loves being a mother. Her children are bright and precious and adorable. Cassie and her husband decided that she would stay at home while her children are too young to be at school. They scrimped and saved so that Cassie would be able to quit her job, and they accepted the fact that their lifestyle would change dramatically. Yet Cassie is having a hard time with this decision; she is filled with ambivalence. She deeply loves her children, of course, and is grateful for the time she's having with them now, when they're so adorable and change so dramatically with each passing day. At the same time, though, they're exhausting! Rewarding and wonderful, too, of course. But because the skill it takes to raise children is so undervalued in America, what she does all day is not recognized by many people as the difficult task it is.

Cassie also misses the satisfaction she once found in her job. Instead of spending her days with adults, taking great pleasure in her success, *and* getting paid for her work, she feels isolated from the world she once knew well. While on one level she feels good about making the choice to stay at home with her young children, on another her frustration sometimes spills over into her relationship with her husband and her kids.

Trying to be a super-mom has driven plenty of women to the brink of exhaustion. It's hard enough to divide your energies between keeping your marriage healthy and raising a family . . . going to work just adds another log to the fire! You have to find the balance that works for you. And it helps a great deal if you're able to be flexible and open in the way you structure your life.

Cassie is committed to staying home with her children—for now. But some days she wonders if it's worth it, if her children can sense that she's often miserable being home with them.

For many women, balancing children and careers means asking for help and enlisting whatever support you can find. It also means coping with guilt on several different levels. You want to be home with the kids *but* you need (for financial reasons) or want (for emotional reasons, like me or Cassie) to work. Can you do it? Yes, women everywhere do it every day, but each one finds her own comfort level.

Here's what I advise:

◆ Try to deal with the guilt first. Look for the answers within yourself. Trust your instincts and your innermost desires. Don't make decisions because you think you're supposed to, or because there is relentless pressure from family members.

◆ Make a list of every possible alternative. Can you work a flexible schedule, work from home one or two days, even share a job with another working mother?

◆ Make sure the people around you, particularly your husband, know what your dilemma is. Talk about whether he can shoulder more of the burden than he has so far. Don't allow resentment or fury to build up inside until it explodes. Be willing to ask for help. Admit that you can't do everything. Banish the super-mom fantasy from your life right now!

◆ Use this situation to draw your family together. Work together as a unit. Allow your husband to be your partner. Above all, *ask your children to help*. Tell them that you are all going to pull together as a family, and see how they react. I think you might be amazed. Children desperately want to feel that they belong, that they're an integral part of any family. Even very small children like to feel that they're contributing, even if it's only to keep you company when you're dusting. (This doesn't mean screaming at the kids to clean up their rooms!)

I'm convinced that the greatest gift you can give your children is to not let your marriage suffer as a result of your struggle for balance. More than any amount of "quality" time, they need to know that their parents have a strong relationship—and that they can rely on you. If you and your husband communicate well and try to find solutions together . . . if you make your children active participants in your family council, then you can cope with all the rest.

You're married to your husband, not to your career or to your children. Devoting yourself to him, your first priority, will make everything easier and ultimately more satisfying.

TIME MANAGEMENT BY TOVA—OR HOW I STAY ORGANIZED (MOST OF THE TIME!)

Have you ever wished for a magic wand to wave over you and make you instantly more organized? Most of us have. Maybe you feel you could do more if you had the time, but you don't. I've learned that when you don't want to face a particular problem, saying you don't have the time is a handy (and believable) excuse! But that's usually what it is—an excuse not to make necessary changes.

When you're trying to get organized, remember my mother's words: It can be done. But don't try to do it all in one day. Don't take the superwoman approach and decide to clean the whole house. By the end of the day the entire house will be in an uproar and all you will have done is make a bigger mess—and your husband will be home in an hour!

I'm exhausted just thinking about it!

Here are some ideas that have worked for me. I bet they can help you become and stay organized.

Tova's Strategy 9:

Follow six simple rules to help you get organized and stay organized.

1. **The "Touch Once" rule:** Any mail, papers, you name it, gets either filed or tossed after one touch. If you touch it, you must do it. Enforce this rule and it will soon become a habit. Your children can treat it like a game. Why, you and your husband can treat it like a game, too. I'm for anything that involves touching!

2. **Whoever starts, finishes.** Again, no exceptions. And no arguments. This applies to everything from doing the dishes to paying the monthly bills.

3. **Put things back in place immediately after use.** You'll find this much easier to do if you . . .

4. **Have a place for everything.** (Do remember to let your husband know where things are hidden!)

5. **Spring cleaning is not just for spring.** Try to do a spring cleaning for every season. The more often you do this, the less often you'll have to worry about big cleaning chores. Regular desk cleanings and closet cleanings are a must.

6. **Arrange things so that certain tasks are done regularly, and in the same way.** Then you don't have to constantly reevaluate how to deal with these tasks. Often, thinking about what to do takes more time than actually doing it.

Don't you feel more organized already? Now that your space is under control, let's tackle your schedule.

Tova's *Strategy* 10:
Create a Master Calendar together.

Here's another strategy that really worked for us. Ernie and I found that dealing with our constantly shifting schedules was a nightmare. When you have to travel as much as I do, and you balance and juggle so many things, details certainly have a way of getting away from you. So I have a huge Master Calendar at work, where all the things I have to do are marked with erasable pens in different colors. I update it frequently, because my schedule always seems to be changing at a moment's notice. One color pen is for my Los Angeles meetings; another, for my out-of-town trips; one for special projects (like this book); one for charity events; and one, of course, for Ernie's schedule.

Ernie and I also have a smaller version of my office Master Calendar at home. He marks in the dates when he's working or busy, and we swap. This way we always know where the other person is and what's going on during the day, so we can plan our time together accordingly. (And because, as you know, I believe in dating my husband, I mark my dates with Ernie in indelible ink. I treat these dates as if they were crucial business meetings—you wouldn't dream of not showing up for one of those, would you?—and I never cancel them.)

You can easily set up a Master Calendar in your office or home. Use one color pen for your projects and schedule, one for your husband, one for each of your children, and one for you as a couple. Have your kids be responsible for filling in their own sections of the Calendar. You're never too young to start learning how to be organized!

ORGANIZING YOUR LIFE ON PAPER

I like to write things down. Well, okay, I really need to. There's so much going on that if I *don't* write things down, I tend to forget them all. Here's what works for me:

Tova's *Secret* 17:
You can never have too many lists.

Every day, as soon as you've had a cup of coffee or gotten into the office, make a list. Write down whatever you want or expect to accomplish that day. But don't make your list so long that you can't possibly get through it that day. Keep it short. That's the whole point. This way, crossing off each item on your list, or even putting a little X in a box next to it, can give you a wonderful sense of accomplishment.

Lists don't just have to be about things you have to do. Why not list your dreams, or make a wish list of where you'd like to go on vacation, or a list of events you'd love to share with your husband? How about making a list of your husband's favorite things to do, to see, and to eat?

Pro and con lists can be very useful. For many people, considering both sides of a problem provides perspective as well as potential solutions.

A feelings list is indispensable, especially during times of crisis. Sometimes this list turns into a diary. Just make sure to do all of your writing out of sight of your husband, as he might be too curious and want to read what you've written. Even though you have every right to set down your ideas in the privacy of a journal, keeping one can make your husband feel left out.

I love finding old lists. They almost always make me laugh. How much I always want to accomplish in one day!

MONEY AND YOUR MARRIAGE

Ernie is very generous, and has been since we met. But he is also very conservative with his money. He still can't get over the fact that coffee now costs two dollars a cup when it used to cost ten cents.

Money is such a stressful subject for most couples. It triggers all sorts of emotions, most of them negative. Everyone worries whether they have enough of it, especially in Hollywood, where people use what you're paid as a measuring stick. Thinking about money tends to make us crazy, either because we're not getting enough of it, or the IRS is trying to take away what we do have. The struggle over money can kill love, and it can certainly screw up your life and your marriage if you give it that power.

Think of how it feels for a man to say to his wife, "Look, this is how much I make, and that's all there is for now." If that amount isn't judged sufficient, it puts a man under tremendous pressure to either bring home more or feel like a failure.

Where does the money come from, and where does it go? Your husband goes grocery shopping and spends twice as much as you usually do. He asks you to get the car washed on your way home from work, and you ask him to pick up your dry cleaning. The VCR dies one rainy Saturday night, and then your boss is fired and you're worried about your job. Then an unexpected dividend check arrives on the same day your husband gets a large bill from the IRS for a miscalculation on last year's return. Who pays for what, and why?

Too many couples avoid talking about money. The issues are complicated, there's often not enough to go around, and it can be hard to find good advice on how to tackle your family finances. But don't let the topic scare you off. It's too important!

CONQUERING YOUR APPREHENSION
ABOUT MONEY

Too often, women handle money as if it doesn't belong to them. Maybe we feel that somehow the dollar bill given to us is different from the dollar bill given to our husbands. Or that we don't deserve it, so we're afraid to deal with it in a straightforward manner. So we go to someone else to handle it, but don't pay attention—and all of a sudden it's gone. You can't manage your money if you let the idea of money scare you.

You owe it to yourself to be an active participant in the management of your family's finances. It doesn't matter what your net worth is—billions or pennies—the principle is the same. There are absolutely no excuses not to understand how money works and what to do with it. Don't wait until something drastic—downsizing at work, separation, illness, a sudden emergency—happens to figure it out!

I've seen too many of my friends suffer because their bank accounts were jointly designated as Mr. *and* Mrs. John Doe. What if Mr. or Mrs. dies? Will the surviving spouse still have access to the account? (What do you think?) How simple it would have been to set this account up as Mr. *or* Mrs. John Doe. When the husband of a dear friend of mine died suddenly, the next morning my friend found that she was denied access to her own bank account. She couldn't drive her car because it wasn't registered in her name. She actually didn't have the right to live in her own home because the mortgage and deed were in her late husband's name.

Why did this happen? Because money was a subject this couple could not bear to discuss. Neither of them knew how to talk about it. They were *scared*.

But money is scary only when you don't know anything about it. I've so often heard women say, "Oh, dear, how do I read these bank statements? Who am I going to ask to help me with this? I don't want my husband to think that I'm stupid."

That's the key: *"I don't want my husband to think I'm stupid."* Let me tell you right now: There is no such thing as a stupid question when it comes to something as important as your finances. Besides, it's not that difficult to understand the basics; no matter what any financial wizard says, two plus two will always equal four.

(Did you hate math in school and vow never to think of it again once you graduated? I cringe when I think back to geometry class—and algebra was even worse. I did have one math teacher who had every single student totally enthralled with numbers. What he did was make us look at numbers as a fun adventure. I've never forgotten one of his secret formulas: Think of a number from one to infinity. Now double it. Now add ten. Divide by two and subtract the original number you thought of. You'll always get five!)

BEING SMART ABOUT MONEY

Obviously, the ideal time to start talking about money is before the wedding, but if you're already married, don't worry. It's never too late to start managing your money properly. With time, it should be as easy for you to discuss money as you do your friends or the temperature outside or who's going to walk the dog.

This is what I suggest:

1. Set Aside Time

Like my math teacher, make this time fun. Set a weekly or monthly date—which means you can't cancel it. Break out the chocolates or a steaming order of Chinese food, but skip the great bottle of wine. This is not a night for fuzzy thinking. Open a dialogue by flattering your husband. Ask him for his advice and guidance. Make a deal with your husband that playtime comes after bill time; hopefully he'll plow through the paperwork in a new world record!

Why not sit down and make a list of five frivolous items you both want, as well as five serious items that are important to both of you? List the reasons for each, and discuss how and when to save for them. Review this list again and again, crossing items off the list as you acquire them or replacing one wished-for item with another.

2. Set Up a Budget

Stop throwing all your receipts in a shoe box and stop paying no more than the minimum balance due on your credit cards. Don't assume that if you're earning X amount of money and your husband is earning XX amount, collectively you should be on Easy Street. Unfortunately, joint finances aren't that simple, or people would never fight about money.

The bottom line is that your budget is a tool to help you live within your means, not over them. It'll help you plan for unforeseen expenses and set aside a percentage for savings. By being prepared, you'll feel more in control of the money you have—and you'll be able to take advantage of good investment opportunities that arise.

As soon as either your or your husband's financial situation changes—a raise, a bonus, scheduled overtime, or loss of income—adjust your budget.

3. Set Up Your Bank Accounts

While some couples prefer to pool all their assets, what has worked best for us is to have a joint account for the household expenses as well as separate accounts for each of us. Separate accounts are a must in my book: They offer convenience (no one writes a check against money the other has spent!) and safety (if something dreadful suddenly happens to one of you, access to your joint account could be a problem). Just as important, separate accounts help remind you and your husband that even though you are married, you are also individuals with your own responsibilities and interests.

I can speak from experience on this topic. When Ernie and I were first married, I discovered that all his finances were handled by a business manager. While Ernie had every credit card in the world, this business manager kept him on a weekly stipend of only fifty dollars in cash. Also, he had a habit of referring to Ernie's money as "their" joint money. As in: "We're going to do this with our property here."

I was in a bind. I didn't want to offend Ernie's judgment, nor did I want to start barking about what he should or should not do with his money. (You know by now that you can't tell your husband, "You must change this or else!" Or: "Listen to me, because that's wrong!") That would have caused real harm to our marriage before it even had a chance to get started.

Instead, I gently said to Ernie, "Honey, I didn't know you and your business manager owned property together." He got my point. Eventually, Ernie decided to take a more hands-on approach to his money, and a potential crisis was averted.

Here are few tips about how to manage these different accounts:

◆ You decide to paint the wall of your brand-new house as a surprise to your brand-new husband before you move in. A gift like this comes from your personal account. If, on the other hand, you and your husband together decide to have the walls painted, then you should pay for this from your brand-new joint account you've set up to handle household expenses.

◆ You and your husband live together, you eat together, you entertain together—so that means you also "cat" together. If you marry a person with a pet, you adopt the pet as well, and these costs come from the joint account. No meowing about it—feed the cat!

◆ If you both share one car, then the cost of maintaining it comes from the joint account. Your own car should be paid for from your own account. (Unless you and your husband decide that it's easier for all transportation to be financed from one account.)

◆ One couple I know has an account for entertainment, gifts, and clothing. Both have set amounts that they must work with, and as long as they stay within those limits in each category, they don't have to ask permission from each other before making a purchase.

Talk about what works best. Be open to the possibility of changing the way you handle your money, especially once you have children. You'll see over time what makes the most sense for you—and it may not be the same method that works for your friends.

4. Do Your Homework

It's not a difficult or time-consuming chore to find an expert or group to help you learn about finance and understand your investments. How will you know what you can do with your money if you don't ask? Do you want Uncle Sam to take all of it because you were too embarrassed to talk about it? I don't think so.

Here are a few suggestions:

◆ Sign up for courses in finance or money management at your local community college or YMCA.

◆ Check out the latest computer software. Some software programs such as Quicken or Excel can automatically balance your checkbook, provide you with a budget, and do projections for your household expenses as well as your taxes.

◆ Get to know your banker. Ask questions. A friendly face is much easier to talk to about savings and investment options than a nameless stranger. Banks are often happy to explain the basics and risks involved in money management. Do not take it personally if your banker's manner is no-nonsense, or you are turned down for a loan. A bank is a business. If, however, you don't think you are being treated with proper courtesy, look for another bank.

◆ Talk to an accountant or certified tax planner. Both can save you a bundle. No matter how much money you're earning, spending some on professional advice can have a considerable impact on your budget.

◆ Look for a broker who speaks your language. Many large brokerage houses will take on couples with modest assets or erratic income (if you're self-employed, for example).

◆ Interview financial planners the same way you interview babysitters, a massage therapist, or a new employee; ask for their résumés and for personal recommendations. Talk to friends and colleagues who are happy with their financial management about whom they consult.

Go armed with a list of questions; if you don't write down your queries, it's easy to forget them. And don't leave the office until your questions are answered. Remember what I said—there is no such thing as a stupid question about money.

◆ Try to have as few credit cards as possible. Always do your utmost to pay the balance each month. More couples lose thousands of dollars every year by mismanaging their credit cards; it's way too easy to pay the minimum and forget just how much you're paying in outrageously high interest charges.

◆ If for some reason you have a windfall, I suggest the first thing you do is pay off all your bills. Nothing kills romance more quickly than worry about debt. Agree—compromise if necessary—on how much you will allow yourselves to spend, and if you go over budget, try to enforce a dry spell where credit card use is off-limits until the balance is down to zero.

Do not, under any circumstances, overcharge and hide the bills from your husband!

5. Set Your Goals for the Future

I'm a firm believer in having many different savings accounts. There can be one for your retirement, one for your kids' college education, one for vacation, one for emergencies, one for frivolity. Discuss your goals and decide which investments should be in safe, untouchable accounts (such as long-term bonds) and which can be slightly riskier (such as stocks and mutual funds). See what kind of plans your employer might have for matching your contributions to a 401(k) account. Do you lower your tax bill by contributing to an individual retirement account (IRA)? Should your money be in real estate or certificates of deposit, or both? How much cash flow do you need? How much do you need to set aside for a "cushion" to make you feel safe? Or if you plan to buy a house, what's the best way to make that dream a reality?

Whatever you do, make sure your health insurance is up-to-date.

Both you and your husband must not hesitate to outline a plan in case of unexpected illness or even death. This means that there must be no secrets, that you must find a way to carry on an open, honest dialogue about wills, trusts, property, safe-deposit boxes, burial plots, insurance, all those tough-to-talk-about but absolutely vital subjects. Don't put this off because it seems morbid or unbearably intimate (it can be much easier to talk about sex than money!)—and don't wait for a tragedy to make you face the realities of life. Plan carefully so that your family will inherit what's yours, or Uncle Sam will gladly remove it from the premises.

This is a perfect time to state that any man who insists on handling *all* the money and not letting you near the books is trying to control *all* of your life. And if you are dependent in your mind or your heart on your husband for money, you will never really find your own voice or your own power. You give up your freedom for the "security" this dependence creates. And you'll pay and pay, and be constantly angry about your powerlessness, whether you can voice it or not.

RETIREMENT: THE QUICKEST WAY TO RUIN YOUR MARRIAGE

"Retirement" is a word that should be stricken from the English language (as well as the Norwegian!). You see, after retirement, the next step is death.

I remember sitting with the brilliant actor Henry Fonda just before he was about to start filming *On Golden Pond*. He had just finished another film, and he said to me, "You know what, I've had this all my life . . . when I finish one job, I go from thinking, *Oh, thank God that's over,* to telling myself, *Oh, my God, what am I going to do? Will anyone hire me ever again?*"

I looked at him, shocked, and I said, "But, Hank, you're *Henry Fonda!*"

His reply? "That doesn't mean anything to me."

Ernie is exactly the same. He loves his work and he loves *to* work. He can't imagine retiring, and I certainly can't, either.

There's a myth that work should be over at the age of sixty-five. I've known so many men who were very active, very driven, very career-oriented, and very happy—until they retired at age sixty-five (or at whatever age they were forced out). A year later they were dead.

Work keeps us focused. It keeps us busy. It keeps us youthful. These men suddenly found themselves in that most unfortunate, vulnerable position of wondering, *Now what am I going to do?* Because they couldn't figure it out, the life force just seemed to leave them. Boredom and disinterest set in, a boredom that I believe can be equated with stopping the heart.

I know many women with husbands who've just retired, only to discover it's the worst thing in the world for both the man and the woman. All of a sudden this formerly vibrant, busy husband begins climbing the walls in the house, a lump, underfoot, and in the way. He's always hanging around wondering what she's doing that day or why she does this or why she does that and can he go with her. He asks, "What's for lunch? When is lunch? Where are you going? Well, aren't you happy I'm home?"

What he does not want to hear is a deafening no.

If your husband does retire, I advise you to work out boundaries so that he stays out of your space in the house and quickly establishes his own space. You've entered a new stage in your marriage, one where finding the right balance may not be easy. You can fight it, or you can communicate and compromise and look to the future with joyful anticipation.

Remember numbers eight and nine on my list of Borg-Nine Principles? Being a Mentor and Giving Back. Retirement is the ideal time to start doing both.

When you suddenly aren't working anymore, it's so good to find something that you're truly committed to, some way you can make a difference. It's a perfect time to apply all your knowledge and experience, all those years of learning, exploring, and digesting the world. Now you're ready to take advantage of your many interests and talents because you finally have TIME.

Retirement is your opportunity to do something you've always felt truly passionate about. Study sculpture. Open a bed-and-breakfast in the country. Devote time to young people, or to people older than you are. Whatever you decide to do, set aside a certain portion of your time to give of yourself to others. The goal is to keep you focused and active and busy living your life. The minute you sit down and just stare into space, you're finished.

Of course, you won't figure out what to do with your future all in one day. But don't lose sight of the opportunity you've been given to fill those years ahead of you. And don't deny that you've got a challenge that must be faced. The more you try to sweep it under the carpet, the bigger the bulge is going to be.

Brainstorm together and offer suggestions to your husband, encouraging him to do the same for you. Explore your options—there are so very many. One of the great things about volunteer work is that you're under no obligation to continue if the organization you've volunteered for turns out not to be right for you. Find another group that needs help, one that will welcome you with open arms. There are so many fantastic places and people who will use and cherish your expertise and wisdom.

Age doesn't mean physical infirmity is inevitable, or that your mental faculties will become less acute. (That's not to say health concerns don't exist, but many older people are as dynamic and as full of life as they ever were—some even more so!) Seniors are the fastest-growing segment of the population in America, and they have so much to offer.

Ernie is a great example of this. He has a true youthfulness and enthusiasm. He's very happy to be where he is and to see what he has accomplished in his life. And he loved the opportunity to work with a bunch of adorable young actors on his sitcom, *The Single Guy*. These actors idolize Ernie, and clearly they feed off one another's energy.

Ernie is still full of pep. His excitement over the deck we were building never waned all through the time it took to actually finish the project. In fact, he enjoyed it so much that our contractors are now like a part of the family. Sometimes I wish I could borrow a little of his energy when my own supply is running low.

Here's Ernie on work: "Do I want to stop working? Well, it all depends, because I really enjoy it. Show business is always crazy, but it gets me out of the house and out from underfoot for a while. Tova's glad about that!

"Do you know how I got my last job, on *The Single Guy?* Tova stumbled over me one day and said: 'You, get a job!' So I called my agent, and she got me a part in a pilot, which I told myself was just a thing they were shooting. It'd be nice to work, I figured, but that was as far as it would go.

"Well, one day I'm out in my bus, and Tova calls me. 'Hi, honey, how are you?'

" 'I'm fine, darling, how are you?'

"Everything was fine, and we chatted for a while, and then she said, 'Remember that little thing you did called *The Single Guy?*'

" 'Yes, I sure do.'

" 'Guess what,' she said. 'You've been picked up.'

" 'Oh, my God,' I said, 'that means I've got to go to work!' "

" 'That's right. Not only that—you're going to be on between *Friends* and *Seinfeld.*'

"I burst out laughing. And then I said, 'I wonder who the producer went to bed with!' "

I hope you know he's kidding!

◆ 11 ◆

Heart and Home:
Cherishing Your Loved Ones
and Creating a Safe Haven

An IMPORTANT PART OF
making a good marriage better and a healthy marriage even stronger is
learning to cope, individually and as a couple, with the other important
relationships in your life: your children, your parents, your in-laws, your
extended families, ex-spouses, and all those people who will definitely
make demands on your time and emotions.

Let's begin by considering the most challenging and potentially
wonderful roles you two will ever take on, that of parents to your children. I've already told you that my philosophy when it comes to children is simple:

◆ You're married to your husband, not your children. No matter
how much you love them (and you will), he needs to come first—
and to know that he does.

◆ If you make your husband your priority in your marriage, your children will benefit by growing up in a home where their parents devote themselves to each other as well as to their family.

◆ When you and your husband have a strong, loving marriage where communication is constant and open, your children will grow up with those same values. After all, children learn more about how to live from their parents than from anyone else, so what kind of role models do you want to be for your children?

What's hardest about parenting is that we don't learn it in school. We get mostly on-the-job training for this lifelong challenge and responsibility. And some of us are instinctively better at it than others. To understand what can help you approach this time in your married lives, it's important to keep several things in perspective.

First and foremost, never forget that it's not just your child you're carrying during those nine months of pregnancy. That precious life carries part of both of you. Your husband must be involved in all your decision-making about your child's future. Now, more than ever, you need to function as a couple.

If you already know you have trouble communicating with your husband, consider how much harder it will be to find common ground when there's a needy, hungry, crying infant in the house. Before the baby arrives, you and your husband need to make your commitment to each other as strong as you possibly can. Use your pregnancy to open new paths of communication. Instead of feeling separately terrified and overwhelmed by what's about to transform your lives, give each other encouragement and the strength to plan for your future. (Of course, no matter what plans you've made, realize that once the baby arrives, nothing is going to be the way you imagined it!)

Obviously the dynamics of any marriage change when you have children. There's this amazing new person, this wonderful new source of energy in your lives. But the tiny creature you've fallen utterly in love with will also make demands on *your* energy, as well as your time—time you used to be able to spend with your husband. As luscious and remarkable as your baby is, never forget how luscious and remarkable your husband is, too!

Encourage your husband to be as involved as possible in the day-to-day care of your child. I think one of the most wonderful sights in the world is a father cuddling his own little baby. It brings tears to my eyes, it is so dear. I can almost imagine the baby saying, "It's okay, Daddy, I know you won't drop me."

And if your husband doesn't change the diaper exactly right, so what? Laugh together as you both struggle to learn all these new parenting skills. And look for ways to share this experience of child rearing. Talk about what he remembers learning from his father about being a parent, and get him to write up some of the memorable episodes in your child's keepsake baby book. Most of all, as hard as it will be to do so, make a special effort to keep your role as a parent from completely overshadowing your relationship with your husband. If you end up living for your children, you don't need me to tell you how your marriage will suffer.

> ◆ **Amanda:** The first six months were the worst because my son never slept. Henry was a naturally crabby, colicky, very alert baby who wanted to be a part of everything. His fussing drove me so crazy, I almost began to hate him. But as soon as he got a little older and started talking enough so that we could communicate more effectively, I was completely smitten. I love this little boy so much that I can't imagine not ever thinking of him as anything other than the precious joy that he is.

But what happened to Amanda's husband when Henry was fussing and crying all day and all night? How did he feel? Utterly miserable. Amanda's angst and exhaustion because of their child nearly drove him out of the house. Only when Amanda confessed her fears and anxieties to her husband, finally asking for his help, was their marriage able to survive.

Communicate! Talk about what you're feeling! I just can't say it enough.

A friend of mine recently divorced her husband after fourteen years of marriage. They have a five-year-old son they both love dearly. She told me, "You know, we had all sorts of problems that we thought were manageable until we had our son . . . and then these little sort-of-manageable problems instantly were magnified into catastrophic ones. The issues you think you can shove under the rug and ignore suddenly sprout like Jack's bean stalk. They eventually drove us apart. Mostly because we realized we really didn't like each other anymore."

Did she regret having her son, I asked her. "Absolutely not," she replied. "Do I wish I weren't a single mother? Most of the time. Do I wish my husband and I had communicated better when we had the chance? You bet. But now I have to look forward and not dwell on it, or I'll be a wreck for my son, and that's the last thing I want to do to him."

GIVING YOUR CHILDREN WHAT THEY NEED MOST

Children must be nurtured and loved but also disciplined. The greatest gifts you can give your children are stability and unconditional love, coupled with clear-cut rules and boundaries. That way, they can develop their own sense of self and self-worth. Children respond to limits; they crave them. They can learn early on what's right and wrong when you help them understand, and when you don't contradict what you teach them by your own behavior. Children learn so much by watching and listening to their parents.

Living in Beverly Hills, the capital of conspicuous consumption, I often see parents who are unwilling to discipline their children and say no when it's called for. Sometimes I just want to shake the mother or father and say, "You are ruining this child. He'd be better off figuring things out for himself." But I can't. I can only shake my head and hope for the best.

Without healthy discipline, your children will not grow up to be healthy adults. If you are constantly letting them set their own limits (giving them power they're too young to handle) or worried about hurting their feelings (will they hate you for sending them to bed at eight instead of eight-thirty?) you must get over it right now.

Children are highly adaptable creatures and can adjust to nearly any routine. If they are used to both Mommy and Daddy going off to work, then it will seem perfectly natural to them. If each day they are cared for after school by a baby-sitter, then that will seem perfectly ordinary and safe. (It'll be harder for them to adjust if Mommy decides to go back to work after ten years at home, but they'll soon adjust.)

After all, how can you have a happy marriage if your children make the rules of the house? How can your husband be number one in your life if your children control the time you spend together?

◆ **Margaret:** It nearly breaks my heart when my husband tells me that he knows he comes last—well, second. But we know that our children won't always need so much from me, and we have enough faith in our future together to wait it out. There is simply no way to find a balance when the kids are this age. We keep reminding each other . . . soon! After all, parenting is a short period when you consider your entire lives together. We try to be flexible. We stay up late and often chat over a snack and a cup of hot cocoa, and use this time to catch up with each other.

Margaret and her husband have made a decision to communicate. They chose to be realistic, to set goals together, and to let humor save the day. It's a constant struggle, but the alternative is unthinkable for them. Their appreciation for each other will keep them together forever.

Of course, sometimes people use their children as an excuse not to deal with their problems. The children are the glue that holds the marriage together, but it's a sticky situation that keeps two people who should no longer be together bonded in an unhealthy place. The woman usually tells herself, "If I focus all my attention on the children, then I don't have to figure out how to give my husband what he says he needs."

And the children pay the price.

Divorce is an unfortunate fact of life in our society. Given my own experiences growing up, I feel that no matter how painful a divorce may be, children are much worse off when their parents have a volatile, unstable relationship. Children know when there are problems in the house. They become afraid. They blame themselves. They act out. They *suffer.* And hearing their parents say that they've stayed together only "because of the children" leaves their young ones with a terrible legacy of guilt and shame.

(This issue is complicated and can't be fully discussed within the scope of this book. Let me just say this: Not every marriage can be saved, or should be. And whatever we can do to keep our children from being overwhelmed by guilt and regrets, we must.)

Speaking of regrets, I must confess to one that Ernie and I will always have: not having our own child. When Ernie and I first talked about it, he was pushing sixty and already had three children (as well as an ongoing custody battle that had brought him much heartbreak), while I was still struggling with my secret burden of shame and guilt.

Thinking about what might have been is an exercise in futility, I know. I'm certain if we'd had a child, I would not have wanted to leave him for a second. And I can see that giving my energy and devotion to my business helped fill the hole in my heart left by my giving up David.

FIGURING OUT YOUR PARENTS
AND IN-LAWS

Long after I'd left childhood behind, my mother remarried again, and the wonderful man who became my new stepfather was not only kind to my mother and me, he taught me so much about love and fearlessness. This man dared to follow his dreams no matter what the obstacles were. It was through him that I finally found a positive role model in a male parent. (More about this darling man later!)

Our relationship with our parents has a tremendous impact on our emotional development and our attitude about what makes a good marriage work. Your relationship with your parents changes as you grow older, but nothing transforms it more completely than when you get married. And whether you live minutes away or miles apart from your parents, you can't escape having to deal with them.

When you get married, you have to recognize that you and your husband are your core family now. It's important to set new boundaries in your relationship with your parents. No matter how much you love them and cherish their advice, it's time to cut the umbilical cord for keeps. Of course, this is easier said than done! Whether you're ninety-eight or nineteen, you'll always be their baby.

Tova's Secret 18:

**You're married to your husband, not your parents.
And not his parents, either.**

It's necessary to your survival as a couple to be able to live your lives separate from their influence and control. You need to be able to say no to your parents sometimes—and to handle the guilt they may try to place on your shoulders when you choose what's right for your marriage over what would make them happy. Learning to say no takes practice, so start with something small. See what happens. Then take it from there.

Your husband must always come first. Your husband needs to feel the same way: You must always come before his parents.

I know it's hard. (Who ever said it was going to be easy?) Sometimes a daughter-in-law is made to feel that she's an unwanted interloper in the family, that nothing she does is right. (Other times, of course, the relationship a woman establishes with her mother-in-law is far better and less critical than the one she has with her own mother!) Form a united front when dealing with his parents or yours, and make sure that you discuss how best to handle them *before* you leave the sanctuary of your home. These conversations will forge yet another link between the two of you.

This means that when your husband complains about his father's overbearing ways or his mother's terrible cooking, you should cheer him on and support him. But do this in a way that does not insult your in-laws; your husband might end up disagreeing with you. He does love them; it's just that they drive him crazy sometimes. Even though you're grown up now, it's easy to feel like a child again around your parents.

Because you're the woman, the responsibility for keeping the channels of communication open will fall on you. You'll have to remember the birthdays, his Mother's Day cards, their anniversaries. Don't look at this as a chore or a bother, but as something that will bring you closer to them. As the years go on and his parents understand that you love their boy as much as they do (and as they grow to accept that you're the only one who can jolly him out of his terrible moods), they'll be less nervous about turning over their caretaking responsibilities to you.

EXTENDED FAMILIES AND STEPCHILDREN, OR EXES WITH AXES (TO GRIND)

When I was fourteen, my mother decided to move back to Oslo for a year. Despite the fact that I hadn't seen my real father in seven years, he was not thrilled to see me. Neither was his wife, my stepmother. One night, my stepmother ordered me to wash the stairs . . . to put me in my place, and to keep me there. These were the kind of broad stairs you find in old European buildings, and I remember crouching down, crying, with a pail and a little mop as I scrubbed. I felt like Cinderella.

(I shall spare you the conversation my mother had with my father when she found out what had happened. Believe me, I never forgot those stairs when I became a stepmother myself.)

When you marry a man who's been married four times before, there's no such thing as a clean slate. Divorce may end a marriage, but when children are involved, there's always unfinished business (which can be painful for everyone involved). Ernie's first wife was a good woman and a good mother to their daughter, Nancee. It's not for me to explain why some marriages just don't survive; theirs just didn't. Neither of Ernie's next two marriages produced children, just fireworks. Ernie describes his second wife, actress Katy Jurado, as a "spitfire that somehow or other I happened to get together with—through mutual respect and admiration, I suppose, then, *bam,* that was it, we got married." Obviously a lot of planning and careful thought went into that one!

Ernie's third marriage, to Ethel Merman, lasted only thirty-two days. "I was standing there minding my own business," Ernie claims, "and this woman is belting out these songs and I said, 'Gee, isn't that nice,' and she looked at me and I told myself, 'Hey, a newfound friend.' We got along fine until the day we were married. Boy, that was it." Another case of impetuousness rather than logical thought. Oh, well . . . who ever said men were logical when it comes to love?

Ernie's marriage to his fourth wife lasted longer and produced the wonderful Cristofer and Sharon, but it was extremely volatile—and it did not end well. "I came back from making a movie in Mexico to find several large trucks parked in front of our house. Moving van–type trucks. And there was my Oscar sitting right on top of one of the trucks. I recall my ex-wife saying, 'There, that's what you loved all the time'— meaning my Oscar—'so take it and get out!' Two armed guards were standing there with their guns drawn, and I was forced to move out of my own house. Before I even had a chance to talk to my lawyer, I was barred from my own home and from my own children."

I met Ernie not long after this happened, and he was shattered. Not only because his marriage had ended in such a manner, but because of how bad it was with his children, who were still living with their mother. One day, Ernie remembers his eight-year-old looking up at him when he arrived for his usual visit, and saying, "Daddy, we don't want to see you anymore." Ernie just died inside. He kept replaying that scene over and over in his head. His children were so young, and he loved them so much, and they had been taken away from him.

"She pulled me back out of it, Tova did," Ernie says now. "She told me, 'Honey, they're young, it's not them speaking. They've been coached to say that.' Deep down I knew she was right, but it didn't make my pain any less unbearable."

The only positive thing that came out of this dreadful situation was that it brought Ernie and me closer together. I'd known that we were in for a bumpy ride, because even though Ernie and his ex-wife separated in September and we met the following March, we heard rumors that I would be named as correspondent in their divorce.

Ernie wasn't given the chance to see Cris and Sharon again for seven years. The anger and frustration Ernie felt wasn't going to go away. It became part of our relationship, and we had to deal with it. At times it was absolute hell, but we really had no choice. Oh, we could have chosen to ignore the problem, living with constant bitterness and anger. But we chose to get through it together. Mostly what we did was talk. And talk and talk some more. Even when it was terribly uncomfortable—remember, I was still not able to talk about David!—we kept on talking.

By the time Ernie's ex-wife decided he could see the children again, they were both teenagers, angry and confused. Surprisingly, at first Ernie was afraid to see them since he knew he couldn't bear to be rejected by them again. I told him that he must see them. "Start out slow," I told him. "Meet them for coffee, to break the ice."

I became the intermediary. It was one very slow step at a time, because the kids were a little bit mixed up, too. They resented their father; they resented having to restart a relationship with him after all this time. They were also angry at both their parents for putting them in this situation.

It was tough going, but these children were too important not to fight for. "Tova seemed to understand them far better than I did. She made it as easy as she possibly could when they were teenagers," Ernie says.

Maybe because I had given up my own son, I overcompensated at first with Ernie's children. I wanted to do anything to bring them together.

HOW TO AVOID BECOMING AN EVIL STEPMOTHER

It's up to you as the adult not to let the thorns of a former relationship keep pricking you until you bleed. This is especially hard when there are children involved. And the reality of that former marriage is nowhere clearer than in the way your husband's children behave when they're with you.

At the beginning, a divorced man's children will usually despise you. The children will likely see you as the person responsible for taking one of their parents away (even if this is completely untrue, and the marriage ended long before you arrived). That's all the children can understand at first, no matter what you say or do, no matter how loving you are. They are also likely to say, when you correct some behavior, "You can't tell me what to do, you're not my mother." They're right, of course, but that doesn't mean they shouldn't be taught to respect you.

Dealing with your husband's children definitely puts an added stress on a marriage. Even the best of kids can be manipulative. And they usually are. Some kids take to their stepparents right away, while others look for ways to make trouble. Try to see the humor in what they say and do, even when it's hurtful to you. Laugh at the situation (not at the kids, of course) and do your best to step back from it. Your husband's children were there before you were!

But let's say that you've just been annihilated by your husband's young daughter all weekend. There were tantrums and screaming and "I hate you's" echoing through the house, and then she broke your favorite lamp on purpose and tried to erase your files off the computer. She's finally gone home, and all you want to do is scream at your husband: *"This child is a monster! You don't understand what she did to me, the spoiled little brat! I hate her and never want to see her again!"*

Please, whatever you do, don't! Zip your lip; drinking glass after glass of water will help keep you from blurting out what you really want to say. If you have to go outside and scream, pound a pillow, hit a punching bag, do it. Do whatever it takes to get the rage and frustration out of your system.

But—

Please don't blame your husband when his visiting children behave badly. He's going to love them and defend them, no matter what they do. Instead of sharing your impatience with his children's tantrums . . . he'll become impatient with *your* tantrum. He's so vulnerable, he just can't cope with their neediness *and* yours. So don't make him the target of your anger; don't lash out at your husband because your feelings have been hurt.

I know it's not fair. It's not fair at all, but it *is* the reality of your life with the man you chose to marry. So grow up, grit your teeth, and deal with it. See it as an area where you can practice giving up your need for control. If your love for your husband is strong and true enough and you continue to communicate without blame, you'll both get through it. And eventually, so will the children.

◆ **Brenda:** The hardest part about being married to a man who isn't the father of your children is that you want your own special "alone time" with him. But it's difficult with children always around. It's easy to lose sight of your relationship, of each other. You're caught up in your own need and you forget that your husband might have had a bad day at work, that he might need someone to talk to him and make his dinner or maybe give him a back rub . . . because you've had your own bad day at work and then your kids are screaming . . . and you just want to crawl into bed at nine-thirty and forget all about everything. Don't lose sight of the fact that the man you love needs you. And you want to be there for those needs.

You can learn so much from children, even if they aren't yours. From Ernie's children I learned tolerance. You see, if they're given un-conditional love and attention and are not criticized, stepchildren will almost always stop testing a stepparent, much in the same way that Ernie eventually stopped testing me.

But if you fight these children, they'll know you're not on their side, and they will fight back. It's up to you not to give in to childish emo-tions. If you can be calm and patient and loving, even when confronted by the superbrats of the century, eventually they will come around.

Ernie and I persevered through this crisis involving his children be-cause I made the decision to put my husband first, no matter how awful or frustrated or stymied I felt. My ultimate responsibility was to him. My job was to comfort him, to be there for him. I had to ignore whatever his ex-wife was saying about me, and I learned not to take whatever his children did as a personal attack. His ex-wife's opinions and behavior were not relevant to how I saw myself or how I chose to lead my life. I knew what my relationship with Ernie was, and I cherished every sec-ond of it.

I also knew that my relationship with Ernie was different from all of his other relationships. Whatever love had once existed between him and his ex-wives existed no longer. It had nothing to do with me.

The point is this: If you want to obsess over your husband's ex-wives, go right ahead. Just be aware that every night you'll be dining with a ghost—a ghost that you've invited to sit down with you at the table. Is this what you want in your house? I bet it's not!

A man is so vulnerable when it comes to his ex and their children. But it's excruciating for him to acknowledge it. For a man to admit that he doesn't know how to handle his own child when the little one comes for a visit, or for him to tell you he feels terribly frustrated and guilty, he needs to feel safe—and confident of your unconditional love.

Even though this may be one of the hardest tasks you tackle in your marriage, try to be as loving and supportive of your husband as you can be when dealing with his ex and his children. If there are still financial issues to be negotiated such as alimony and child support, the outcome of which affects the future of your own relationship, it's natural to feel frustrated or angry sometimes. But try to act like a queen, untouched by such crises. Your husband will love you even more for it. And at the end of the day, that's the most important thing in the world to you, isn't it?

All three of Ernie's children now have unique and individual relationships with their father. They're an important and integral part of my life as well. I see myself more as a mentor to them than as a stepparent. We talk all the time, and they know I will go to bat for them if they need me. I can't imagine life without them!

SECOND CHANCES: HOW TIME TRANSFORMS YOU AND EVERYONE ELSE

There's something vital we can learn from even the most harrowing marital situations, and that is the notion of second chances. After all, I'm Ernie's *fifth* chance! So how can I not believe in *second* chances?

As I told you earlier, Ernie's marriage to Ethel Merman lasted a mere thirty-two days, one of the shortest in history. At their wedding, Ernie's friend Sid took all the pictures. One photo—of Ernie, his father, his sister, and Ethel and her parents—was particularly interesting. In it, you see, Ernie's looking at his watch.

Well, Sid decided to put all the photos together in a book as his wedding present to them, and he slaved over it for weeks. As soon as his labor of love was finished, and Ernie and Ethel were back from their honeymoon and settled in a little bit, Sid decided to surprise them with a visit and their present. Driving over to their house, he was just so excited—until he turned on the radio in his car, and suddenly heard a news flash: Ernest Borgnine and Ethel Merman were getting divorced! Sid looked at the wonderful memento he'd created of their wedding day and thought of all the work and love he'd put into it. And then he threw it out the window.

Years later, I asked Sid why he'd thrown it out. He replied, "I don't know—I was so mad. And it's too bad, because it would have been worth a lot!"

Especially the photograph of Ernie looking at his watch!

Never forget that time can transform you and everything else. It can soften even the most painful memories. It can sometimes make you fall in love all over again with the same man. With forgiveness comes a second chance. It all depends on how much you want to hold on or how much you want to let go. If I'd stayed bitter after my divorce, I never would have found Ernie. If I didn't believe in second chances, I wouldn't have dared to marry him.

As for Ernie, after all those failed marriages, he never dreamed that he'd marry again. Or that when he did, he would find true happiness. Take it from us: It's never too late to make a success of marriage!

Speaking of second chances . . . years after my mother divorced my wicked stepfather, she finally met the man of her dreams, a rancher named Bill. He came from a very, very old family with very, very old money, and they expected him to go to a prominent university and then into the family business. But Bill really wanted to be a cowboy. He went to Princeton for a year, couldn't stand it, left, and never went back. His father disowned him, but Bill didn't care.

My mother met Bill in a bar, and they clicked right away. I was so happy when they were married, because they had a great passion, and he was a wonderful guy. I really loved Bill, who sadly is no longer with us. He was one of those guys who had a marvelous twinkle in his eye and a great deal of dignity. He loved life and never felt sorry for the decision he made to be a cowboy and leave his family behind. He found the courage to follow his dream—and by doing so, he found happiness and love too! If you want to be a cowboy, then for goodness' sake, go out there and *be a cowboy!* If you want to be an adventurer, don't live it through a movie, go out in the world and be one. Far too often we lose ourselves in dreams and fantasies instead of experiencing all that life has to offer.

Ernie and I have another friend whose beloved wife of many years died. He was bereft. We worried that our friend would soon pass away from a broken heart. Well, this man did all of his banking with a lovely woman, who had become very close to this couple over the years. Gradually, the professional relationship between our friend and his banker evolved into an incredible love relationship. In her abundant, nurturing love, he found a wealth more valuable than all the money in the bank. It's not that our friend didn't love his first wife—he adored her—but she was gone. And now our friend has been married to his wonderful second wife for more than fifteen years.

Second chances are available to everyone—if only you have the guts to grab them.

◆ **Vanessa:** I decided I wanted to learn how to play the piano at the age of forty-seven, and practically everyone I knew told me that it was impossible and that I couldn't do it. I'm an accountant, so what do I know about music? I was very discouraged, until a girlfriend told me to stop listening to these fools (they were just jealous anyway, she said) and ignore what they were saying. She explained to me that learning to read and play music is a lot like math. The notes, the beats, all that. You deal with figures all day long, she told me, so just look at the notes on the pages as if they were figures and you'll be fine. She made me realize I could do it! And I did! So—don't let anyone tell you that you can't do something.

No matter what has happened in the past, you and your husband can wipe the slate clean and start all over again . . . if both of you are willing. Remember that good marriages go through so many different phases. Many couples look back at their early days, when they were struggling and working so hard to raise a family, as some of the most fulfilling and happiest of their lives. Take an evening to reminisce about when you first became husband and wife, working toward the same goals, delighted by and thrilled to be in each other's company. You were living your own grand adventure then, and the future looked so exciting.

Why not rediscover those emotions together, and restore the magic to your marriage? It *can* be done.

MAKING YOUR HOME A SAFE HAVEN

"After Tova and I were married, I wanted to move out of the house I'd been living in (the same house I'd first lost in the divorce settlement but bought back afterward) because I'd known so much unhappiness there with my former wife," says Ernie. "Tova looked up at this house one day—and I'll never forget this as long as I live—and she said, 'Why do you want to sell this house?'

" 'Because it just reminds me of something that was bad, something terrible, and I don't like it anymore,' I replied.

" 'No, Ernie,' she said, 'you don't understand—it's just that this house has never had any love.'

"I looked at her and said, 'What do you mean?'

" 'Look at it, there's no smile on this house. But it's so beautiful. You just need to love it. If you just love it and say, "Hi, little house, I love you," it'll be okay.'

"You know something—to this very day, whenever we leave the house, we say, 'See you later, little house.' And when we come home, we say, 'Hi, little house, how are you?' I swear, our house has got the biggest smile in the world. That's a fact."

I think you can tell that Ernie loves our house deeply. I love it, too, but I must confess that I'm not as *in* love with it as he is. He believes that a house should be lived in and comfortable. I wouldn't want to suggest that I want mine to be more like a museum. Let's just say that we have very different tastes. That's true of many couples.

Creating your own space together is a major test of marriage. Something as seemingly innocuous as choosing a couch or a lamp or deciding on the color of a wall can cause tremendous friction between husband and wife.

One of my friends told me that her husband sees his home as his closet. That, unfortunately, sums up their marriage (which is not a happy one) in a nutshell. If all you do in a house is change your clothes there, how can it nourish your relationship? It's so important for a couple to see their home as their castle, a place of refuge, a haven where they feel safe and protected from the world. Your home is the one place where you're allowed to express *all* your feelings and be yourself.

But creating a home where you *both* will feel comfortable involves real communication and a willingness to listen without criticizing your spouse's ideas. It doesn't necessarily mean you have to spend a lot of time or money, but doing it right will take some work. Besides sharing ideas, one of your main goals is to find a way to give each other the space you both need. Even the tiniest apartments can still have "his" and "hers" corners.

When I want to redecorate, I think more about color and grace and luxurious fabrics, that sort of thing. Ernie is more interested in practicality, efficiency, and cost factors. The trick for us is to blend the two. One of the ways we did this is by having separate rooms that we each decorated to our own taste. Ernie has his Lincoln Room, which is full of marvelous memorabilia and history. He also has his own office, lined with bookshelves and photographs, while I have my lovely closets that are organized and spacious.

We also deal with our taste differences in our bathrooms. Ernie's has a toilet stall decorated to look like an outhouse. Very cute and funny, but not exactly my kind of throne room. My bathroom is much more feminine and elegant, with thick carpeting, well-lit mirrors, and softly colored wallpaper. It's a place where I can luxuriate in my bathtub, surrounded by the candles Ernie loathes, a stack of magazines, and peace and quiet.

Think of decorating the way you view your hair: No matter how bad your haircut, your hair is going to grow again. And if you hate the color of your hair, you can change it. The same is true in your house: If your husband insists on a particular item—let's say, maybe an especially hideous sofa given to him by his aunt—tell yourself *and* your husband that you are willing to live with this splendid specimen of seating for the next few years . . . but that when it's time to redecorate, it will definitely be your turn to choose the sofa!

I've always believed that filling your house with treasured objects and displaying mementos of your marriage—photographs, little gifts you've bought each other, beloved wedding presents—is far more important than any decor. Those pieces make your house into your personal environment, your private escape. Another way to do this is by creating special "house" rituals together.

Every night before we go to bed, Ernie and I say good night to our wooden dog, Bali. (Guess where we bought him?) Yes, we found Bali when we were on a cruise—one of our marriage renewals, actually. We went ashore looking for something ceremonial to commemorate our latest wedding, and as we walked into a store, Ernie nearly tripped over this dog, who appeared to be lying down asleep. Ernie looked down at him, realized the dog wasn't real but beautifully carved from wood, and decided he had to have it. They told him it belonged to the store owner and wasn't for sale, but Ernie, great actor that he is, finally convinced them to part with it. He had to carry this massive thing, which weighs about two hundred pounds, all the way home. But he didn't mind a bit!

Now Bali guards the entrance hall of our house. He's Ernie's pet. Trust me, if your husband wants a carved wooden dog, let him have one. Don't try to talk him out of it or it will just grow into something bigger than the dog.

(I must add, though, that Bali has the biggest pair of balls I've ever seen on a dog, alive or wooden! Do you think Ernie was trying to tell me something?)

MAKING PEACE WITH WHAT YOU CAN'T CHANGE

No matter how much we want to, sometimes there are certain things we just can't remake about ourselves or our spouses. Some of my girlfriends, who know their plumbers' phone numbers by heart, wish they had a husband who was more handy around the house. Others wish their husbands were less handy and more interested in going to the theater.

In my case, I'd like to be Julia Child, but the truth of it is, I just can't cook. The thought of baking a cake sends me into a cold sweat. I think this stems from growing up with a mother who was a housekeeper and a cook; I knew way back then I never wanted to do what she did. Luckily, Ernie doesn't mind doing the cooking. I can't imagine what our marriage would be like if he did!

I'll never forget the one and only time I decided to use the kitchen to cook him a beautiful dinner. I bought *The Joy of Cooking* and planned our meal perfectly: delectable leg of lamb (complete with its own cute little meat thermometer so I would know when it was done), steamed vegetables, new potatoes, a little gravy. Lovely and simple, right? Wrong!

I got to work, slicing and dicing. I remembered to preheat the oven. I set our dining room table with our best china and silver, arranged the flowers, and lit the candles. The aromas were fabulous and my mouth was already watering. I was so proud of myself! Ernie was also thrilled, so when he offered to help me, I said, "Don't you dare get up!" and went into the kitchen to bring out my feast.

Well, as I was heading toward the oven with one of my china platters, I slipped on a bit of grease (no surprise, I had left the place in a bit of a mess!) and went down in a heap. The china platter slipped out of my hands and broke into shards and wedges all over our slick Spanish-tiled floor. So there I am, sliding on our tile, worrying about my beautiful leg of lamb . . . and one little wedge of broken china slices neatly into my instep and it starts gushing like an oil well.

My darling husband came rushing in to find me in a hysterical heap on the floor. He tied a tourniquet around my foot, which was covered in blood, picked me up, and hurriedly drove me to the emergency room, where I was promptly given eleven stitches.

Well, I told myself, this is a sign that I am not yet ready to cook. I know that for some people it's a real pleasure to create elaborate and delicious meals. I think I'll stick to my cosmetics! (And do something else with all those cabinets . . .)

Tova's *Compromise* 6:

If cooking isn't your thing, turn your kitchen into a den.

Why is it that so many happy memories center around food? For most people, the aroma of a particular food they once enjoyed at a family gathering can click them right back to an event that took place dozens of years before. Scent memory is amazingly strong. I think that's why so many men like lavender; it reminds them of their grandmothers.

FAMILY RITUALS

One of my favorite memories is of Christmas in Norway. The tradition was that children could not see the tree itself until the dusk on Christmas Eve. Then, thrilled beyond measure, we placed candles in their little holders on the tree, and lit the tapers. (It's a good thing Ernie wasn't Norwegian, or he'd have gone crazy with all *those* candles!) There was something so magical about the cold air and the spruce tree, the aromas and the sounds so rich and so warm and so loving. I always felt as if they'd wrapped their arms around me. Later that evening, after all the church bells in Oslo started to ring, resonating all through the town, we'd sing carols around the tree.

No matter where your family is from or what time of year it is, rituals and traditions are important. You want to create something unique, something everyone in the family can participate in, something that makes you all feel special.

You already know how much Ernie and I believe in rituals to celebrate our marriage. Well, it's just as important for *families* to establish their own rituals. You don't have to wait for a holiday to roll around to start one. Rituals can be as simple as going on vacation with the family to the same cabin on a lake every summer. Or stuffing a Thanksgiving turkey together with your cousins from Milwaukee. Or walking to the ice cream store at twilight for hot fudge sundaes. Or ordering double-cheese pepperoni pizzas to munch on whenever you rent videos for family movie night. Card games on a Saturday afternoon or picnics before a football game—they're simple, familiar activities, but they make memories that last. A ritual can be as simple as making cards for each other and leaving them all over the house, the way Ernie and I do.

Use your imagination, and have fun!

GIVING YOURSELF THE WORLD

One ritual I started for myself goes back to 1981. I'd always had a yearning to see and experience the world, so I told myself, "Okay, Tova, give yourself a trip somewhere for your birthday." I picked up a dart, and I literally threw it at a large map of the world hanging on my wall. Wherever that dart landed, I decided, would be my destination (except if it landed in the water, obviously; then I'd just throw it again!).

Ernie thought I was crazy at first, but I've been going on my yearly trips ever since. Sometimes he comes with me and sometimes he doesn't. He knows it's my unique birthday ritual, and he wouldn't dream of asking me not to go.

Naturally, I hope my dart lands on Tahiti or some other lovely tropical island—it's landed on Fiji twice—but I'm ready to go wherever it takes me. This past year it fell on a place called Warnabul, Australia, a tiny town in the middle of nowhere. My darts take me to places that I would never, even in my wildest dreams (and even with Ernie's adventurous nature), think I'd end up!

So if you or your mate imagines a ritual that's maybe a little bit off the wall like mine, allow it to happen. Sometimes you throw a dart and take a journey to a place you never knew you wanted to go!

Tova's *Secret* 19:
Celebrate your birthdays with a dartboard and a dream.

(Happy?) Holidays

Holidays can be a time of wonderful celebrations with the people you love best. But I bet that most people, if pressed for an honest opinion, would have to admit how stressful they find them. Do any of these comments sound familiar?

- ◆ "I'm not going to my mother's house for Christmas ever again."
- ◆ "I hate your sister. And her husband is a drunk."
- ◆ "No, we went to her house *last* year. This year we're going to my family!"
- ◆ "If you don't want to spend Christmas there, you can just stay home."

You get the idea. Are holidays ever like the warm and cozy commercials that start bombarding us earlier and earlier every year? Watching these make-believe, perky families practice all that goodwill toward men certainly sets us up to feel disappointed and guilty when our own family gatherings are anything but happy.

At holiday time (as well as all year long), you want to put your husband first. But that doesn't mean you always go to his parents' house. And it doesn't mean you don't get a vote. It means you communicate and compromise and set boundaries. Ask your husband what he really wants to do. What if he hates going to his aunt's house but feels obliged to because of family pressures? If you stand by him and back him up, you can help him remove guilt from the equation.

Maybe it's time for you to start a new holiday tradition together that brings the family to your house. Or maybe, like some couples, you reserve this family holiday for just the two of you—and fulfill "family obligations" to others in another way.

GETTING AWAY FROM IT ALL, OR JUST FROM EACH OTHER

Vacations often can be as stressful as holidays, sometimes even more so. Expectations are so high, and there are no buffers. You're together in one room; there's no office to escape to; there are no friends handy to keep you company when you want a break from each other. Everything is intensified and a bit unreal. Especially if you've been looking forward to this trip as a way to rekindle your romance . . . or have fantasized that this vacation will be just like your honeymoon. Maybe you hope the resentment you've stored up and all your other problems will magically disappear after a week in Cancun.

But moments after you arrive, exhausted and disheveled, your husband drinks a margarita and falls asleep two seconds after his head hits the pillow. You go to bed mad, you wake up mad, and there goes your vacation.

Recognize that it always takes several days to unwind when you first arrive anywhere. Give yourselves some time to adjust. Find a vacation spot within your budget with activities (or peace and quiet) that suit both of you. If your husband likes to play golf, for instance, and you don't, try to find a vacation spot where he can tee off to his heart's content and you can relax or shop or do what you like to do. This doesn't mean you have to spend a fortune on a fancy resort, merely that you find a location that pleases you both. Make the search for the perfect spot a project you do together as a couple. The anticipation and planning are part of the fun.

Many families like to create their own traditions by spending vacations with the same friends in the same spot every year. This can be wonderful, especially if it gives your children something to look forward to, but what if your friends sometimes drive you crazy or you're tired of going to a familiar location all the time? If these trips become too much of a chore or feel like an obligation, don't feel guilty about not wanting to go year after year (and don't forget that your relationships with your friends go through ups and downs just like your marriage). If you take a "vacation from your vacation" one year, I'll bet you return to it with renewed interest the next time.

Nor do you have to do every single thing together when you are on a holiday. If your husband wants to lie on the beach and you don't, let him lie on the beach! Don't sulk that he's not paying attention to you. It's his vacation, too. Go do something you enjoy, maybe relax with a good book, or do some plain old people watching.

Compromise! Ernie likes to go on vacation to places that are not necessarily on my top ten list of destinations. Once I flew from my exquisite hotel in Paris, France, to Ernie's not-so-exquisite fishing site in Homer, Alaska, to join him. Did I really want to go? No. Did I wish he were flying from Homer, Alaska, to Paris, France? You bet. Did I mope and complain? A little (to myself). Then I got on a plane. More than one plane, as I recall.

Because if I'm not there for my husband, shame on me.

This is not about "I did it for you, so now you have to do it for me."
You do these things for your husband because you love him and you
want to. You want your husband to be happy, and deep down, you know
that it'll take a lot less energy than you first thought. Once you get over
your initial resistance, you'll find that sharing your husband's interests on
vacation will become a delightfully intimate part of your life together.

HIS HOBBIES AND YOURS

Ernie loves his work, but he also loves his weekends. Saturday is his
time to unwind, and for him that usually means the golf course. Luckily he doesn't expect me to go with him, so I use that time to do whatever I want to do for myself. I feel sorry for football widows . . . but even
they can get a lot done while their dearest spouses turn into seasonal
couch potatoes! On the other hand, if your husband makes it clear he
would appreciate your company during the pigskin season, don't act like
a martyr. Try to find something that's satisfying to do at his side while
he's watching the game. You can knit or embroider or read or talk on
the phone as long as it doesn't disturb him; you can pay the bills or read
a book; you can curl up next to him and try to take a nap. And once the
season ends, make sure he joins you in some of your favorite activities—
not as a payback, but in order to keep you close.

Don't mope or begrudge your husband his hobbies. And don't be
offended if his hobby doesn't include you. It doesn't mean your husband
doesn't love you and want to be with you; it just means he likes pursu-
ing his own interests on his own. Give him the space he needs to do
what he loves.

Men can be so grateful when you encourage their hobbies. Try it, and you'll see. He's probably so afraid that you're going to squawk when he heads out for poker night that he'll be thrilled to pieces when you send him out the door with a kiss and a hug instead of a frown and a pout. Oh, the relief he'll feel, and the gratitude. Chances are, he'll fall all over himself in the future to please you. All because you pleased him.

EXHAUST FUMES, OR ERNIE AND THE BUS

Some husbands take their wives to the country, or to Florida, or wine tasting in Tuscany. Some plan camping vacations or set off on cruises. Others prefer to explore romantic little bed-and-breakfasts in offbeat little towns, or simply unwind in a desert motel. Not my Ernie.

My beloved husband has a bus. A forty-foot-long Greyhound, a monster eighteen-wheeler whose insides could appear in a Southwest-theme issue of *Architectural Digest*.

When I first heard about this thing, I said to the aforementioned beloved husband, "What part of me looks like she belongs on a bus?" The only kind of Greyhound I'm interested in is at the dog track.

Oh, well. Some women are football widows; I'm a bus widow. In fact, if I made a list of 100 things I want to do in this lifetime, spending time on a bus would be number 101.

If, however, Ernie really wants me to go with him on a bus trip, I go. I don't sit on the bus and moan, "Why am I here? Why are you doing this to me? What kind of vacation is this supposed to be anyway?" If I stayed so attached to my own needs, then I wouldn't be able to see anything beyond them—like my husband's needs. And I must confess that I almost always enjoy it more than I thought I would. Part of that is because Ernie holds court in every truck stop in America. He loves to explore, meet people, and find things for our home on these trips.

The bus is a ritual for Ernie. It's his way of relaxing. And to tell you the truth, most of the time he doesn't mind my not going with him. It's his time with the guys, his own little world.

The bus Ernie has now is actually Bus 2. Bus 1 didn't talk to him. When he turns Bus 2 on, it says, "Systems all okay. Checking . . . blah, blah, blah." It's voice activated.

I'll never forget when Ernie called me from Oregon, where Bus 1 was having a maintenance check. (I called it going to the bus doctor.) "Honey, I'm only here to do this maintenance," Ernie told me. "But they just showed me this new bus."

"Yes?" I said. I had a feeling. . . .

"Well," he said, "you won't believe it, but there's another bus here, one that talks to you. See, it's very important when you're out there in the dark and you don't know what's wrong with the systems and, well, you know how everything is computerized, it's so technical, and here you have a voice-activated thing. Because of that, you're always in touch."

I'm thinking, *Yes, honey, um-hmm, and now for the punch line.* . . .

"I'm really thinking of getting it," Ernie goes on.

"So," I said, "when do you expect delivery?"

"Well, actually it's coming a week from Thursday."

"Oh!" I said, "Great!" Great, obviously, is not what I was *thinking*.

Ernie named Bus 2 the *Sun Bum*. He has a *Sun Bum* logo and hats and jacket. Now he's the Ralph Lauren of the bus world.

I have to tell you one last funny story about Ernie and his bus. Ernie was out on one of his trips, and another driver gets on the CB. Ernie answers, and this man says, "What does *Sun Bum* mean?"

"Oh, it's the guy I drive for," Ernie replies. Pause . . . pause.

"Who do you drive for?"

"Just some broken-down actor." Pause . . . pause again.

"Who's the broken-down actor?"

"Ernest Borgnine."

"He's not broken down!" the other driver insisted. "He's pretty darn good. So how long you been driving for him?"

" 'Bout a year and a half."

"And what's your name?"

"Ernest Borgnine."

"Yeah, right! I don't believe you," the driver said.

"Honestly, it's me," said Ernie. "Don't you recognize my voice?"

"Nah. I don't know. Wait—there's a truck stop coming up soon. Pull up in there and let's see if you're for real."

In the meantime, he gets on the CB to talk to every other trucker in the vicinity. By the time Ernie pulled up to this truck stop, there was a convoy pulling in to see if it really was Ernest Borgnine in the bus—and they were delighted to see that it was.

That's my husband!

· 12 ·

Body, Mind, and Spirit: Glowing from Within

W HEN I WAS LOOKING
for a name for my second fragrance as well as for my salon, I didn't have
to look very far. Body, Mind, and Spirit celebrates the unique creatures
we are, and it incorporates every aspect of what makes us whole human
beings. By recognizing that each element of the three is as important as
the other two, we strike a perfect balance.

BODY: FEELING GOOD IN YOUR OWN SKIN

The goal of getting married is not to be able to say, "Well, I've got
him, so now I can wear my ratty old chenille bathrobe all day to hide

the fact that I've gained a few pounds, because he'll love me no matter what." You owe it to yourself—and to your husband—to look your best and maintain your health at any age. If you look good, you feel better about yourself. And if you feel your best, you'll look your best, too. We all know that a little effort goes a very long way.

Accept no "maybes" when it comes to your body. No "maybe I'll start a diet" or "maybe I'll start an exercise regime." How you feel about your body is how you feel about yourself. And when you take care of it, it will take care of you.

Before we go any further, I want you, in the privacy of your home and when you know you won't be disturbed, to strip nude and stand in front of a full-length mirror. Examine your body. This is no time to be shrieking "Ohmigod, I've got to lose fifteen pounds," or "I hate my hips." Instead, look at the marvel that is your body and scrutinize it carefully. Think about the parts of your body that you really enjoy and admire. This can be something as small as beautiful fingernails or long eyelashes, or some larger aspect of your femininity: the roundness of your breasts, the soft curves of your belly. Admire everything that makes you a woman. Your body is the temple of your self. You should love it and want to take the best possible care of it. When you do, everyone around you will notice. Especially your husband.

CREATING A BEAUTY RITUAL

Maintaining your body and your health need not take a lot of time, energy, and money. Of course, some women will spend every moment of the day and every cent they have fighting the natural aging process. The bad news is, all the high-priced creams and all the scalpels in the world can't stop it. But you can *retard* the aging process when you take good care of yourself. And a strong, healthy body is your best defense against developing health problems later on.

What I suggest you do is create your own beauty ritual. Take it from me—makeup and skin care are my business, after all—this can be quick, fun, and effective. I have my daily routine down to a science. Here's what I do every morning:

Exercise: First come the toning exercises, such as sit-ups and stretches. This takes less than twenty minutes. I begin by stretching, and then I do my abdominal exercises, which are especially crucial for good posture. Let me share my most important exercise, which will greatly improve your posture and alignment:

◆ Stand with your back against a door that is slightly ajar. Your feet are one inch from the door and shoulder width apart. Hook one of your thumbs around the side of the door that is ajar, at about ear-height. (This will stabilize the door as you lean into it.) Press your body to the door, tilting your pelvis forward until your body is flat against the door.

◆ Feel the position, then step away from the door. (It's not the most comfortable position in the world because we're so used to slumping.) Slowly walk away, still holding that aligned position. Hold your body in this position as you carefully walk around the room.

This is much more difficult at first than it sounds. It took me ages to get to the stage where I felt comfortable and knew my posture was aligned. It also takes strong abdominals. This simple exercise can do wonders for your back. And when you walk tall and strong, you'll feel tall and strong! Since I live in high heels—don't dream of asking me to wear flat shoes!—I'm always glad to have a few more centimeters added to my height.

The rest of the good news: As soon as you start to work out, your body will respond. You'll feel tighter and stronger because you *are* tighter and stronger.

Bathe: As soon as I finish my exercises, I take a quick shower or bath.

Skin care: My skin care regime is simple: I use my Beauty Bar, followed by a cleanser. Rinse with warm water and pat dry. Never rub your skin. (At night be sure to remove all your makeup first!) Then I use my

Cactine Skin Refresher, which is cool and wakes me up. I follow that with moisturizer, day *and* night. Our skin dehydrates and loses elasticity as we age, so it needs to be replenished with as much moisture as we can give it. And I'm not just talking about your face. Your entire body needs moisture, so don't forget to slather on body lotion, paying special attention to your hands, elbows, and feet. If you're going outside, applying a sunscreen is a must.

Several times a week I also use one of my cactine masques, which stimulate, exfoliate, tone, and leave my skin glowing.

Makeup: I prefer an understated look with my makeup and use mostly natural hues. Some women make the mistake of using far too much foundation and other makeup as they mature in a misguided attempt to cover their wrinkles. This is wrong; on your face, *less is more*. A thick layer of foundation will only call attention to what you're trying to diminish.

Hair: My hair is easy to take care of, because I have a low-maintenance haircut. Getting a good haircut is a must, and I suggest you save up for the very best you can afford, just as you'd save to buy an outfit for a special occasion. Your hair is often the first thing people notice about you, so there's no excuse not to have it styled properly. I also have my hair colored about once a month—and I'm proud of it! Adding a bit of color or highlights helps enhance a woman's natural beauty.

Style: I know what looks good on me and is appropriate for my workday or QVC appearances, so getting dressed is a snap. I'd say that my style is conservative with a lot of panache, and will stay that way forever. I love accessories, which update any outfit. My most important advice about clothing is to stick to whatever best suits your figure type. Avoid trends. If you find a suit, for instance, that you particularly like, getting a good seamstress to copy it for you can save you hundreds of dollars.

♥

Once I get to the office, I try to drink at least six to eight glasses of water each day, and I keep a lovely silver Thermos of hot spring water on my desk. I like to sip hot lemon water from one of my favorite porcelain teacups. This way I encourage myself to drink my daily quota of water (which also helps keep my skin hydrated) and do it with style.

This beauty ritual works for me and helps me start my day in a way that nourishes body and soul. Nobody should tell you that you don't deserve this time for yourself. In fact, taking time for yourself will enable you to make other aspects of your life better. And when you feel better, everybody around will, too. That includes your husband!

Which brings me to a last point. Your husband should also have his own beauty ritual; his skin needs attention as much as yours does. I'm fortunate that Ernie loves my products and has been using my masques religiously for years; he knows how effective they are. Many men, though, are not as open to taking care of their skin—at least, not until they wake up one day and realize their skin is as rough as a Brillo pad. At which point much of the damage has already been done.

My suggestion is to turn the lights down low and put some soothing music on. Give your husband a massage with some lovely skin cream. If you start a beauty ritual for your husband in this way—in a romantic and pleasurable setting—he'll be much more amenable to following it up himself . . . especially when you tell him how his skin is improving. Trust me, men are twice as vain as we are!

A word of warning: It's important to care for your skin, but not at the expense of your marriage. A friend recently told me about a woman she knew who used a rather unique moisturizer every night: *mayonnaise!* She might be convinced it's doing wonders for her skin, but can you imagine how her husband feels when he gets into bed next to that face? I don't think he got married to sleep next to a salad!

Tova's *Secret* 20:

Don't believe in beauty fads.

My dear friend Joanie used to be a big believer in fitness and beauty fads. She went to see the latest facial exercise guru in Hollywood, who was seriously displeased with the state of Joanie's jawline. "I'm failing chin!" Joanie wailed to me one day. "I'm not even getting an F in chin— I'm getting a Z!"

"How can you fail chin?" I asked her. Joanie just shrugged. Her facial guru had given my friend chin exercises to do, and Joanie couldn't quite get it right. How could she? She was supposed to accentuate her chin, mumble, and pull her lip up over her bottom teeth, and so on. Frustrated, the facial guru told Joanie to practice these exercises in her car every time she came to a light. (In Los Angeles, that's about once a minute.)

So there's Joanie, mumbling and doing her chin exercises at a red light in Beverly Hills, when a car pulls up alongside her. The driver sees what she's doing, panics, leaps out of his car, runs to her door, opens it, and tries to drag her out. "Don't worry, lady," he shouts. "My brother is an epileptic." Joanie's screaming, "Leave me alone! Who are you? Are you crazy?"

He wasn't crazy—he thought she was having a grand mal seizure.

The moral of this story? Stick to a good skin-care routine and you won't have to worry about failing chin!

(Of course, don't forget I live in the city where people will pay just about anything to look firm and young. When Dustin Hoffman's character was advised to go into "plastics" in *The Graduate*, I don't think the man who told him so was thinking of plastic surgery, but it can be pretty frightening out here. I've seen enough plastic faces and bodies in Hollywood to open a recycling center!)

HEALTHY COUPLE, HAPPY MARRIAGE

Health was the last thing on my mind when I was trying to hide my pregnancy all those years ago. I actually wore a girdle—size Tiny, mind you—and literally squeezed myself into it as long as I could. Squeeze, squeeze, squeeze. Breathing was out of the question.

Looking back, I absolutely cannot believe what I did to my body and my baby!

I've known for years it was important to eat smart and exercise smart and keep up with what's happening in the worlds of science and healing. But even healthy habits can't always protect you from getting sick.

I was too busy to have breast cancer. My feeling before my diagnosis: I have a business to run and Ernie to take care of, so please don't bother me with something as pesky as a lump in my breast.

My reaction was very common. I was in denial. I think it's why I had a hard time telling Ernie, and also why I didn't cancel the oral surgery I'd scheduled so many weeks before. I just wanted to get it over with, so I went ahead with this minor operation the day before I was scheduled to have the lumpectomy. Did I think about how dumb this was? No. Did I tell the oral surgeon? No. Did I tell my oncologist? No. Not until the anesthesiologist came over and told me what he was about to do, that he'd be putting a mask on my face, did I speak up. And that was only because my face was swollen. "Oh, no," said I, "you can't put that thing on my face, I just had oral surgery."

He cleared his throat and asked me when, and I said, "Yesterday." He got a most peculiar look on his face and said, "Would you excuse me, please." My surgeon stormed in a moment later. I shall spare you the details of our conversation . . . except that I thought he was going to blow a gasket!

As I recuperated from the operation, I did as much research into breast cancer as I could. I particularly wanted to try and combat the side effects of the radiation treatments I had to have. I started taking a lot of vitamins, especially antioxidants. I used my Cactine emollient to protect the tender skin of my breast. (I was grateful my skin never got any burns from the intense radiation—two minutes a day of concentrated rays for six weeks.) I even made friends with the two X-ray machines, naming them Victoria and Albert, after the queen of England and her husband. I tried to keep a positive outlook throughout my treatment, and I'm sure it helped.

In fact, Ernie and I consider ourselves lucky when it comes to feeling well. He is a marvel of good health and vitality, and has been most of his life. But we have to watch what he eats. Ernie can breathe in and gain weight. I like to call him a consummate actor and a consummate eater. So in order to keep his weight manageable, he's made a rule, and he sticks to it: Once he brushes his teeth, no more food will touch his lips.

My problem, of course, is getting him to brush his teeth at six o'clock at night. Why, I often wonder, are all those lavishly photographed food commercials on television *after* the dinner hour?

For me (and most diet professionals agree), there is no such thing as an effective diet. Instead, I follow certain guidelines that help me maintain my weight. Try these:

- ◆ Avoid eating late at night.
- ◆ Avoid fried foods.
- ◆ Don't mistake thirst for hunger.
- ◆ Don't go food shopping when you're starving.
- ◆ Give yourself a day once in a while to eat anything you want. Having a a few treats to look forward to will help you eat healthy the rest of the time.

- ◆ Watch portion control. Just because your plate is overloaded doesn't mean you have to eat it all.
- ◆ Eat slowly and chew your food well.
- ◆ Eat as little salt and sugar as possible.
- ◆ Nibble on healthy snacks when you're hungry.

Overload and overkill seem to be the American way. Overload the plate in the restaurant with food; overload the mind with too much to do; overload the body with "no pain, no gain." My advice is to try to set some limits; don't take on *too* much, or you'll give up before you get going.

That's why my preferred form of exercise is walking. Not a leisurely stroll, but a brisk walk. Swift walking has the same aerobic benefits—which you need for cardiovascular health—as running. I see my walking as a bit like the fable of the tortoise and the hare. The hare says, "I'm going to beat you." And the tortoise says, "Have a wonderful trip." Remember who wins?

Why not make exercise a family time? Go out for walks with your husband, and you'll both benefit by better health. You can include your children in your stretching and toning sessions—make them seem like family games. Just don't make excuses not to do them.

One last thought: Why are men such babies when they're sick? Is it because taking to their beds reminds them of when they were little, and Mommy took care of them, spoon-feeding them chicken soup? Is it because women are biologically programmed to endure the pain of childbirth, so we're more stalwart? Answer this question and you get a prize!

A friend told me a funny story about the first time her husband ever got, well, seriously intoxicated. He woke up with such a bad hangover that he begged his wife to drive him to the emergency room. He was sure he was dying. She assured him he wasn't, and told him no one ever died from a hangover. But he wanted a doctor to reassure him he'd pull through, just in case. Men!

MIND: FINDING YOUR OWN VOICE

When I first married Ernie, I was extremely introverted and shy. Can you believe that I spoke only when spoken to? Ernie refers to this as his quiet period. Let him explain:

"For the first two years of our marriage, Tova barely said a word," he claims. "We'd go to a party, she'd just sit there, and I'd beg her to say something. Then someone would greet us: 'Hello,' he'd say to my wife. 'What's your name?' 'Tova,' she'd reply. That's it. Just Tova.

"The man would keep trying. 'Tova is a lovely name.' 'Yes,' she'd agree. That's all she'd say. And then one bright day, she opened up—and hasn't stopped since!"

I can remember the exact moment when I found my voice. It was at a dinner party held for the stockholders of 20th Century–Fox after a preview screening of some footage from *The Poseidon Adventure*. Irwin Allen, the producer/director, was there, as well as the president and CEO of Fox, and they were talking about how they hoped the film would recoup their investment. And I said, "Are you kidding? You're going to do $134 million with this."

I don't know how it happened, but that figure simply popped into my head. Irwin Allen never stopped talking about it. That was what the film earned (almost to the penny) during its initial release!

I've thought a lot about how hard it was for me to speak up. It's still true that when I get stressed out or feel overwhelmed, my instinct is to shut down and stop communicating. My mother, on the other hand, initiates conversation no matter where she is or who's nearby. For years, especially when I was younger, it would irritate me no end. I found it embarrassing. I think the phrase I said to her more than any other (except I love you, of course) is "Mother, would you *please.*" Even now, I still catch myself saying it to her.

I realized that I'd started to find my voice when I unexpectedly ran into Lou again. I was in a restaurant with a girlfriend, and when Lou saw me, he came over and asked if he could sit down. I told him that I would really prefer it if he didn't. Was I proud of myself for doing that! I was no longer the girl he had abandoned; I was a self-supporting woman who lived by herself in the big bad city and had acquired a certain amount of street smarts. I was far more capable of asserting myself, but I was not yet sure who I was. It took years for me to develop confidence in myself and learn what I was capable of doing. Having a successful business helped, of course. So did a loving husband who accepted and loved me unconditionally.

Finding your own voice comes with experience. I think I had trouble finding mine because I was always so worried about what people might think that I was unable to be myself. I was too busy inventing scenarios about who these people were, or imagining what they were telling themselves about me, to focus on what they *really* were like or what they *really* were saying.

Once you find the real "you," all kinds of lovely and interesting people will find you, too. Let's say, for instance, that you're at a party and terrified of having to meet all these new people. One of the most endearing things you can say to a stranger is, "You know, these parties always make me so nervous, but you look so calm. How do you do it?" I guarantee you will make an instant ally.

Remember, people love to talk about themselves. Ask their advice, ask what they do and where they grew up, ask where they live and how they know their hostess. As soon as any conversation gets going, you'll think of plenty of interesting things to say, and your worries about meeting new people will be forgotten.

YOUR GIRLFRIENDS AND THEIR OPINIONS

I didn't have many girlfriends during childhood to teach me about trust and friendship. I still remember when a little girl who lived in the house where my mother was working asked me if I wanted to taste some sarsaparilla. What she gave me to drink was Benadryl! I didn't know any better; I was just so thrilled to be included. (I also remember she had a swing set with monkey bars; one day she threw one of the bars at me and broke my tooth. No wonder I kept to myself most of the time!)

As I grew older, though, I learned how important and delightful a trusted girlfriend could be. Some of the most wonderful women in the world have become my friends, and they've taught me so much. And I know one of the things that helped me recuperate from breast cancer was friendship. I had the greatest support not just from my staff and everyone at Cedars-Sinai, but especially from my friends. My beloved friends Pat Mitchell and Laraine Gerber drove me to the hospital nearly every day, then sat there and waited for hours so that they could drive me back home again. For them it really was a labor of love.

Yet even the closest friends can get into trouble by offering advice without knowing all the facts. You need to be careful about listening to your girlfriends' opinions. No matter how much you care for your friends, they're not living your life and can't possibly understand the dynamic of your marriage. Too often we let our friends' opinions undermine or even poison our relationships.

I mention this because it happened to me. When I came back from California and found out that Lou had been sleeping with another woman in our bed, I went in hysterics to my best girlfriend, who had been baby-sitting my store for me while I was away. She went to my house to get my clothes and things, and she provided a warm shoulder to cry on.

But in the midst of my terrible shock, when I was feeling so vulnerable and confused, my friend said to me, "Well, dear, I meant to tell you this sooner, but . . . and *this* happened, and *that* happened." She told me things I really did not need to hear, things I wasn't able to deal with then. She told me unequivocally not to go back to Lou. "I wouldn't stand for it. He is such a bastard and I can't believe what he's done to you," she said. "You can stay here as long as you like and—oh, my goodness—what a snake that man is. He is so awful." And on and on.

Of course she really did think she was helping me. I can't blame her because she meant well, but in retrospect I see what I let her do to me. I was so angry already, and my friend fueled that anger until I was out of control and even more hurt.

Girlfriends usually speak with the best intentions when you need help, but never forget that you are the only one qualified to make important decisions about your life. A friend's comments and concern cannot and should not be seen for anything more than it is: one person's advice, filtered through her own experience.

It took me a long time to learn the dangers of counting on my girlfriends' opinions. When my company started to grow, I paid through the nose for several consultants because I wanted my products to be sold in Saks Fifth Avenue and Neiman Marcus. Not just because these posh department stores were important outlets—but because my girlfriends said, "Can't we say you're at Saks? Do we have to say you're in mail order?" Mail order in those days was simply too tacky, you see, and these friends' main concern was what they could say about me. Reflected glory, that sort of thing. It didn't matter how hard I was working to establish myself; they needed to be able to boast, "My friend just stepped on the moon. Isn't that nice? Wow!" Saying that "My friend Tova Borgnine works in mail order" didn't have the same kind of ring to it. I had to do a lot of growing up before I could see those "friends" for the shallow ladies they really were. I also learned to let go of my own ego and value my work for itself.

I think the best way to give advice is to say something like, "I can't tell you what to do. Only you can make that decision. I'm here to listen to you and to hear you out, so take your time. You can cry, you can scream, you can take as long as you want. Most important, you can say terrible things about your husband, and then when you kiss and make up, you won't have to be embarrassed that you told me you hated him and you wanted a divorce and were never going to see him again."

During a crisis or any tough situation, professional counseling from a competent neutral party will be much more beneficial than advice from well-meaning friends. Your girlfriends may love you and confide in you, but even someone who loves you will always have her own agenda. Your friends' opinions are just that. *Opinions.*

Tova's *Secret* 21:

True friends want what's best for you, but they don't necessarily know what the best for you is.

Ask for advice, accept advice, weigh the advice, then do what you think is best for you.

MANAGING STRESS

Carl Jung said that life is what happens to you when you are busy doing other things. When I got a wake-up call in the form of breast cancer, I began to ask myself some tough questions: What is it I am not nurturing? Why am I going so fast? Why can't I slow down and take time for me? (And if I can't take time for me, who will take it?) If taking time for me means I take two days off from work so that I can just stay in bed and watch old movies, well, would that be so awful?

Isn't it ironic that marriage, divorce, birth, death, moving into a new home, losing your job, and changing your career all deliver about the same level of stress? It's because they're all about *change.*

Men deal with stress very differently from the way women do. They often try and hide the fact that they're feeling stressed. They don't want to admit they're not big and strong and able to handle everything. It's usually up to us to worry about healing them—but then trying to find the time to heal ourselves just creates more stress.

Stress must be tackled from the inside, on an emotional level, even if external forces are causing it. I've learned a lot from a year of experience working on live television. What works for me when I'm in a stressful situation like that? I start to put my makeup on, and a half hour later the stress is gone. Vanished, just like that. It literally melts off my face.

The first step in managing stress is asking yourself these questions about the situation you're in:

- ◆ Is what some other person is doing bothering me?
- ◆ What hard evidence do I have (besides my own feelings) that this is true?
- ◆ Do my fears seem logical and realistic in the context of the situation? Why?
- ◆ What does this person stand to gain, and what do I stand to lose?

◆ What would happen if I decided to relinquish my fears about this person and get on with my life? Would I feel more relieved or more anxious?

Are you ready to take action? Good. Then:

◆ Make whatever decision you think best to change in some way.
◆ Select the change you want to make.
◆ Decide on a plan to accomplish this change.
◆ Anticipate your reaction should this attempt fail.
◆ Get to work changing. It can be done.

(Notice that I didn't say change the other person or situation. You can only change your reaction to it. But that's enough.)

My favorite way to handle my stress is to pound a pillow. I have my very own nice pounding pillow, and I pound it to death. I picture the face of the person or thing that has gotten me distressed . . . then go to it. It works wonders!

I'm also a big believer in the stress-relieving powers of a nice hot bath. Run one that is as warm as you can tolerate. I like to add mineral salts to the water; preferably sea salts, which have the same composition as our blood plasma. Don't stay in your bath until you get nauseated or headachy or faint, but only to the point where you are perspiring. Then you'll be ready for a lovely long sleep.

Here are some more suggestions you might find useful:

◆ **Monica:** If I'm on the way home from work and I'm feeling stressed, I drive with the windows open and the music real loud so that I can't hear myself thinking. The louder the music is, the more soothing! I need to be able to scream along with the music. I do worry sometimes about someone in the car next to me, calling 911 on their car phone and reporting: "There's a very sick woman on the road. She doesn't look drunk, but there's something very wrong with her—she's screaming out her window!" But it works for me.

How about some other strategies to combat stress?

◆ Take a physical break. A walk around the block will clear your head and burn a few calories in the process. Or go to the gym. Some women like to lace up boxing gloves and hit a punching bag.

◆ Take the phone off the hook or leave your answering machine on and the phone's ringer off. If you're expecting an important call, let your answering machine screen the calls you don't want to take.

◆ Listen to audio books. When a person with a really interesting voice is reading the story, you'll be transported.

◆ Soothe your senses with the sound of running water. You can buy small (and inexpensive) desktop fountains to place on your desk at home or at work.

◆ Get a manicure and pedicure or make an appointment for a massage and facial. Pamper yourself. Go to the hairdresser. It's especially lovely when someone else is washing your hair.

◆ Rent the saddest, sappiest, biggest tear-jerker of a movie you can think of. Or else pick up a silly movie you loved as a kid.

◆ Do anything you know will make you laugh, such as going to a comedy show or watching a video of one.

◆ Take yoga classes and practice breathing exercises.

◆ Spend time with your pet if you have one. (If you don't, maybe you should!) Go for long walks with your dog, or play with your cat. Pets are known to lower an owner's blood pressure, and a healthy dose of a pet's unconditional love is a wonderful mood soother.

◆ Try aromatherapy. The fragrance of many essential oils has a very therapeutic effect on your mood. My own Tova scent refreshes and revitalizes me. When I travel, I like to spray the inside hem of my hotel room drapes, and tuck a few sachets into my suitcases and dresser drawers. Sometimes I spray the cover of the ironing board. I also put a mixture of baby powder and a few drops of my perfume on starchy hotel sheets to make them smoother and delicious-smelling.

◆ Make love, as long as the source of your stress isn't your spouse. Sex is a great tension–reliever, and can often get rid of headaches and body aches as well as the blahs.

Whatever you choose to do to manage your stress, remember how important it is to take time for yourself. I know that is easier said than done, but *you're* worth it.

LETTING IT ALL GO

Sometimes, of course, the only release that really works is a good cry.

Did you know we are the only species on earth that cries? Maybe that's why crying can make people feel so uncomfortable. People are afraid of intense emotions, and when they are forced to confront sadness, it taps right into their feelings of vulnerability, their worries about losing control. They'll back away from a woman in tears, not knowing what to do.

Think about when and where crying is sanctioned. At the movies or in a theater, you can sit in the dark (where nobody can see you) and emote to your heart's content. When you see something heroic or tragic on television, it's considered okay to cry. But most of the time, tears make people very uncomfortable.

Yet crying can be very therapeutic. It rids the body of tension and often leaves you in a state of calmed exhaustion, so you'll fall right asleep and then wake up refreshed. Tears are a necessary part of life, an outpouring of real emotion, so never be ashamed of your crying.

When husbands cry, though, most wives know something must be *very* wrong. If you see tears in your husband's eyes, I'll bet your gut reaction is to say, *"Oh, my God, he's crying!"* You'll do anything you can to comfort him.

But your husband might find it hard to comfort you when you're upset and in tears. What I suggest you do is explain to him what you need at times like that. When you are in a comfortable, intimate place, say, "Honey, when I was crying last week, it would have meant so much if you could have come over to comfort me. I really need you to give me a hug when I'm crying. Please don't be afraid when you see me in tears, because a good cry often helps me get over what's making me upset in the first place." Men usually respond well to specific instructions, so next time, he'll know what to do.

Tova's *Strategy* 11:

Cry when you need to—it's good for you!

FINDING YOUR BEST TIME

Every person has an internal body clock. Ernie happens to be the most alert and raring to go early in the day. *Very* early in the day. He gets up with the sun. "Hello, sun," says he, while I am still mumbling under the covers.

When we were first married, Ernie's early rising was a problem for me. When you're courting and all full of adrenaline, with waves of love energy enveloping you, the clock doesn't seem to matter. You're on the same wavelength and living by the same clock. But once you settle in together, your natural sleep patterns become obvious. (Especially if your beloved husband snores!) If only I could have slept until the last possible second in the morning, gotten up, thrown on my clothes and makeup, and still been able to pull everything together, I would have been quite content. But Ernie made sure that was not to be.

Gradually, over the years, I have become more of a morning person. *Because* of my husband. I could have said to him, "Don't wake me. Don't talk to me till noon. Leave me alone in the mornings; you know what I'm like." But I didn't. I wanted to spend that time with my husband, to have breakfast with him and be there with him. So because I was motivated to change my morning mood, my body eventually learned to adjust.

Understanding your body's rhythms (and your husband's) will help you pick the best time to discuss certain issues and problems with him. If he is super-grumpy in the morning, obviously that is not the moment to bring up any important topics. This sounds so simple, but it's something we often forget. It's all part of the learning process of being together as a married couple.

Tova's *Compromise* 8:

**Don't fight your body's internal clock—
make the rhythms work for you!**

SPIRIT: SAYING YOUR PRAYERS AND EXPRESSING GRATITUDE

I can't imagine my life without prayer. Prayer is like absolute meditation for me; it's all about Heart Feeling. And I do believe in a higher power, no doubt about it. Otherwise, all of us who live in this wonderful, wacky world would not be here. And we would not be moving on to whatever it is we go to when we die.

Ernie and I both believe in acknowledging what is wonderful in our lives. His sense of wonder allows him to constantly be surprised and touched. If he sees a flag flying at day's end, he will weep openly; when he sees a rosy sunset or the stars by night (and I don't mean Hollywood stars) he'll go oooh and aaah in pleasure, no matter how many times he's seen them before.

Why not go ahead and make a list of all that is good in your life and acknowledge it? Saying your prayers can take only a few seconds or as long as you like. Nor do you need to say your prayers before or in bed. Try saying them while you're brushing your teeth or taking off your makeup. Create a ritual for yourself that is special to *you*. I have gotten so used to saying "Thank you, God, for my blessings" that it comes as naturally to me now as does saying "I love you" to Ernie at the end of a phone call.

Prayer is all about *us,* in the world. And in us, there is no *you.* There is only the pure world of the spirit.

FINDING YOUR PEACE

Meditation quiets me mentally. (Most of us do need time alone to quiet our thoughts, even if we think we don't.) It brings me into my Heart Feeling, where I can deal much more effectively with the stresses that life presents. One of the wonderful things about meditating is that it helps me to understand how much I don't know, and how much I don't need to know. Meditation is so important for me, not just psychologically but physically, too. It slows me down and improves my immune system. It gives me a few minutes to, literally, *breathe.*

When I meditate, I like to listen to different tapes, with music that I've found helps put me in a reflective state. I do deep breathing exercises I've learned from doing yoga. It doesn't involve a lot of time; you can do it in five minutes if that's all the time you have to spare. You can actually put yourself into a meditative state while you're standing in line at the supermarket!

You can learn how to meditate by reading books about it, or taking a few yoga classes, which will show you how to do specific kinds of breathing. You can meditate to music that you like, or you can do it in silence, if that's what you prefer. But it's all about doing something good for you.

Tova's *Strategy* 12:

Meditate, and breathe new life into your life.

GLOWING FROM WITHIN

For me, marriage is like a road. I can't see the road as it curves around the mountain but the road is not going to stop. It'll keep going on and on. And if I keep driving I'm going to stay on the road. I don't know what's going to come at me, but I'm going to enjoy the trip.

Don't forget to have fun while you're driving! Whatever comes your way, try to laugh at yourself and laugh at life. That way, when sticky situations present themselves (and they will), you'll be ready for them. You can say, "Well, okay. This isn't what I thought my life was going to be right now but this is what it *could* become . . . and I'm going to flow with it."

Your marriage will be what you are willing to make it. There will be beautiful moments and infuriating moments, loving moments and hellacious moments, humorous moments and touching moments—and some will be all of these at once. But each one will become a treasure to share with your husband, and these unique memories will warm you inside and out for the rest of your lives together.

It Can Be Done!
The Lessons We Learn

ONE MORNING THE PHONE rang in my office. My brand-new receptionist picked it up and said, "Good morning, the Tova Corporation." The voice on the other end said, "Good morning, I have the President of the United States for Tova Borgnine. This is the White House calling."

My receptionist said, "Excuse me, the president of what?"

Naturally, I wasn't in the office at the time, but I called the White House back as soon as I could and, my voice trembling, asked for the President. To my amazement, I was put through right away and heard the unmistakable sound of Ronald Reagan's voice greeting me. (It turned out he was calling to thank me for some products I had sent him and Nancy.)

"I am so happy that you sent me these products, but I have one question," said our commander-in-chief. "Should I put the masque on before or after the other creams?"

So I told him how to apply my products, and what an honor it was to know he was using them!

He replied, "I just want you to know I'm really enjoying everything and already seeing some benefits. Nancy and I really appreciate your kindness."

Well, when I hung up the phone I was still awestruck. He'd called me himself! To talk about cosmetics!

Shortly after this, Ernie and I received an invitation to a dinner at the White House, and we were thrilled to fly to Washington. As we stood in the reception line in the East Room along with everyone else, the President passed by and shook Ernie's hand, then mine. As I finished murmuring how privileged I felt to be there—me, little Tova from Norway!—the President leaned forward and whispered, "I just want you to know that today was my masque day."

My feet didn't touch the ground for the rest of the evening.

Isn't this a terrific story? The President of the United States had called me to ask for instructions about a facial masque, when obviously he had a few other things to do. Which just goes to show, give a busy person something to do, and he'll do it.

It can be done!

THE LESSONS WE LEARN

The big earthquake in Los Angeles in January 1994 was one of the most frightening experiences of my life. In fact I don't think I can live through thirty-seven seconds like that ever again.

Once the shaking stopped and Ernie and I realized we were still alive (although the twenty-six-inch television in our bedroom came flying out of the armoire and hit the wall about an inch from where my head had been lying about a minute before, nearly decapitating me), we groped for the flashlights. Which were exactly where they should be. Except for one small little problem—the batteries were dead. Because my security-conscious husband hadn't changed them for months and months. (Not only that, but as safety-aware as my beloved Ernie is, he's equally as intense regarding the extremely high cost of earthquake insurance in a city as fault-prone as Los Angeles. I'll bet you can guess what I'm about to say: Yes, about sixty days before the big one hit, Ernie decided to cancel our policy. Brilliant, Ernie, just brilliant!)

Ernie finally figured out where the new batteries were; we fumbled around in the drawers that had all fallen out of the desks and dressers; and we got the flashlights to work. In the meantime, there were aftershocks every few seconds, and some of them felt as big as the initial quake. It seemed that every possession we owned had fallen in a jumbled mess on the floor, and there was broken glass everywhere. The house was a complete shambles.

When we got outside, Los Angeles was enveloped in utter blackness. We could see nothing; there were no lights at all, nothing except for an occasional terrifying burst of a gas fire. Both Ernie and I thought that it was the end of the world.

(By the way, it *is* darkest just before dawn, in case anybody wanted to know!)

Los Angeles is not a town where you often go over to your neighbors' house to get acquainted. On the morning of the big earthquake, though, all our neighbors were huddled together outside, bound to each other by the terror of the moment and worry about what might be coming next.

What I remember most about the earthquake was the *emotional* aftermath. All of us who lived up there, famous or not, rich or poor, old or young, bonded in the dark. We were panic-stricken and flooded with adrenaline, and no one had a clue whether this really was the end of the world or not. We weren't focused on such typical Hollywood concerns as whose car is more expensive, whose part in the movie is bigger, whose tailor is more exclusive, or whose driveway is longer. Life was stripped down to its essentials: being alive, and being grateful for it.

So I'd like you to do a short exercise. Ask yourself this question: If this were your last hour on earth, how do you want to leave it?

In other words, how much do you have to be grateful for?

I've been thinking about this a lot, especially since I started working on this book. Not that I'm ready to leave this world, mind you, but I have lived the most incredible life. I've done so much that other people may never experience. I have, literally, danced with Fred Astaire. I have been to the White House and had the President of the United States whisper in my ear that that day was his masque day. I have traveled around the world and met incredible people in so many different walks of life. I have been lucky enough to work at what I love, and to experience so many facets of life.

Most of all, I have been blessed with the two great loves of my life: my darling husband, Ernie, and my darling son, David. I see them both as miracles: the love I found with a man when I wasn't looking, and the love I found with the son I gave away and found again. I keep learning from this love. It's a process of evolution. I know how I have grown; I have figured out how to set boundaries and stick to them. I am now able to say, This is what I am and who I am . . . and I am never going to make myself feel bad or guilty because I'm not something else.

When you marry too young, as both Ernie and I did with our previous relationships, you and your spouse don't grow together—and your marriage doesn't last. But when you're older and wiser and clearer about what you expect and what you want to give, you let go of so much you thought was necessary to make you happy.

Sometimes I look back at old pictures and I can't believe the woman in them was me. She's so unlike me now, from the look in her eyes to her demeanor, clothes, everything. I was so timid, so unsure, not yet myself. Who wants to look back with regrets? *Not me.* I want to live fully, in the moment, no matter how difficult this might be.

I'd like to tell you the story of a dear friend of mine who was very depressed after her marriage of more than thirty years ended. She packed up and moved out of state to be near her elderly father, and she had completely given up on love. But as soon as she went off in a new direction, unlike any she'd ever tried before, this man appeared. He is quite possibly one of the nicest human beings I've ever met. They fell in love and were married, and they adore each other. It has been the best thing for both of them, and they are deliriously happy. Their marriage only gets better and better.

What's the point of my story?

Tova's *Secret* 22:

Never stop working at keeping the love around you.

❖ **Elaine:** You're never too old to learn. I grew up in a house where I was constantly told, "If you climb up that tree, you will fall down and break your neck." I was convinced I was completely clumsy, that I would be all my life. Plus, I have a real terror of heights. Well, I learned a very painful and enlightening lesson when I went to a hiking spa in the desert. We climbed up to these marvelous Native American caves and ruins I wanted very much to see, and after I got up there and was admiring the beautiful vista at my feet, I suddenly realized I had to get back down. My heart froze. How on earth was I going to be able to do it? I was in such a panic that my thigh muscles seized up, and I had to slide part of the way on my rear end. The trail guides stayed calm and were with me all the way. "Put your foot here, put your foot there," they said, while I was in tears, hyperventilating while I screamed at all of them that I couldn't do it.

But I got down. I made it down the hill without killing myself. I really thought about this lesson, because it had been drilled into me all my life that I was incapable of making this kind of physical journey. For once, I had been fully living in the moment. The moment was about pure survival, about putting one foot in front of the other, and nothing else. I had no choice but to move forward. I finally understood the meaning of a hike like that. It's not about the physical exercise, but about the *journey*.

Yes. Life is a journey. Marriage is a journey, too. I think we should all try to focus on putting one foot in front of the other, on the path before us. Don't look down and don't look back. That's not where you're going.

There's always a new lesson to learn. I found this out when I went to Harvard in 1983 for an accelerated MBA course for executives, sponsored by the Young Presidents Organization. This is a terrific group that has helped me tremendously (especially in such areas as organizational skills and how to delegate—not my strong suit, as you already know!). To be a member, you have to be under forty, the president of your company, have at least fifty employees, and gross over $5 million a year. Back then, not many women were eligible, and I was the only female present for this course session.

As soon as I arrived, my insecurities kicked in. When anyone asked me what university I'd gone to, I was intimidated and a bit mortified instead of being proud that I'd accomplished so much *without* a degree. (Trust me—I don't have *that* problem anymore!)

I checked in and registered, and then called Ernie as I always do. I told him that I thought we'd be studying in our rooms after dinner, and asked him to call me then. At dinner, though, we were told that we'd be studying in the communal living room instead. All twelve of us, a lovely dozen. Eleven men, and me.

I assumed that if Ernie called me, there would be no answer in my room, and he could leave a message with the switchboard. What I didn't know was that the phone would ring first in the dorm room, and then automatically shift over to the living room. There we were, deeply involved in our case studies, when the phone rang. I didn't pay much attention to it because I assumed it wasn't for me. One of the men answered with a hello. There was a very long pause, and then a scream that everyone could hear came crackling from the phone, "WHAT ARE YOU DOING IN MY WIFE'S ROOM?"

The man holding the phone went absolutely white. "But . . . but I'm not in her room," he sputtered. "She's *here.*" Poor thing, he looked as if he had just been caught with his pants down.

Well, I immediately knew who was calling! But anytime you try to explain this kind of setup from a distance, it usually just gets worse.

"Hello, darling," I said to Ernie. "Actually, I'm here with eleven guys."

"Oh, is that so?" he replied.

"Yes, honey, we're studying."

"Uh-huh."

"And we're all in the living room."

"What do you mean, the living room?"

The conversation went from bad to worse. At least at this point we were all laughing. Once Ernie calmed down, we had him to thank for breaking the ice. Everyone teased me after I hung up, telling me not to answer the phone, no matter how many times it rang. What would they do if one of their wives called and heard *my* voice?

I learned an especially valuable lesson from the YPO. I'd been feeling, at this particular stage of my business, that no one else had ever gone through what I was going through; that no one else had ever felt exactly as I did. But of course they all had.

Running your own business is not that different from entering into a marriage. No one can teach you the ropes or predict what's going to happen. It's something that you have to work at, to embrace, and to figure out as you go along.

What I can predict, though, is that if you really love the man you married, if you try your best to treat him like a king, if you do all you can to communicate and compromise and be there for him, you can be truly happy in your marriage.

GOING ON TOGETHER

I've always tried my best to remain open to each new experience, even in my life's most painful moments. From the betrayal of my first marriage came the happiness of my second. From that dismal day when I cried all the way to work, I learned to conquer a crisis and face my demons. I no longer waste my time fantasizing and then getting angry because reality does not live up to my expectations. But my reality is better than I ever imagined it would be. Ernie knows I love him with all my heart, and I am so grateful to have a husband who is a true life partner, because I know how rare that is. I've found depths in both of us that I hadn't known were there. My marriage has been a gift.

At the same time I've learned how to express my own needs. I've figured out how to give 100 percent to my relationship and still run a company. Most of all, I've learned to fill every day of my life with meaning. I hope this book has given you some ideas about how to do this for yourself. I ask you to try them and then watch what happens. You'll see how your life will begin changing the minute *you* change what you want.

If I were to give you one last list (and you know that I feel you can never have too many!), it would be this one:

WHAT IT TAKES TO HAVE A HAPPY MARRIAGE

Appreciation	Commitment	Communication
Compassion	Confidence	Diligence
Empathy	Encouragement	Flexibility
Forgiveness	Fun	Humor
Imagination	Kindness	Passion
Patience	Physical attraction	Playfulness
Respect	Shared interests	Togetherness
Trust	Understanding	

Plus a good hairdresser, two bathrooms, time to yourself . . .
And of course you must love the man!

♡

Alan Shepard, one of the Apollo astronauts who walked on the moon, is a good friend of ours. One day Ernie asked him, "Could you tell me what it was like for you, up there?"

Alan turned to him and replied, "I looked down to see how vulnerable the earth was. And then I cried like a baby."

All of us on earth are alone and vulnerable out there in the dark. But marriage brings the light and the dark together, the happiness along with the heartache. Marriage should give you a delicious, secure feeling. No matter what happens, you and your husband will continue to live in each other's hearts, minds, and souls.

Now I want you to set aside all the lists, the secrets, the strategies, the compromises, and the rules. There's just one thing to remember:

How you feel about your husband is unique. And when a man knows who you are—and loves you for it—it's a miracle. Stay true to your heart, keep your indomitable sense of self, lose your ego—and really love your husband.

It's time to embark on your own great adventure. You too can be married happily forever. It can be done!

$\mathcal{S}$pecial $\mathcal{M}$oments

❖

During the writing of this book the topics of love, romance, and marriage were often discussed over dinner and at parties with friends and colleagues. Of all the wonderful stories that I heard, perhaps this one, from my dear friend Peggy Briggs, whose husband, Doug, is president of QVC, rates as one of the most romantic. I share it with you in the hopes that you too will know the meaning of "double happiness."

"There's no question that my husband is a romantic. Doug was still in college when we decided to get married and he felt badly that he couldn't afford to buy me a diamond engagement ring. From time to time we talked about getting something less expensive but I said I would be just as happy to wait till we could afford a diamond.

"One of these discussions took place while we were driving one evening and Doug abruptly turned into a shopping center and parked the car in front of a supermarket. With barely a word of explanation, he ran inside. A couple of minutes later he came out with the biggest grin on his face. When he got back into the car he presented me with not one but two glittering rings—you know, the kind that come in big plastic bubbles from the gum machines. He didn't want me to go empty-handed. I felt extra special because now I had two engagement rings!

"And I still have them today. Whenever I come across them in my jewelry box, the sight of them makes me smile remembering that wonderful romantic gesture."

Iova's 22 Secrets

◆

1. Men want the same things women do—but they don't know how to get them.
2. If you're not paying attention to your relationships, they can run right away from you.
3. Happiness is all the more sweet because it so often comes after heartbreak.
4. Trust each other enough to talk about everything.
5. Age is a state of mind.
6. Men can think about only one thing at a time.
7. You have to tell your husband how much you love him.
8. The only person you can change is yourself.
9. Small steps can take you further than you think.
10. If you don't take care of yourself and your needs, nobody else is going to do it for you.
11. The best way to click yourself out of a mood is to do the opposite of what you usually do.
12. Focus your attention on your husband.
13. Trust your intuition.
14. Changing your actions will change his reactions.

15. Never talk about money after ten P.M.
16. As soon as the courtship stops, the magic stops.
17. You can never have too many lists.
18. You're married to your husband, not your parents. And not his parents, either.
19. Celebrate your birthdays with a dartboard and a dream.
20. Don't believe in beauty fads.
21. True friends want what's best for you, but they don't necessarily know what the best for you is.
22. Never stop working at keeping the love around you.

$\mathcal{J}$ova's 12 $\mathcal{S}$trategies

◆

1. Use my "Five Ways to Be Sure He's the One."
2. Figure out the elements that make a good marriage work.
3. List what you believe is absolutely essential for you to have in a committed relationship.
4. Practice the vocabulary of love and marriage.
5. Learn the Rules of Marriage and do all you can to follow them.
6. Write down the best things about your husband and refer to them often.
7. Create a scrapbook of your marriage that holds your memories.
8. Celebrate your love as often as you like with "Monthaversaries."
9. Follow six simple rules to help you get organized and stay organized.
10. Create a Master Calendar together.
11. Cry when you need to—it's good for you!
12. Meditate, and breathe new life into your life.

Jova's 8 Compromises

◆

1. Give your husband the one thing he wants, then make yourself happy, too.
2. Ignore your husband's moods and let him work it out for himself, or else try to help him—it's your choice.
3. When you give your husband freedom of choice, he won't feel that you are trying to tell him what to do.
4. Letting go of your need for control will give you more.
5. Persuade your husband to let you burn candles occasionally, as long as he's around to put out the flames!
6. If cooking isn't your thing, turn your kitchen into a den.
7. Try your utmost to share whatever your husband loves to do.
8. Don't fight your body's internal clock—make the rhythms work for you!

Author's Note

♦

You've reached the end of the book—congratulations! Did you realize that you had joined me in practicing the Borg-Nine Principles?

- You tapped into the **inspiration** that made you want to get and stay married.
- You recalled the **passion** that you first brought to your relationship.
- You chose to read each chapter of this book because you **hoped to accomplish something worthwhile**—the preservation of your marriage.
- You understood that examining your relationship closely is a bit of **risk-taking**.
- You kept coming back to the book even when distractions called you away—**persistence**.
- Your **perseverance** in practicing each strategy showed real dedication.
- You gradually learned that **patience** is more than a virtue—it's a promise of good things to come.

Now you're ready to finish up with the last two—**being a mentor** and **giving back**.

How? Don't keep my secrets and strategies to yourself. Share them with your girlfriends, your sisters, your mother—anyone you know and love enough to want to help get the best out of their marriages!

Dearest Readers:

Throughout this book I have tried to show how our relationships reflect our inner sense of self. And in both my personal and professional endeavors, I have searched for ways to help women realize and uncover this true beauty within. I hope that my book and my TOVA products have gone some way to fulfill this mission. If you would like to learn more about how you can experience the "Tova difference" please call us at 1-800-852-9999.

And I would love to hear from you. Please send your letters to:

Tova Borgnine
The Tova Corporation
192 N. Canyon Drive
Beverly Hills, CA 90210